# Introduction to
# Curriculum
## Design
## in
## Gifted
## Education

# Introduction to
# Curriculum Design
## in
## Gifted
## Education

Edited by
Kristen R. Stephens, Ph.D.,
and Frances A. Karnes, Ph.D.

PRUFROCK
PRESS INC.™

PRUFROCK
ACADEMIC
PRESS

A line of materials supporting scholarship and research-based practices in education

Library of Congress Cataloging-in-Publication Data

Introduction to curriculum design in gifted education / edited by Kristen R. Stephens, Ph.D., and Frances A. Karnes, Ph.D.
    pages cm
ISBN 978-1-61821-479-9 (pbk.)
1. Gifted children--Education--Curricula--United States. 2. Curriculum planning--United States. I. Stephens, Kristen R., editor of compilation. II. Karnes, Frances A., editor of compilation.
LC3993.9.I67 2016
371.95--dc23
                    2015029568

Copyright ©2016, Prufrock Press Inc.

Edited by Lacy Compton

Cover and layout design by Raquel Trevino

ISBN-13: 978-1-61821-479-9

Printed in the United States of America.

At the time of this book's publication, all facts and figures cited are the most current available. All telephone numbers, addresses, and websites URLs are accurate and active. All publications, organizations, websites, and other resources exist as described in the book, and all have been verified. The authors and Prufrock Press Inc. make no warranty or guarantee concerning the information and materials given out by organizations or content found at websites, and we are not responsible for any changes that occur after this book's publication. If you find an error, please contact Prufrock Press Inc.

Prufrock Press Inc.
P.O. Box 8813
Waco, TX 76714-8813
Phone: (800) 998-2208
Fax: (800) 240-0333
http://www.prufrock.com

# TABLE OF CONTENTS

## Section IV: The Role of Assessment in Curriculum Development

## Section V: Trends and Future Directions for Curriculum for the Gifted

# Introduction

**Kristen R. Stephens and Frances A. Karnes**

Curriculum is a fundamental component of our educational system serving to guide both teachers and students through the teaching and learning process. In recent years, the examination of what and how we teach has intensified with the introduction of the Common Core State Standards in Mathematics and English Language Arts. Although conversations pertaining to these and other standards can be quite contentious, these new standards have encouraged critical reflection around what is important for students to know, understand, and do within and across grade levels.

As modifications are made to the general curriculum, educators of the gifted must closely analyze the implications of such changes for the curriculum for gifted students. As curriculum reformers tout the implementation of these new standards as providing a more rigorous curricular experience for students, gifted education advocates must acknowledge that these more rigorous standards will still require adjustments to address the educational needs of our gifted learners. The idea of a "one-size-fits-all" curriculum is not only impractical, it is disingenuous given the unique learning needs of each student in our classrooms.

The goal of this text is to present the current thinking and scholarship regarding curriculum development for the gifted to assist educators in developing new and/or modifying existing curriculum for gifted learners. The text is organized into five sections: Foundations, Survey of Curriculum Models, Curriculum in the Core Subject Areas, The Role of Assessment in Curriculum Development, and Trends and Future Directions for Curriculum for the Gifted.

**Section I: Foundations** provides the reader with the essential background knowledge needed to develop curriculum for the gifted.

# Introduction to Curriculum Design in Gifted Education

In Chapter 1, Angela Housand highlights the characteristics of gifted students and their implications for curriculum development. Components of the curriculum that are responsive to the curious, creative, capable, connected, and conscientious leader—all aspects of the gifted learner—are examined.

Chapter 2 by Elissa Brown provides an overview of the history of curriculum theory and practice. Social and political tensions as well as advancements in our understanding of the development of human cognition are all explored in relation to their influence on curriculum development in both general and gifted education.

Jessica Hockett and Catherine Brighton present the principles and best practices of general curriculum design in Chapter 3. The source and organization of the curriculum, the goals and priorities of the curriculum, and the tailoring of curriculum are all discussed in the context of developing high-quality curriculum for all students.

In Chapter 4, Susan Johnsen outlines how to approach the aligning of curriculum to relevant standards. Three alignment models are presented and consideration is given to how curriculum documents can be appropriately differentiated for gifted students.

**Section II: Survey of Curriculum Models** is comprised of Chapter 5 by Ann Robinson and Audrey Tabler. This chapter surveys the major curriculum models and frameworks currently in use to guide curriculum development. Descriptions of selected models, a summary of efficacy research, and examples of projects currently implementing each model are provided.

**Section III: Curriculum in the Core Subject Areas** examines curriculum development from the perspective of specific content areas—English language arts, mathematics, science, and social studies.

Elizabeth Fogarty, in Chapter 6, describes the characteristics of gifted English language arts students, explains why they require different experiences in the classroom, and offers suggestions for modifying curriculum to better meet the needs of these students

In Chapter 7, M. Katherine Gavin highlights the essential components of an effective mathematics curriculum for gifted students. Instructional strategies and sample curriculum materials are shared to support the development of students as mathematicians.

Chapter 8 by Michael Matthews provides contextual considerations for developing science curriculum for the gifted and suggestions for modifying, evaluating, and selecting existing instructional materials in the sciences. The role of argumentation in the science classroom and recommendations for Science Olympiad preparation are also offered.

Developing rich and challenging experiences for gifted students in the social studies is the focus of Chapter 9 by Shelagh Gallagher. The components of a differentiated social studies curriculum and ideas for enhancing learning experiences in social studies through problem-based learning are shared.

**Section IV: The Role of Assessment in Curriculum Development** includes Chapter 10 by Carolyn Callahan and examines curriculum implementation, management, and assessment. All of the processes necessary to ensure that the curriculum is achieving desired outcomes are detailed in this comprehensive chapter.

**Section V: Trends and Future Directions for Curriculum for the Gifted** explores special areas of consideration in the curriculum development process, including creativity, technology, service-learning, social-emotional development, and cultural responsiveness.

In Chapter 11, Bonnie Cramond and Sarah Sumners address several critical questions that have implications for curriculum development: Why teach creativity? Can creativity be taught? Should we infuse creativity into the current curriculum or design a stand-alone creativity curriculum? Creative dispositions and instructional models focusing on the creative process are also detailed.

Chapter 12 by Brian Housand examines the role of technology in curriculum for the gifted. From seamlessly integrating technology into the curriculum to examining the ways students engage with technology in the classroom, a variety of considerations are discussed. Access to technology, use of technology for creative expression, and responsible use of technology are additional topics explored in this chapter.

Kristen Stephens, David Malone, and Alissa Griffith introduce the reader to service-learning in Chapter 13. The chapter summarizes the research supporting service-learning experiences for students, highlights the role service-learning plays in curriculum development for gifted learners, and shares teachers' experiences with implementing service-learning in schools and classrooms.

In Chapter 14, Jean Peterson provides an overview of affective curriculum that addresses the social and emotional development of gifted students. Strategies for incorporating affective components into existing curriculum as well as developing "stand-alone" affective curriculum are presented.

The development of culturally responsive and relevant curriculum is examined by Donna Ford and Michelle Trotman Scott in Chapter 15. The revised Bloom-Banks Matrix is shared. Although Bloom's taxonomy addresses the rigor required of gifted students, the Banks Multicultural Curriculum Model ensures relevancy is equally considered in developing curriculum for gifted students.

It is our hope that each chapter in this text provides the reader with the necessary knowledge and tools to create new or adapt existing curriculum for gifted students. The development and refinement of curriculum is an ongoing process that not only demands staying abreast of the most current research to ensure implementation of evidence-based practices, but also requires educators to come together, share expertise, and reflect deeply about what is essential for students to know, understand, and be able to do across grade levels and content areas. Curriculum is our guide, so we must ensure that it is always directing us to our desired destination.

# SECTION I
# Foundations

# CHAPTER 1

# In Context

## Gifted Characteristics and the Implications for Curriculum

**Angela M. Housand**

## Introduction

Numerous perspectives within the literature on giftedness and talent development attempt to characterize giftedness. Listings of characteristics often include intellectual attributes, creative characteristics, domain-specific behaviors, affective characteristics, and trait comparisons, to both illustrate similarities between gifted students and eminent producers as well as to highlight differences between gifted students and their nongifted peers (Davis, Rimm, & Siegle, 2011; Reis & Housand, 2007; Renzulli, Siegle, Reis, Gavin, & Sytsma-Reed, 2009; Renzulli et al., 2013; Sternberg & Davidson, 2005). The purposes for listing such attributes vary from simply trying to broadly define manifestations of intelligence to informing procedures for effectively identifying gifted students. Recurrent across both purposes is the suggestion that gifted and talented students are atypical learners, capable of advanced performance, and qualitatively different from their nongifted peers in their cognitive abilities, personality traits, past experiences, and/or affective characteristics (Clark, 2002; Renzulli, 1978, 1996; Treffinger, Young, Selby, & Shepardson, 2002).

VanTassel-Baska (2011) contended that three characteristics of gifted and talented students—complexity, precocity, and intensity—are critical for curricular planning and development. Complexity as a characteristic refers to gifted students' abilities to grapple with complex ideas, reason abstractly, engage in higher order thinking, and enjoy challenging activities. This ability to enjoy complexity stems from their precocity or evidence of advanced performance in a domain as well as their emotional responsiveness and capacity for intense focus on topics they find interesting. Although consideration of these characteristics certainly leads to outstanding curriculum for gifted students, it does narrow the focus and limits attention to the influence of environment, thus potentially advancing the belief that giftedness is static or unchanging and that once a student is identified as gifted, he or she will always display these unique capacities.

Increasingly, however, experts suggest that the characteristics of gifted individuals are not static in nature and no one individual possesses or displays all of these characteristics consistently across time or content areas (Renzulli, 1986, 2005; Sternberg, 1997; Treffinger et al., 2002). It has been known for decades that giftedness varies among individuals; across gender, cultures, and socioeconomic status; and across disciplines and time (Bloom, 1985; Frasier & Passow, 1994; Reis, 2005; Treffinger et al., 2002). Further, gifts and talents may be manifest and apparent, emergent and ill-defined, latent and hidden, or camouflaged by a learning disability. To further complicate matters, many conceptions acknowledge that giftedness and gifted behaviors manifest as a result of the dynamic interaction between internal factors, such as motivation, persistence, or interest, and external factors, such as access to resources, enriched learning opportunities, or support (Mönks & Katzko, 2005; Renzulli, 1996, 2002), and research supports that giftedness is developmental and fluid or less fixed than previously believed (Dweck, 2006).

The general agreement within the field of gifted education seems to be that giftedness is a multifaceted construct and no singular definition or clear consensus exists about the exact nature of giftedness. A position statement by the National Association for Gifted Children (2010) advances the idea that gifted individuals are those who demonstrate outstanding levels of aptitude or competence in a given domain. Within education, these exceptionally able learners progress in learning faster than their same age-peers, are found in all segments of society, and require differentiated educational experiences with opportunities for advanced levels, depth, and pacing of curriculum. Regardless of the complexities, some consideration of these characteristics is fundamental for designing and planning curriculum for gifted and talented learners (VanTassel-Baska, 2011).

Curriculum has to address the variability in the development of gifted behaviors and be prepared to support a broad range of developmental stages and individual characteristics even within the narrower population of students who have been identified as having the potential for advanced performance. Examples of some generally accepted and often used differentiated learning experiences for gifted students include acceleration in domains of talent or by grade-level; grouping practices that are flexible and cluster gifted students together by talent area or for advanced instruction; inquiry-based strategies that rely on seeking answers to open-ended problems or questions; embedding higher order thinking and problem solving into core subject areas; and focusing on curricular content and processes that are based on student interests, have applications outside educational settings, or have personal meaning for students (e.g., relevant to their sense of identity or future goals; Assouline, Colangelo, VanTassel-Baska, & Lupkowski-Shoplik, 2015; Ackerman, 2014; Colangelo, Assouline, & Gross, 2004; Renzulli & Reis, 2014; Rogers, 2004; VanTassel-Baska & Brown, 2007). Of paramount importance within these differentiated educational experiences are the curricular decisions: the consideration, determination, and description of what students ultimately are *expected to be like* and *be able to do* (Stahl, 1994) or as Tomlinson (1999) would suggest, what students *should know, understand,* and *be able to do*.

This provides the platform for thinking about curriculum as a means to serve not only the internal characteristics of gifted students, but also develop talent traits that are instrumental for advanced achievement such as intellectual engagement (Goff & Ackerman, 1992), openness to experience (Costa & McCrae, 1992), perseverance and passion for attaining long-term goals (i.e., grit; Duckworth, Peterson, Matthews, & Kelly, 2007), a need for Ascending Intellectual Demand (Tomlinson et al., 2009), and intense focus in areas of personal and "professional" interest (Housand, 2014; Renzulli & Reis, 2014). What then are the attributes of gifted and talented students in our classrooms that can be leveraged to support growth and achievement for these individuals? In other words, which traits of giftedness are most important to consider in decision making about high-quality curriculum, and what constitutes "high-quality curriculum"?

Gifted students are curious, creative, capable, and connected. They also have the potential to be the future leaders of society. These characteristics can be used to great advantage when designing curriculum (see Table 1.1). Curiosity, for example, is a hallmark of giftedness that naturally results in engagement as gifted students seek answers to their questions. Each discovery provides the fodder for deeper questioning or a new line of inquiry altogether. Gifted students' capacity for advanced performance and creative productivity are demonstrated when they find and solve challenging problems and these students enjoy the challenging work and opportunity to be productive. Therefore, curriculum must be responsive to this need to ensure they still love the challenge even after they leave the academic setting. These students, quite simply, have the capacity to go deeper and further than their nongifted peers, and curriculum must support and stretch these advanced capabilities to help them be competitive in a globally connected society and become the compassionate and conscientious leaders that society needs.

# Connected

## Context

First, consider the milieu of gifted students today. This generation of students is connected like no other generation before (Pew Internet Research, 2010). The Internet and social media have transformed not only how people communicate, but also the *ways* they acquire, create, and share information. Although the characteristic of connectedness is not unique to gifted students, it *is* fundamental to who they are. No longer is technology merely a tool, it is *the medium* for attaining knowledge, collaborating with peers, exchanging ideas, creating products, and sharing knowledge and insights. It is imperative that any consideration of curriculum assumes that the use of technology tools is fundamental to the learning process, with an awareness that students today are adept at socializing via the Internet, but may yet require instruction about effective research skills, professional communication protocols, presentation modalities or tools, and responsible digital participation (i.e., digital citizenship). The implications of this

## Table 1.1
*Components of Effective Curriculum That Are
Responsive to Gifted Student Characteristics*

| Gifted Student Characteristic | Effective Curriculum |
|---|---|
| Connected | • Connects to students' lives<br>• Is real and useful beyond the classroom<br>• Allows for meaningful collaboration<br>• Is sensitive to global concerns<br>• Provides authentic audience<br>• Requires authentic outcomes (e.g., products)<br>• Focuses on real problems and processes<br>• Utilizes the conventions of a discipline<br>• Guided by habits of mind<br>• Provides opportunities for connecting with intellectual peers |
| Curious | • Promotes inquiry-based learning<br>• Requires problem solving<br>• Connects to students' lives<br>• Reflects interest-based content<br>• Supports persistence through emotionally compelling topics<br>• Engages the learner through sufficient challenge<br>• Requires effort |
| Creative | • Nurtures problem definition<br>• Requires problem solving<br>• Utilizes divergent thought as a problem-solving strategy<br>• Provides opportunities for original, creative, and practical work in the disciplines |
| Capable | • Provides cognitive challenge<br>• Challenges beliefs<br>• Addresses profound ideas<br>• Requires growth on the part of the student<br>• Provides an authentic audience<br>• Requires authentic outcomes (e.g., products)<br>• Focuses on real problems and processes<br>• Utilizes the conventions of a discipline |
| Conscientious leaders | • Requires self-reflection<br>• Requires reflective practice and metacognition<br>• Considers self within the world<br>• Sensitive to multicultural and global concerns<br>• Requires students to be respectful of others' needs and contributions<br>• Requires decision making |

connectedness are multifaceted and serve to address logistical, process, and content concerns in decision making about high-quality curriculum.

## Curricular Considerations for Connected Students

**Logistical concerns.** For example, a unique logistical challenge in addressing the needs of gifted students is helping them connect with peers who have similar interests and abilities. Finding this type of connection is particularly important to gifted students' sense of identity, establishing feelings of belonging and acceptance, their ability to maintain engagement in and motivation for learning, and self-determination for achieving successful outcomes (Baylor, 2011; Phillips & Lindsay, 2006; Reynolds & Caperton, 2011; Ryan & Deci, 2000). Technology and access to the Internet provide unique curricular opportunities to connect youth to communities where they can find individuals who share their interests, advanced knowledge, and insights, and find mentors who can serve to advance gifted students' knowledge to expert levels while encouraging continual advancement in fields of interest. Take, for example, one student in a pilot study of FutureCasting® (Housand, 2014), who generated professional-level blog posts that garnered, within a 24-hour period, 273 "hits" and opened an international dialogue with participants from the United States, Germany, Malaysia, and Singapore about achieving quality photographic images with a specific camera using various lenses and aperture settings. This example illustrates several things about high-quality curriculum. According to experts, high-quality curriculum should connect with students' lives, seem real and useful in contexts beyond the classroom, allow for meaningful collaboration, and be sensitive to global concerns. Experts also agree that high-quality curriculum should be authentic—focused on real problems and processes, using the conventions of the discipline, and guided by habits of mind (Hockett, 2009; Kaplan, 1986; Renzulli, Leppien, & Hays, 2000; Renzulli & Reis, 2014; Tomlinson et al., 2009; VanTassel-Baska, 2011). Therefore, it is imperative that curriculum incorporate opportunities for students to make connections to intellectual peers (not necessarily age peers) who share their interests and ability to explore a topic with commensurate levels of intensity and focus.

**Process concerns.** Another indicator of high-quality curriculum is a flexible curriculum that gives consideration to individual student differences. It has already been established that gifted students are qualitatively different than their same-age peers and that they require curricular adjustments, but it is important that these adjustments are sufficient. Once again, the connected nature of gifted students' experiences provide opportunities for accommodations such as progressing through the curriculum at a faster or slower rate; access to curriculum, courses, and mentors who enable gifted students to participate in sufficiently challenging learning experiences; and the provision of myriad choices related to process, pace, and content of learning. In other words, technology and access to the Internet provide the opportunity for curriculum to focus on process skills, such as effective research strategies, and remove limitations curriculum can inadvertently create by allowing students to explore as much and as many content resources as deeply as their interests require and in the contexts that are most meaningful to their lives.

**Content concerns.** Content is also an area where the ability to connect via digital technologies provides affordances for high-quality curriculum. Most curriculum experts agree that effective curriculum should be integrative, emphasizing connections between domains of knowledge and across and within disciplines (Kaplan, 1986; Renzulli et al., 2000; Renzulli & Reis, 2014; Tomlinson et al., 2009; VanTassel-Baska, 2011). Fortunately, gifted students "connected" lives provide ready access to information and function to support both deeper levels of exploration and connections between disciplines. No longer is a content question something that needs to be memorized. Instead, ready access to content knowledge through laptop computers, iPads, and smartphones moves information-level learning into the role of deeper and more complex meaning making (Housand & Housand, 2012). With this scaffolding of information-level knowledge, curriculum can focus on requiring students to make connections, transfer ideas within and across domains, apply knowledge at multiple levels, identify patterns, and understand the depth and complexity of disciplines of study. Further, an integrative curriculum focusing on connections between disciplines allows students to find different points of entry, connect their interests to the academic content, and combine information from a variety of fields to develop novel and insightful solutions to problems they encounter within sufficiently advanced learning opportunities.

# Curious

## Episodic Nature of Curiosity

Gifted students are curious by nature, but curiosity does not automatically progress to a well-defined interest area or advanced levels of engagement in curricular content. Students may be curious, but without access to resources to satisfy initial states of curiosity, episodes of curiosity will not lead to continued interests or desired outcomes such as advanced achievement. Put simply, curiosity is a cyclical process that when satisfied leads to a desire for new information (i.e., curiosity begets curiosity). According to Arnone, Small, Chauncey, and McKenna (2011), when curiosity is satisfied, it becomes a multistage episode that can lead to deepening levels of interest and vice versa. The first stage of episodic curiosity is the trigger, which is a "stimulus characterized by uncertainty" (Arnone et al., 2011, p. 185). This is followed by reaction and a resolution. Learning is dependent upon whether the episode of curiosity was satisfied or not. If the curiosity is not satisfied, learning in that instance does not occur and the impetus for the next episode of curiosity is negated. Moreover, gifted students are able to acquire deep content knowledge and maintain intense focus when seeking answers to questions of interest, suggesting that gifted students may be uniquely able to benefit from curriculum that supports open-ended exploration and the cyclical processes that underlie curiosity. In turn, such curiosity may also be hindered when curriculum does not provide the freedom for deep exploration in areas of personal and "professional" interests that help learners make sense of ideas and information by building upon previous knowledge, skills, and understandings (Housand & Housand, 2012; Tomlinson et al., 2009; VanTassel-Baska, 2011).

## Curriculum Considerations for Maintaining Curiosity

Fortunately, gifted students' connected lives provide ready access to information and function to support both episodic curiosity as well as deeper levels of exploration. No longer is a question something deemed to be addressed at some future time, but instead, with access to the Internet, curiosity can be satisfied immediately, providing the impetus for deeper and more complex exploration of information, thus helping sustain curiosity (Housand & Housand, 2012).

Therefore, decisions about curriculum should serve to support students' curiosity by promoting inquiry-based learning and problem solving, connecting with students lives, motivating students via interest-based content, and providing learning opportunities that are compelling and satisfying enough to encourage students to persist despite frustration so that they may understand the importance of effort (Collins & Amabile, 1999; Csikszentmihalyi, Rathunde, & Whalen, 1993; Renzulli & Reis, 2014; Tomlinson et al., 2009; VanTassel-Baska, 2011).

# Creative

## Creativity in Gifted Students

Creativity is often identified as a defining characteristic of giftedness. Sternberg and Lubart (1993), for example, provided a conception of creativity as a separate type of giftedness, proposing that an individual interactively combines separate personal resources to enable the process of creative production. Specifically, they suggested that intellectual processes, knowledge of a domain, intellectual styles, personality attributes, task-focused orientation, and one's environmental context enable individuals to define problems, solve problems, utilize divergent thinking, think abstractly, tolerate ambiguity, take reasonable risks, and persevere in the face of obstacles. Gardner's (1983, 1993) conception of a creative individual is one who produces novel products or solutions within a domain that is recognized by members of the respective field. Renzulli (1986) and Tannenbaum (1986) also see the creativeness of individuals as a form of giftedness, as each have separately distinguished between the traits of individuals who excel in academic settings and those who produce original knowledge, materials, or products. The Munich Longitudinal Study of Giftedness (conducted from 1985–1989; Perleth, Sierwald, & Heller, 1993) provides support for "creative" being a unique characteristic of giftedness, as they found clear differences between students who demonstrated creative productivity as opposed to high academic performance. Regardless of the perspective on creativity, one characteristic is common: Creativity results in a product, some tangible outcome that is novel, unique, or insightful.

## Curriculum Considerations for Supporting Creative Productivity

What then are the curricular decisions that would nurture and support the development of creative characteristics? According to Sternberg and Lubart's theory (1993), it would involve creating curricular opportunities that nurture problem definition, require problem solving, and utilize divergent thought as a problem-solving strategy. Therefore, curriculum should provide students with opportunities for original, creative, and practical work in the disciplines (i.e., utilize the conventions of a field to create new and original works); should stretch students beyond where they currently are in terms of content knowledge, process skills, and level of productivity; and nurture personality attributes such as tolerance of ambiguity, moderate risk-taking, and willingness to surmount obstacles and persevere (Renzulli & Reis, 2014; Tomlinson et al., 2009). To achieve these goals, curricular settings need to provide students with the requisite tools and skills to engage in authentic processes.

# Capable

## Gifted Students and Challenge

Gifted students pose a unique opportunity for educators as it relates to challenge. Because gifted students are capable of gaining deep background knowledge and achieving at high levels, have a rapid capacity for learning, and are capable of accelerated growth compared with their same age peers, the challenges they encounter need to escalate with a steep trajectory. Unfortunately, the ability of gifted students to persevere when faced with challenges that truly stretch them can be underestimated. When this happens, there is no difference between high-quality curriculum for all students and curriculum being delivered for gifted students, yet the purpose of curriculum for gifted students is to provide optimal educational experiences to enable gifted students to develop their talents and fulfill their potential by providing services or activities that are not ordinarily provided by schools.

Take for example the concept of differentiation, which seeks to meet students where they are by implementing curriculum that addresses different learning modalities, appeals to students interests, and uses varied degrees of complexity to meet students' needs within educational settings. Conceptually, differentiation is an ideal approach to serve the needs of *all* students including gifted and talented students; however, differentiation that provides the rigor, challenge, complexity, and opportunities for creative productivity that are commensurate with gifted students' abilities is rarely present in heterogeneously grouped classroom settings where gifted students spend the majority of their time (Latz, Speirs Neumeister, Adams, & Pierce, 2009; Reis et al., 2004; Westberg, Archambault, Dobyns, & Salvin, 1993; Westberg & Daoust, 2003; Whitton, 1997).

## Curriculum Considerations for Providing Sufficient Challenge

Tomlinson and colleagues (2009) suggested that effective curriculum that addresses a student's needs for sufficiently advanced, complex, and in-depth learning should be both mentally and affectively challenging, deal with profound ideas, and stretch the student beyond where he or she is now or where he or she has been before. One way to accomplish this kind of challenge is to provide opportunities for gifted students to create authentic products, participate in authentic processes utilizing the conventions of a discipline, and solve authentic problems (i.e., real-world problems, the solution to which have implications beyond the classroom walls) that are driven by meaningful outcomes (Hockett, 2009; Little, 2012; VanTassel-Baska, 2011). Not only do these modifications provide the opportunity for growth, challenge, and to grapple with complex ideas, they can also be highly motivating and engaging for gifted students (Hockett, 2009; Little, 2012) and are worthy of the time and attention they receive from gifted students.

# Conscientious Leaders

### Defining Leadership

Leadership is generally defined as one's ability to influence others, but a quality that is rarely intentionally developed within schools today (Sternberg, 2005). Yet, gifted students are often characterized as the leaders of tomorrow or expectations of leadership are placed upon them based on characteristics such as being creative problem solvers, having strong communication skills, or staying motivated when faced with a challenge. Leadership skills are not necessarily innate characteristics and leadership opportunities are not necessarily something that all gifted students seek. However, for the advancement of society, it is important that our future leaders be intelligent, make effective decisions, be persuasive, have the ability to achieve at high levels, persist when faced with obstacles, and have a strong concern for those less fortunate (Judge, Colbert, & Ilies, 2004; Renzulli, 2002).

**Leaders for today.** Gifted youth today are members of a generation who, more than any other generation before, are primed to make positive change in the world because as a group, they value learning and growing over self-promotion, they pursue work that is personally fulfilling rather than merely for financial gain, and seek change that leads to community engagement and equitable treatment for members of society (Pew Internet Research, 2010). Unfortunately, as a group they may seek change for a better society, but as a group they do not want to put forth the effort to instigate that change (Pew Internet Research, 2010). This places gifted students in a unique position within this generation to emerge as leaders. According to Karnes and colleagues (Karnes & Bean, 1990, 1996; Karnes & Chauvin, 1986, 2000; Karnes & D'Ilio, 1989), gifted students possess the traits necessary to emerge as leaders. They defined leadership in gifted students as demonstrating a desire to be challenged, to solve problems creatively, to reason critically, to see new relationships, to be flexible in thought and action, to tolerate ambiguity, and to motivate others. These traits are in keeping with those of an emergent leader, which can be characterized as one who is a role model, motivates a group to continue making progress despite being stalled, and recognizes patterns that enable him or her to pair group members' traits to tasks that need to be accomplished (Guastello, 2002).

**Benevolent leadership.** As mentioned before, there is more to leadership than the skills of effective management. According to Renzulli (2002), there is a need for high-potential students to develop leadership capabilities in combination with a concern for less fortunate individuals. He used the term *social capital* to identify a set of intangible assets that address the collective needs and problems of other individuals and communities at large. Similarly, Tannenbaum (2000) called on a similar disposition for gifted students with the notion of "social leadership" or the ability to enable a group to reach its goal, and in the process, improve human relationships. It is not surprising that leaders in the field have identified aspects of conscientiousness as a requisite quality for effective and benevolent leadership because research by Judge and colleagues (2002) found that among other qualities, conscientiousness had a statistically significant relationship to leadership.

Can these attributes be developed and if so, what types of curricular options need to be made available?

## Curriculum Considerations for Developing Leaders

There is research to suggest that leadership skills *can be developed* (Smith, Smith, & Barnette, 1991) and fairly consistently leadership development programs include instruction on the component skills of leadership, opportunities for students to participate in leadership roles, and instruction about leadership styles and traits (Davis et al., 2011). These however, do not necessarily address the social components of leadership that might enable gifted students to develop conscientiousness and altruistically consider those less fortunate in their decision- making processes.

Therefore, in addition to incorporating leadership skill development into learning opportunities, curriculum should also require students to be reflective. Students must first define their values, priorities, strengths, and weaknesses within the context of the unique circumstances to understand their options. Simply reflecting upon the individual is, however, insufficient and curriculum must require students to consider themselves within the world. For example, curriculum should be sensitive to multicultural and global concerns, while requiring students to be respectful of the contributions, needs, ideas, and products of others and provide opportunities for students to be reflective about how their learning affects their values and belief systems in order to make effective decisions for themselves and others.

# Conclusion

All students benefit from being challenged. Every student should have the opportunity to work within his or her zone of proximal development (Vygotsky, 1978), or at a level of difficulty that is somewhat beyond his or her capacity to successfully complete work without the support or guidance of teachers. That said, what is good for gifted students is potentially good for all students, but what is good for all students may not be sufficiently advanced, complex, in-depth, or encouraging of creativity for gifted students. Gifted students are capable of so much more than most recognize, and all too often, in educational settings, not enough is asked of gifted students.

"Form follows function" is a principle associated with architecture and design that suggests the shape of a building or object should be based upon its intended function or purpose. The same is true for curriculum design. The content and processes of curriculum must be designed to meet the needs of the student for which it is intended to serve. Without an understanding of gifted students' advanced capacities, their ability to grapple with complexity, or the intensity of their curiosity and drive, there is no way that one can design curriculum that will challenge, engage, or excite these unique students to learn.

When considering curriculum to serve the needs of gifted students, there should be ample opportunities that could result in failure if inadequate effort is put forth. When gifted students are challenged at a level slightly beyond their ability, they will be forced to seek help from teachers and mentors, develop strategies and skills that lead to success, experience complexities that stretch them outside their comfort zone, attain levels of "epic" achievement, and grow—beyond where they are now or where they have been before.

# References

Assouline, S. G., Colangelo, N., VanTassel-Baska, J., & Lupkowski-Shoplik, A. (2015). *A nation empowered: Evidence trumps excuses holding back America's brightest students.* Iowa City: University of Iowa, The Connie Belin & Jacqueline N. Blank International Center for Gifted Education and Talent Development.

Ackerman, P. L. (2014). Adolescent and adult intellectual development. *Current Directions in Psychological Science, 23,* 246–251.

Arnone, M. P., Small, R. V., Chauncey, S. A., & McKenna, H. P. (2011). Curiosity, interest, and engagement in technology-pervasive learning environments: A new research agenda. *Educational Technology Research and Development, 59,* 181–198.

Baylor, A. L. (2011). The design of motivational agents and avatars. *Educational Technology Research and Development, 59,* 291–300.

Bloom, B. S. (Ed.). (1985). *Developing talent in young people.* New York, NY: Ballantine.

Clark, B. (2002). *Growing up gifted* (6th ed.). Upper Saddle River, NJ: Merrill/Prentice-Hall.

Colangelo, N., Assouline, S. G., & Gross, M. U. M. (2004). *A nation deceived: How schools hold back America's brightest students.* Iowa City: University of Iowa, The Connie Belin & Jacqueline N. Blank International Center for Gifted Education and Talent Development.

Collins, M., & Amabile, T. M. (1999). Motivation and creativity. In R. J. Sternberg (Ed.), *Handbook of creativity* (pp. 297–312). New York, NY: Cambridge University Press.

Costa P. T., Jr., & McCrae, R. R. (1992). *Revised NEO Personality Inventory and Five-Factor Inventory professional manual.* Odessa, FL: Psychological Assessment Resources.

Csikszentmihalyi, M., Rathunde, K., & Whalen, S. (1993). *Talented teenagers: The roots of success and failure.* New York, NY: Cambridge University Press.

Davis, G. A., Rimm, S. B., & Siegle, D. (2011). *Education of the gifted and talented* (6th ed.). Boston, MA: Pearson.

Duckworth, A. L., Peterson, C., Matthews, M. D., & Kelly, D. R. (2007). Grit: Perseverance and passion for long-term goals. *Journal of Personality and Social Psychology, 92,* 1087–1101.

Dweck, C. S. (2006). *Mindset: The new psychology of success*. New York, NY: Random House.

Frasier, M. M., & Passow, A. H. (1994). *Toward a new paradigm for identifying talent potential*. Storrs: University of Connecticut, The National Research Center on the Gifted and Talented.

Gardner, H. (1983). *Frames of mind: The theory of multiple intelligences*. New York, NY: Basic.

Gardner, H. (1993). *Frames of mind: The theory of multiple intelligences* (10th Anniversary Ed.). New York, NY: Basic.

Goff, M., & Ackerman P. L. (1992). Personality-intelligence relations: Assessing typical intellectual engagement. *Journal of Educational Psychology, 84,* 537–552.

Guastello, S. J. (2002). *Managing emergent phenomena: Nonlinear dynamics in work organizations*. Mahwah, NJ: Erlbaum.

Hockett, J. A. (2009). Curriculum for highly able learners that conforms to general education and gifted education quality indicators. *Journal for the Education of the Gifted, 32,* 394–440.

Housand, A. M. (2014). [Futurecasting: Defining future attainment aspirations through digital portfolio development]. Unpublished raw data.

Housand, B. C., & Housand, A. M. (2012). The role of technology in gifted students' motivation. *Psychology in the Schools, 49,* 706–715.

Judge, T. A., Colbert, A. E., & Ilies, R. (2004). Intelligence and leadership: A quantitative review and test of theoretical propositions. *Journal of Applied Psychology, 89,* 542–552.

Judge, T. A., Bono, J. E., Ilies, R., & Gerhardt, M. W. (2002). Personality and leadership: A qualitative and quantitative review. *Journal of Applied Psychology, 87,* 765–780.

Kaplan, S. N. (1986). The grid: A model to construct differentiated curriculum for the gifted. In J. S. Renzulli (Ed.), *Systems and models for developing programs for the gifted and talented* (pp. 180–193). Mansfield Center, CT: Creative Learning Press.

Karnes, F. A., & Bean, S. M. (1990). *Developing leadership in gifted youth*. Reston, VA: Council for Exceptional Children. (ERIC Document Reproduction Service No. ED321490)

Karnes, F. A., & Bean, S. M. (1996). Leadership and the gifted. *Focus on Exceptional Children, 29*(1), 1–12.

Karnes, F. A., & Chauvin, J. C. (1986, May/June). The leadership skills: Fostering the forgotten dimension of giftedness. *Gifted Child Today, 9,* 22–23.

Karnes, F. A., & Chauvin, J. C. (2000). *Leadership development program.* Scottsdale, AZ: Gifted Psychology.

Karnes, F. A., & D'Ilio, V. R. (1989). Personality characteristics of student leaders. *Psychological Reports, 64,* 1125–1126.

Latz, A. O., Speirs Neumeister, K. L., Adams, C. M., & Pierce, R. L. (2009). Peer coaching to improve classroom differentiation: Perspectives from Project CLUE. *Roeper Review, 31,* 27–39.

Little, C. A. (2012). Curriculum as motivation for gifted students. *Psychology in the Schools, 49,* 695–705.

Mönks, F. J., & Katzko, M. W. (2005). Giftedness and gifted education. In R. J. Sternberg & J. E. Davidson (Eds.), *Conceptions of giftedness* (2nd ed., pp. 187–200). New York, NY: Cambridge University Press.

National Association for Gifted Children. (2010). *Redefining giftedness for a new century: Shifting the paradigm.* Retrieved from https://www.nagc.org/sites/default/files/Position%20Statement/Redefining%20Giftedness%20for%20a%20New%20Century.pdf

Perleth, C., Sierwald, W., & Heller, K. A. (1993). Selected results of the Munich longitudinal study of giftedness: The multidimensional/typological giftedness model. *Roeper Review, 15,* 149–155.

Pew Internet Research. (2010). *Millennials: Confident. Connected. Open to change.* Washington, DC: Pew Research Center. Retrieved from http://www.pewsocialtrends.org/2010/02/24/millennials-confident-connected-open-to-change

Phillips, N., & Lindsay, G. (2006). Motivation in gifted students. *High Ability Studies, 17,* 57–73.

Reis, S. M. (2005). Feminist perspective on talent development: A research-based conception of giftedness in women. In R. J. Sternberg & J. E. Davidson (Eds.), *Conceptions of giftedness* (2nd ed., pp. 217–245). New York, NY: Cambridge University Press.

Reis, S. M., Gubbins, E. J., Briggs, C. J., Schreiber, F. J., Richards, S., Jacobs, J. K., . . . Renzulli, J. S. (2004). Reading instruction for talented readers: Case studies documenting few opportunities for continuous progress. *Gifted Child Quarterly, 48,* 315–338.

Reis, S. M., & Housand, A. M. (2007). Characteristics of gifted and talented learners: Similarities and differences across domains. In F. A. Karnes & K. R. Stephens (Eds.), *Achieving excellence* (pp. 62–81). New York, NY: Merrill/Prentice Hall.

Renzulli, J. S. (1978). What makes giftedness? Reexamining a definition. *Phi Delta Kappan, 60,* 180–184, 261.

Renzulli, J. S. (1986). The three-ring conception of giftedness: A developmental model for creative productivity. In R. J. Sternberg & J. E. Davidson (Eds.), *Conceptions of giftedness* (pp. 53–92). New York, NY: Cambridge University Press.

Renzulli, J. S. (1996). Schools for talent development: A practical plan for total school improvement. *School Administrator, 53*(1), 20–22.

Renzulli, J. S. (2002). Expanding the conception of giftedness to include co-cognitive traits and to promote social capital. *Phi Delta Kappan, 84*(1), 33–40, 57–58.

Renzulli, J. S. (2005). The three-ring conception of giftedness: A developmental model for promoting creative productivity. In R. J. Sternberg & J. E. Davidson (Eds.), *Conceptions of giftedness* (2nd ed., pp. 246–279). New York, NY: Cambridge University Press.

Renzulli, J. S., Leppien, J. H., & Hays, T. S. (2000). *The Multiple Menu Model: A practical guide for developing differentiated curriculum*. Waco, TX: Prufrock Press.

Renzulli, J. S., & Reis, S. M. (2014). *The Schoolwide Enrichment Model: A how-to guide for talent development* (3rd ed.). Waco, TX: Prufrock Press.

Renzulli, J. S., Siegle, D., Reis, S. M., Gavin, M. K., & Sytsma-Reed, R. E. (2009). An investigation of the reliability and factor structure of four new scales for rating the behavioral characteristics of superior students. *Journal of Advanced Academics, 21*(1), 84–108.

Renzulli, J. S., Smith, L. H., White, A. J., Callahan, C. M., Hartman, R. K., Westberg, K. L., . . . Sytsma, R. E. (2013). *Scales for Rating the Behavioral Characteristics of Superior Students* (Rev. ed.). Waco, TX: Prufrock Press.

Reynolds, R., & Caperton, I. H. (2011). Contrasts in student engagement, meaning-making, dislikes, and challenges in a discovery-based program of game design learning. *Educational Technology Research and Development, 59*, 267–289. doi:10.1007/s11423-011-9191-8

Rogers, K. B. (2004). The academic effects of acceleration. In N. Colangelo, S. Assouline, & M. U. M. Gross (Eds.), *A nation deceived: How schools hold back America's brightest students* (Vol. 2, pp. 47–57). Iowa City: University of Iowa, The Connie Belin & Jacqueline N. Blank International Center for Gifted Education and Talent Development.

Ryan, R. M., & Deci, E. L. (2000). Self-determination theory and the facilitation of intrinsic motivation, social development, and well-being. *American Psychologist, 55*, 68–78.

Smith, D. L., Smith, L., & Barnette, J. (1991). Exploring the development of leadership giftedness. *Roeper Review, 14,* 7–12.

Stahl, R. J. (1994). Achieving targeted student outcomes: An information constructivist (IC) model to guide curriculum and instructional decisions. *Journal of Structural Learning, 12*(2), 87–111.

Sternberg, R. J. (1997). A triarchic view of giftedness: Theory and practice. In N. Colangelo & G. A. Davis (Eds.), *The handbook of gifted education* (pp. 43–53). Boston, MA: Allyn & Bacon.

Sternberg, R. J. (2005). WICS: A model of giftedness in leadership. *Roeper Review, 28,* 37–44.

Sternberg, R. J., & Davidson, J. E. (Eds.). (2005). *Conceptions of giftedness* (2nd ed.). New York, NY: Cambridge University Press.

Sternberg, R. J., & Lubart, T. I. (1993). Creative giftedness: A multivariate investment approach. *Gifted Child Quarterly, 37,* 7–15.

Tannenbaum, A. J. (1986). Giftedness: A psychosocial approach. In R. J. Sternberg & J. E. Davidson (Eds.), *Conceptions of giftedness* (pp. 21–52). New York, NY: Cambridge University Press.

Tannenbaum, A. J. (2000). A history of giftedness in school and society. In K. A. Heller, F. J. Mönks, R. J. Sternberg, & R. F. Subotnik (Eds.), *International handbook of giftedness and talent* (2nd ed., pp. 23–53). New York, NY: Elsevier.

Tomlinson, C. A. (1999). *The differentiated classroom: Responding to the needs of all learners.* Alexandria, VA: ASCD.

Tomlinson, C. A., Kaplan, S. N., Renzulli, J. S., Purcell, J. H., Leppien, J. H., Burns, D. E., . . . Imbeau, M. B. (2009). *The parallel curriculum: A design to develop learner potential and challenge advanced learners* (2nd ed.). Thousand Oaks, CA: Corwin Press.

Treffinger, D. J., Young, G. C., Selby, E. C., & Shepardson, C. (2002). *Assessing creativity: A guide for educators* (RM02170). Storrs: University of Connecticut, The National Research Center on the Gifted and Talented.

VanTassel-Baska, J. (2011). An introduction to the Integrated Curriculum Model. In J. VanTassel-Baska & C. A. Little (Eds.), *Content based curriculum for high-ability learners* (2nd ed., pp. 9–32). Waco, TX: Prufrock Press.

VanTassel-Baska, J., & Brown, E. (2007). Toward best practice: An analysis of the efficacy of curriculum models in gifted education. *Gifted Child Quarterly, 51,* 342–358.

Vygotsky, L. S. (1978). *Mind in society: The development of higher psychological processes.* Cambridge, MA: MIT Press.

Westberg, K. L., Archambault, F. X., Dobyns, S. M., & Salvin, T. J. (1993). An observational study of classroom practices used with third- and fourth-grade students. *Journal for the Education of the Gifted, 16,* 120–146.

Westberg, K. L., & Daoust, M. E. (2003, Fall). The results of the replication of the classroom practices survey replication in two states. *The National Research Center on the Gifted and Talented Newsletter,* 3–8. Retrieved from http://www.gifted.uconn.edu/nrcgt/newsletter/fall03/fall032.html

Whitton, D. (1997). Regular classroom practices with gifted students in grades 3 and 4 in New South Wales, Australia. *Gifted Education International, 12,* 34–38.

# CHAPTER 2

# History of Gifted and Advanced Academic Curriculum Theory and Practice

**Elissa Brown**

## Introduction

The history of gifted education curriculum has been idiosyncratic. Some curriculum emphases have been embedded and entwined within the history of general education curriculum, while other emphases have been outside, or in spite of, general education curriculum.

Curriculum as a social institution has been analyzed in a series of studies (Baker & LeTendre, 2005; Meyer, 1992) as having two distinct elements; one is the idea of the institutionalism of the curriculum itself, primarily driven by external curriculum policy makers and school reform mandates that our students should know a body of knowledge and subject-specific content throughout their academic preparation, K–12. With this idea of academic preparation was also coupled the idea of young people as future citizens and mass schooling being broad socialization of future citizens. The other distinct element is the idea for a growing and global emphasis on the curriculum as personally relevant, including student choice and responding to the needs of the individual learner or child.

# History of General Education Curriculum Emphases

In order to understand the history of gifted education curriculum, one must first begin with an historical understanding of general education curriculum emphases over the last century. Kelting-Gibson (2013) conducted an analysis of curriculum design and provided a historical overview of the evolution of general education curriculum. By understanding the primary authors and emphases over time, one can begin to speculate how the history of gifted and advanced curriculum emerged over time and the degree to which it dovetails or diverges from its general education curriculum predecessors. Table 2.1 describes the primary authors and curriculum emphases of the 20th century.

General education curriculum emphases over the last century have swung from a focus on curriculum as a science with steps, processes, and outcomes to curriculum whose goals are to engage and deepen the understandings of the learner and allow the teacher to determine the best avenues to reach the student. Curriculum for gifted learners has in some instances been directly linked to general education emphases. An example of this is the utilization of Hilda Taba's framework, which forms one of the key components of the Center for Gifted Education at William & Mary's English language arts units of study. In other instances, curriculum in gifted education has taken more of a buffet approach, picking and choosing aspects of different emphases, such as Gardner, Bruner, or Wiggins and McTighe's work and incorporating it within a local context. This approach is more heavily teacher dependent.

# Table 2.1

*Major Historical Curriculum Emphases of the 20th Century*

| Timeframe | Primary Author(s) | General Education Curriculum Emphases |
|---|---|---|
| Early 1900s | Franklin Bobbit | • Published a book in 1918 called *The Curriculum* which viewed curriculum as a science, "which children and youth must do and experience by way of developing abilities to do things well and make up the affairs of adult life" (Bobbit, 1918, p. 42).<br>• Bobbit's premise was to outline the knowledge that would be important for each content area, and then develop activities to train the learner and improve his or her performance. |
| Early 1900s | William Kilpatrick | • Published an article, *The Project Method*, in 1918 arguing that each child should have considerable input in the planning of curriculum along with the teacher.<br>• "We saw how far intent and attitude go in determining learning" (Kilpatrick, 1932, p. 119). |
| 1920s–1930s | Harold Rugg | • Chaired a committee that developed two volumes of *The Twenty-Sixth Yearbook of the National Society for the Study of Education* (NSSE); *Part I: Curriculum-Making: Past and Present* (1926) and *Part II, The Foundations of Curriculum Making* (1930).<br>• Role was to plan curriculum in advance and include four tasks: (1) A statement of objectives, (2) a sequence of experiences, (3) subject matter to be found, and (4) outcomes of achievement derived from the experiences. |
| 1920s–1930s | Hollis Caswell and Doak Campbell | • Thought curriculum represented a method of incorporating the scientific process, organization, instruction, and evaluation.<br>• Caswell was the curriculum advisor for the state of Virginia from 1931–32. He created a statewide course of study for elementary education. |
| 1940s–1950s | Ralph Tyler | • Played a key role in evaluating the *Eight-Year Study*, which was an ambitious effort to determine if a progressive or traditional curriculum was more effective.<br>• Wrote a book in 1950, *Basic Principles of Curriculum and Instruction*, which covered four basic questions curriculum developers need to answer when writing curriculum and planning instruction: (1) What educational purposes should the school seek to attain? (2) What educational experiences can be provided that are likely to attain these purposes? (3) How can these educational experiences be effectively organized? (4) How can we determine whether these purposes are being attained? |

**Table 2.1,** *continued*

| Timeframe | Primary Author(s) | General Education Curriculum Emphases |
|---|---|---|
| 1960s | Hilda Taba | • Colleague of Ralph Tyler, expanded Tyler's model and developed her own.<br>• Taba's approach (1962) included seven major steps to curriculum design: (1) diagnosis of needs, (2) formulation of objectives, (3) selection of content, (4) organization of content, (5) selection of learning experiences, (6) organization of learning experiences, and (7) an evaluation. |
| 1970s | Jerome Bruner | • Constructivist theory became the general framework for instruction based upon the study of cognition.<br>• A major premise of Bruner's work was that learning was an active process in which the learner constructed new ideas based upon his or her current or past knowledge while interacting with new information. |
| 1970s–1980s | Madeline Hunter | • Began her work with colleagues at UCLA and developed a set of prescriptive teaching practices designed to improve teacher decision making and thus, enhance student learning.<br>• At the forefront of Hunter's teachings was student motivation and staff development.<br>• Hunter's 7-step model guided views of teaching in the 1980s and started a trend focused on staff development, which continues today. |
| 1990s | Howard Gardner | • Best known for his theory of Multiple Intelligences but also was involved in *Teaching for Understanding* research.<br>• Conducted research in the area of authentic instruction. Students were given the opportunity to choose authentic instruction in a field of study in their own ways.<br>• Believed that performance of disciplinary understanding occurred when students took information and skills learned, in ways they learn best, and applied them flexibly and appropriately in new and unanticipated situations. |

**Table 2.1**, *continued*

| Timeframe | Primary Author(s) | General Education Curriculum Emphases |
|---|---|---|
| 1990s | David Perkins | • Codirector of Project Zero with Howard Gardner. Brought university and public school teachers together for a series of meetings to arrange research toward pedagogy of understanding.<br>• Placed understanding at the forefront of his research.<br>• Perkins (1992) stated, "We know a lot about how to educate well. The problem comes down to this: We are not putting to work what we know" (p. 2). He stated that it was important for students to develop understandings and not just memorize facts and figures. |
| 1990s–2000s | Grant Wiggins and Jay McTighe | • Backward design is a process of curriculum development that integrates the works of Bruner, Gardner, and Perkins as well as authentic learning by Newmann and Wehlage from the University of Wisconsin.<br>• Designed a procedure to encourage educators to focus on enduring understandings when designing curriculum and to use more standards-based (as opposed to activity-based) instruction.<br>• The backward design approach encourages teachers to think like assessors, not activity designers. |

# Emergence of Gifted Education Curriculum

Curriculum considerations, and research on appropriate curriculum for gifted children did not receive separate attention until the 1980s, even though special classes, a national definition, and acceleration research and practices had been operationalized around the country since the early 1900s (Colangelo, Assouline, & Gross, 2004). According to VanTassel-Baska's (2004) retrospective review of seminal work in curriculum for the gifted, the emphasis of curriculum studies for the past 30 years falls into the following four main areas: (a) the values and relevance factors of a curriculum for the gifted, (b) the technology of curriculum development, (c) aspects of differentiation of a curriculum for the gifted within core subject areas and without, and (d) the research-based efficacy of differentiated curriculum and related instruction. In 1986 and 1998 respectively, *Gifted Child Quarterly* devoted special issues dedicated to curriculum and those who devoted their life's work to curriculum for the gifted, such as A. Harry Passow. In an interview (Kirschenbaum, 2004), Passow explained that as a result of Sputnik, the National Defense Education Act (NDEA) was passed in 1958 and provided the impetus for curriculum reform in science, math, and foreign languages that was originally designed to improve the math and science curriculum for bright students: "The passage of the NDEA was an acknowledgement that bright students needed a differentiated curriculum in the content areas in order to maximize their educational development" (p. 15). According to Passow (Kirschenbaum, 2004), in the late 1950s the focus was on administrative ways of taking care of gifted children, such as enrichment in the regular classroom, ability grouping, and acceleration. Although those foci are still present in today's educational environments, there has been a shift in the last 60 years, to more attention on curriculum differentiation and customization of learning through instructional strategies and numerous gifted program models.

The two macro approaches employed in the gifted field for planning and delivery curriculum has been enrichment or acceleration. Both approaches have been explicitly used in gifted education for the last 40 years for developing curriculum frameworks, student placement arrangements, classroom practice, and teacher training models (VanTassel-Baska & Brown, 2007).

An example of a successful approach in secondary classrooms has been content acceleration for advanced secondary students (VanTassel-Baska, 1998), through the proliferation of Advanced Placement and International Baccalaureate programs over the last several decades. Many educators worldwide perceive the International Baccalaureate (IB) program and the College Board Advanced Placement Program (AP) as representing the highest levels of academic attainment available. These programs are thought to provide important stepping stones to successful college work because they constitute the beginning entry levels of such work. Thus, one approach to curriculum development for the gifted may be seen as a "design down" model, where all curricula at the K–12 level are organized to promote readiness for college and the process is both accelerated and shortened along the way for the most able. Providing advanced-level content to younger students, such as AP courses, represents an accelerative approach in design and delivery.

Accelerative approaches to learning owe much to the work of Terman and Oden (1947), Pressey (1949), and early developers of rapid learning classes that enabled bright students to progress at their own rates. Early applications of accelerative learning can be found in the Johns Hopkins Studies of Mathematically Precocious Youth (SMPY; Stanley, 1976), where the originators called it *fast-paced academic programs* or *radical acceleration*. SMPY offered courses designed for students in the upper 5% of the school population and delivered the courses, typically during the summer, in a telescoping, compressed, accelerated fashion. Today, several talent search programs across the country, particularly in mathematics (Stanley, Keating, & Fox, 1974), still model their summer programs for gifted students based on earlier SMPY accelerative design principles.

Alternatives to this approach tend to focus on learning beyond, or in lieu of, traditional content academics. Many of the gifted education curriculum models ascribe to an enriched view of curriculum development for the gifted, a view that addresses a broader conception of giftedness, taking into account principles of creativity, motivation, and independence as crucial constructs to the development of high ability. These enrichment views also tend to see process skills, such as critical thinking and creative problem solving, as central to the learning enterprise, with content choices being more incidental. Evidence of student work through high-quality products and performances also is typically highly valued in these models (Renzulli, 1977).

Most of the enrichment-oriented approaches to curriculum development for the gifted emanated from the early work of Hollingworth and her curriculum template for New York City self-contained classes. She was strongly influenced by Dewey's theory of progressivism, and organized curriculum units that allowed students to discover connections about how the world worked and the role of creative people in societal progress. She achieved this by having students study biographies, while promoting the role of group learning through discussion and conversation about ideas (Hollingworth, 1926).

Thus, current curriculum gifted education models are grounded in a history of general education curriculum emphases, research, development, and implementation of both academic preparation and responding to the individual needs of the learner.

# Factors Driving the Idea of Appropriate Curriculum for the Gifted: The Learner, the Context, the Teacher

Our perception of appropriate curriculum for the gifted has been guided over time by three primary forces: the learner, the context, and the teacher. Advanced learners, like other learners, need help in developing their abilities. Yet, advanced learners are typically served in general education contexts with limited interaction with like-ability peers. Lastly, without teachers who coach for growth and curricula that are appropriately challenging, these learners may fail to achieve their potential. Figure 2.1 highlights the main influences on the evolution of curriculum for gifted learners.

## The Learner

Advanced learners, like all learners, need learning experiences designed to fit their needs. When teachers are not sensitive to such needs, they may set learning goals for advanced students that are too low or that develop new skills too infrequently. Then, if students are successful anyhow, they

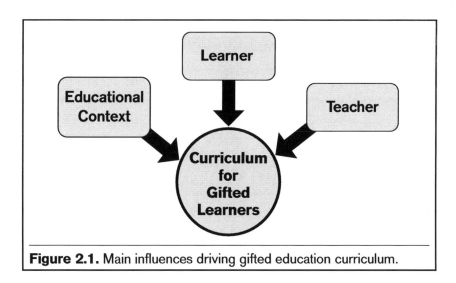

**Figure 2.1.** Main influences driving gifted education curriculum.

often fail to develop the desirable balance between running into walls and scaling them. Advanced learners share other learners' need for teachers who can help them set high goals, devise plans for reaching those goals, tolerate frustrations and share joys along the way, and sight new horizons after each accomplishment. The following factors focused on the learner form some of the rationale for why gifted education curriculum should be differentiated.

◆ **Gifted children's rate of learning is different from other age peers, and accommodating that rate is critical to their development (Keating, 1976; VanTassel-Baska, 1998; Ward, 1961).** It is difficult to generalize about students who are gifted because their characteristics and needs are so personal and unique. However, as a group, they comprehend complex ideas quickly, learn more rapidly and in greater depth than their age peers, and may exhibit interests that differ from those of their peers. They need time for in-depth exploration, to manipulate ideas and draw generalizations about seemingly unconnected concepts, and to ask provocative questions. Feldman's (1986) work on talent development found that gifted children proceed through stages of cognitive development more rapidly than their age peers, and thereby accounted for why a young child can reach adult levels of performance.

◆ **Research in teaching and learning.** Studies of thinking, whether developing expertise in a domain (Bereiter, 2002), intelligence (Gardner, 2000; Sternberg, 2000), or human development of engaging students in optimal learning experiences (Csikszentmihalyi, 2000) have added important contributions to the field of curriculum and allowed gifted education a framework for curriculum planning in response to learner needs. Domains, such as mathematics, incorporate not only subject matter content but also distinct approaches to learning in order to develop expertise and mastery. Research on expertise and creativity has shown that experts and novices differ in metacognitive and executive control of cognition and the talent development process is a multidimensional and dynamic process (Simonton, 2001).

◆ **Advanced learners may become perfectionists.** We praise them for being the best readers, assign them to help others who struggle with math, and compliment them when they score the highest on tests. When people get excited about their performance, these students often assume it's possible to keep being the best. Because they attach so much of their self-worth to the rewards of schooling and because those rewards are accessible for years at a time, advanced learners often do not learn to struggle or fail (Nugent, 2000). Failure then becomes something to avoid at all costs. Some advanced learners develop compulsive behaviors, from excessive worry, to procrastination, to eating disorders, and occasionally even suicide. Many advanced learners simply become less productive and less satisfied.

◆ **Advanced learners may fail to develop study and coping skills.** When students coast through school with only modest effort, they may look successful. In fact, however, success in life typically follows persistence, hard work, and risk. In many cases, advanced learners make good grades without learning to work hard. They may have a fixed mindset that precludes them from hard work or effort (Dweck, 2010). Then when hard work is required, they become frightened, resentful, or frustrated. In addition, they "succeed" without having to learn to study or grapple with ideas or persist in the face of uncertainty. We graduate many highly able students with "evidence" that success requires minimal effort and without the skills necessary to achieve when they discover that "evidence" is invalid.

◆ **Talent can be lost.** The debate about nature versus nurture and the degree to which each is incorporated into the talent development process of an individual continues. Ability does not necessarily translate to performance. Genetic traits do not manifest themselves all at once at birth, and different individuals may begin to exhibit the same talent at different ages. Talent is a dynamic process. Therefore, talent is not stable over time and can be lost. The "promising child" can become a mediocre adult, or in other instances an individual can become a late bloomer in a talent domain. Taken together, the implications suggest that robust, complex curriculum may be the antidote for losing talent over time (Simonton, 2001).

An effective curriculum for students who are gifted is essentially a basic curriculum that has been modified to meet their academic and social-emotional needs. The unique characteristics of the students must serve as the basis for decisions on how the curriculum should be modified (Maker, 1982; VanTassel-Baska, 2004). A program that builds on these characteristics may be viewed as qualitatively (rather than quantitatively) different from the basic curriculum; it results from appropriate modification of content, process, environment, and product (Maker, 1982). Moreover, current research on learning, such as domain-specificity or expertise, informs our thinking about curriculum for the gifted (National Research Council, 2000). Expertise studies have shown that experts and novices differ in metacognitive and executive control of cognition (Bereiter & Scardamalia, 1993; Lesgold, 1984). Therefore, general education curriculum as it is currently operationalized is insufficient to meet the needs of advanced learners. Working like an expert also involves thinking like one. Integrating higher level processing skills in the curriculum—those an expert is likely to use—is therefore crucial. For example, in a typical mathematics scope and sequence, there is too much repetition and practice on procedural knowledge (e.g., computation) instead of conceptual understandings or application of knowledge. Because gifted learners learn at a faster rate, less time is needed for mastery of factual knowledge and more time is needed on deepening the sophistication of knowledge.

## Educational Context

The educational context has driven gifted education curriculum. School reform is more complex because our society is more complex and the implications lead to changes in standards, teacher evaluation, and student accountability measures. Gifted students, while unique and diverse, are part of the overall school population. As such, external mandates from state and federal agencies focused on curriculum have always had, and always will, have implications for curriculum for the gifted. The following external contextual factors have influenced curriculum emphases for the gifted.

- **Field of developmental psychology.** For the last half of the 20th century, when a scope and sequence of K–12 curriculum was formally operationalized, one of the lenses used to determine which grade level certain content, such as algebra, would be implemented was due to the developmental stages of the learner as posited by Piaget's theory of intellectual development (Simatwa, 2010).

- **Infusion of "higher order" thinking skills (Bloom, 1956).** Business decried that our students cannot problem solve, work in teams, or reason deductively. A schema for organizing educational objectives and increasing levels of thinking was fused into curriculum and instruction through the work of Benjamin Bloom and colleagues. Today, curriculum designers and planners still use Bloom's thinking taxonomy as a way to organize instructional processes. Bloom's (1956) taxonomy of educational objectives are ordered from simple to complex and concrete to abstract. It assumed a cumulative hierarchy. Today, that taxonomy has been revised to represent a two-dimensional framework of "knowledge and cognitive processes" (Krathwohl, 2002), still primarily arranged in a hierarchical structure but not a rigidly. Additionally, the revised taxonomy was created to represent a more current view of the empirical evidence of cognitive processing (Anderson et al., 2001).

- **Accountability and No Child Left Behind (NCLB).** Using tests as benchmarks of student competencies for educational progress was the hallmark of the No Child Left Behind Act by focusing educational policy on raising student achievement to proficient levels on state assessments. Legislative measures designed to ensure that all students meet minimal expectations have concerned leaders in gifted education for years because the ceiling has been grade-level expectations with a focus on minimum versus maximum competencies.

- **Common Core State Standards (CCSS).** Typically, the content that the gifted receive in a general school program is minimal compared to what they are capable of learning. The National Governors Association for Best Practices and the Council of Chief State School Officers (2010), developers of the Common Core State Standards, acknowledged that advanced learners may move through the standards more readily than other learners. International studies show U.S. students lag behind students in many other nations in core content areas, which was one of the drivers behind the adoption of Common Core State Standards. In every educational context, gifted learners are expected to learn the content standards and be assessed on them, therefore gifted education can ill-afford not to be vested in CCSS (Brown, 2014).

◆ **School reform initiatives.** One of the social forces driving curriculum reform as a nation is meeting workforce needs whether domestically or internationally. Terms such as *college and career ready*, *internationally competitive*, or *increasing intellectual capital* are all used in numerous reports to document American students' performance. Curriculum planning through this lens is less about classroom activities and more about strategic long-term planning, implementation, and consequences. The mandated curriculum reform plan articulates a set of expectations to gifted students and others. Because gifted students learn high-level material at different rates and levels of proficiency, curriculum planning must incorporate variation and flexibility as a way to balance a focus on the individual and the content. A curriculum plan helps ensure educational quality for gifted students. Curriculum development for the gifted has to be viewed as a long-term process involving adaptation of the general curriculum and/or augmenting the curriculum with robust complex material appropriate to the learner's precocities rather than adding or deleting curriculum. Curriculum for the gifted involves the interaction between the content, instruction, and assessment dimensions as well as the logistical issues of context, scope and sequence, and student outcomes. Curriculum goals, which are embedded or aligned with the school or school system's goals, should be developed, and accountability measures should be in place to determine how these goals are met.

## The Teacher

Every teacher is not able to or interested in being a curriculum writer and developer, yet they are expected to create differentiated experiences for each child based on a generalized curriculum aimed at grade-level standards. The major purpose for developing curriculum for the gifted is based on knowledge that teachers are responsible and accountable for presenting a set of common standards and expectations. Although there may be an understanding that modification to meet the needs, interests, and abilities of individual students is essential, it is naive to believe this occurs (Westberg & Daoust, 2003). Therefore, it is important to recognize that design, intention, and developed curriculum for the gifted matters.

◆ **Expertise.** It is clear that certain instructional strategies and best practices used for gifted students are being increasingly absorbed into general education by reform models intended to upgrade the performance of all students. Subject matter expertise for teachers is essential for gifted learners due to their advanced precocities in content domains. In addition to subject matter expertise, teachers of the gifted are expected to differentiate curriculum. Differentiation is one key strategy that can benefit all learners, but it also is widely known that without specialized training, teachers find it difficult to implement differentiation in a manner that benefits students at all levels of ability (Tomlinson, 2001). Even when training is available, all too often it focuses on simplifying instruction for lower-level learners without a corresponding emphasis on how to make instruction more in-depth and complex for students with high learning potential. Effective teachers guide students to use their ability to explore their interests as deeply as possible to dive into subject matter content.

◆ **Teacher preparation.** The importance of teacher preparation is so critical to the field that accreditation standards for teacher preparation programs in gifted education were developed through a joint effort between the two largest advocacy associations: Council for Exceptional Children (CEC) and National Association for Gifted Children (NAGC). It is this preparation that creates a specialist (Gallagher, 2000). Currently, there is an endorsed set of teacher preparation program standards for institutions of higher education that offer specialized coursework in gifted education. The 2013 teacher preparation standards revise and update the

2006 standards, which have been in use for program development
and NCATE/CAEP reviews since 2007. Each of the seven standards represents important emphases within a program of study
in gifted education for preservice or in-service educators seeking
their initial preparation in this field.

◆ **Advocacy.** Teachers not only have to differentiate and respond to
the diverse needs of gifted learners, they also assume de facto positions of having to advocate, persuade, and collaborate with other
educators, administrators, and the home in order to ensure that
appropriate resources and efforts are provided on behalf of these
learners. Many teachers are not equipped with the skills and dispositions of effective advocates and often may find themselves in
defensive postures with colleagues or as the only point person for
gifted students when parents have questions. Moreover, teachers
may find themselves in classrooms or schools that are ill-equipped
with sufficiently complex materials for gifted students and then
have to divert time from teaching to grant writing, connecting
with local resources such as museums, and finding subject matter
experts to work as mentors in order to appropriately serve gifted
students.

# Conclusion

Gifted education curriculum theory and practice have been influenced
based on social and political forces as well as human development theory in
cognition. This chapter has provided a historical overview of general education curriculum emphases and provided considerations for how those
emphases have shaped our thinking about gifted education curriculum.
It has provided a rationale of factors from three areas (learner, context,
teacher) for why curriculum for gifted students should be differentiated.
The chapter implicitly focuses on the tension between where gifted education curriculum is nested. At times, it is more akin to general education as demonstrated through the implementation of content standards.
At other times, it is more aligned to special education whose emphasis on
the learner is at the heart of differentiation. The application of curriculum

differs across states, local school districts, and even within school districts, schools, and grade levels. Curriculum for gifted and advanced students should contain accelerative and enrichment components. It should be blended with the emphases of general education curriculum while customizing to address the needs of the learner.

# References

Anderson, L., Krathwohl, D., Airasian, P., Cruikshank, K., Mayer, R., Pintrich, P., . . . Wittrock, M. C. (2001). *A taxonomy for learning, teaching, and assessing: A revision of Bloom's Taxonomy of Educational Objectives* (Complete edition). New York, NY: Longman.

Baker, D., & LeTendre, G. (2005). *National differences, global similarities: World culture and the future of schooling.* Stanford, CA: Stanford University Press.

Bereiter, C. (2002). *Education and mind in the knowledge age.* Mahwah, NJ: Lawrence Erlbaum.

Bereiter, C., & Scardamalia, M. (1993). *Surpassing ourselves: An inquiry into the nature and implications of expertise.* Chicago, IL: Open Court.

Bloom, B. S. (1956). *Taxonomy of education objectives: The classification of educational goals.* New York, NY: D. McKay.

Bobbit, F. (1918). *The curriculum.* Boston, MA: Houghton Mifflin.

Brown, E. (2014). Common Core State Standards and gifted education. In F. A. Karnes & S. .M. Bean (Eds.), *Methods and materials for teaching the gifted* (4th ed., pp. 43–65). Waco TX: Prufrock Press.

Colangelo, N., Assouline, S., & Gross, M. U. M. (2004). *A nation deceived: How schools hold back America's brightest students.* Iowa City: University of Iowa, The Connie Belin & Jacqueline N. Blank International Center for Gifted Education and Talent Development.

Csikszentmihalyi, M. (2000). *Intrinsic motivation.* Paper presented at the Northwestern University Phi Delta Kappa Research Symposium.

Dweck, C. S. (2010). Even geniuses work hard. *Educational Leadership, 68*(1), 16–20.

Feldman, D. (1986). Nature's gambit: Child prodigies and the development of human potential. In R. J. Sternberg & J. E. Davidson (Eds.),

*Conceptions of giftedness* (2nd ed., pp. 98–119). New York, NY: Cambridge University Press

Gallagher, J. (2000). Unthinkable thoughts. Education of gifted students. *Gifted Child Quarterly, 44,* 5–12.

Gardner, H. (2000). *Intelligence reframed: Multiple intelligences for the 21st century.* New York, NY: Basic Books.

Hollingworth, L. (1926). *Gifted children: Their nature and nurture.* New York, NY: Macmillan.

Keating, D. (1976). *Intellectual talent.* Baltimore, MD: Johns Hopkins University Press.

Kelting-Gibson, L. (2013). Analysis of 100 years of curriculum design. *International Journal of Instruction, 6*(1), 39–58.

Kilpatrick, W. (1932). *Education and the social crisis.* New York, NY: Liveright Publishing.

Kirschenbaum, R. J. (2004). Interview with Dr. A. Henry Passow. In J. Van Tassel-Baska (Ed.), *Curriculum for gifted and talented students* (pp. 13–24). Thousand Oaks, CA: Corwin Press.

Krathwohl, D. (2002). A revision of Bloom's taxonomy: An overview. *Theory Into Practice, 41,* 212–218.

Lesgold, A. (1984). *Human skill in a computerized society.* Austin, TX: Psychonomic Society.

Maker, C. J. (1982). *Curriculum development for the gifted.* Rockville, MD: Aspen.

Meyer, J. W. (1992). *School knowledge for the masses. World models and national primary curricular categories in the twentieth century.* London, England: Falmer.

National Governors Association Center for Best Practices, & Council of Chief State School Offices. (2010). *Common Core State Standards for English language arts.* Washington, DC: Authors.

National Research Council. (2000). *How people learn: Brain, mind, experience and school.* Washington, DC: National Academy Press.

Nugent, S. (2000). Perfectionism: Its manifestations and classroom-based interventions. *The Journal of Secondary Gifted Education, 11,* 215–221.

Perkins, D. (1992). *Smart schools.* New York, NY: The Free Press.

Pressey, S. L. (1949). *Educational acceleration: Appraisal of basic problems.* Bureau of Educational Research Monograph No. 31. Columbus: The Ohio State University Press.

Renzulli, J. (1977). *The Enrichment Triad Model.* Mansfield Center, CT: Creative Learning Press.

Rugg, H. (1926). *The twenty-sixth yearbook of the National Society for the Study of Education*. Bloomington, IL: Public School Publishing Company.

Rugg, H. (1930). *The twenty-sixth yearbook of the National Society for the Study of Education. Foundations of Curriculum-Making, Yearbook, Part II*. Bloomington, IL: Public School Publishing Company.

Simatwa, E. (2010). Piaget's theory of intellectual development and its implication for instructional management at pre-secondary school level. *Educational Research and Reviews, 5*, 366–371.

Simonton, D. K. (2001). Talent development as a multidimensional, multiplicative, and dynamic process. *Current Directions in Psychological Science, 10*(2), 39–43.

Stanley, J., Keating, D., & Fox, L. (1974). *Mathematical talent*. Baltimore, MD: Johns Hopkins University Press.

Stanley, J. C. (1976). Youths who reason extremely well mathematically: SMPY's accelerative approach. *Gifted Child Quarterly, 20*, 237–238.

Sternberg, R. (2000). *Teaching for successful intelligence to increase student learning and achievement*. Arlington Heights, IL: Skylight Professional Development.

Taba, H. (1962). *Curriculum development theory and practice*. New York, NY: Harcourt, Brace, & World.

Terman, L., & Oden, M. (1947). *The gifted child grows up*. Stanford, CA: Stanford University Press.

Tomlinson, C. A. (2001). *How to differentiate instruction in mixed-ability classrooms* (2nd ed.). Alexandria, VA: ASCD.

Tyler, R. (1950). *Basic principles of curriculum and instruction*. Chicago, IL: University of Chicago Press.

VanTassel-Baska, J. (1998). *Excellence in educating gifted and talented learners* (3rd ed.). Denver, CO: Love.

VanTassel-Baska, J. (Ed.). (2004). *Curriculum for gifted and talented students*. Thousand Oaks, CA: Corwin Press.

VanTassel-Baska, J., & Brown, E. (2007). Toward best practice: An analysis of the efficacy of curriculum models in gifted education. *Gifted Child Quarterly, 51*, 342–358.

Ward, V. (1961). *Educating the gifted, an axiomatic approach*. Columbus, OH: Merrill.

Westberg, K. L., & Daoust, M. E. (2003, Fall). The results of the replication of the classroom practices survey replication in two states. *The National Research Center on Gifted and Talented Newsletter*, 3–8.

# CHAPTER 3

# General Curriculum Design

*Principles and Best Practices*

**Jessica A. Hockett and Catherine M. Brighton**

In many ways, curriculum is the *raison d'etre* of gifted education. Whether by default or intention, gifted students are implied to be those students for whom some aspect of general education curriculum is unchallenging, inappropriate, or unsuitable. These students require curriculum that is tailored to their advanced abilities, so the argument goes, and therefore need or deserve to be "rescued" from the general education curriculum via special programs and classes that will provide "gifted" or advanced curriculum that will help them reach their full potential.

This line of thinking seems reasonable and tidy. Unfortunately, it bypasses several troubling and difficult-to-ignore realities when it comes to actual schools and programs. *Many* students—not just those with advanced abilities—experience less-than-ideal curriculum that does little to help them grow academically from their individual starting points. It is rarely the case that where the general education curriculum can be rightly characterized as disengaging, uninspiring, and lacking rigor and relevance for gifted students, it is otherwise appropriate or optimal for everyone else. And, far too often, curriculum that is reserved for gifted programs is disconnected from disciplinary content and skills, engages students in activities that all students could do, is better-suited to afterschool clubs, or simply gives students "more" work to do. In other words, the curricula that students identified as gifted receive instead of or as a supplement to the general education curriculum does little to solve the problem that the general education curriculum purportedly creates.

Admittedly, comparing low-quality general education curriculum with low-quality gifted programming curriculum creates a kind of catch-22 that pits the worst of both against one another. Do we want students working with low-level, worksheet-driven lessons; fun activities that are disconnected from standards and disciplinary content; or mountains of information to spit back on tests? Of course, the answer is *none of the above*. At minimum, any curriculum reserved for or designated as more appropriate for students with advanced abilities in a discipline must meet *both* quality criteria for general education curriculum *and* quality criteria for gifted education curriculum.

This chapter examines principles and best practices for designing such curricula. We use three categories to discuss curriculum: (1) the source and organization of curriculum; (2) the goals and priorities of curriculum; and (3) the tailoring of curriculum. Within each category, we delineate principles for curriculum design for *all* students based on consensus among professional organizations, standards documents, and curriculum experts in general and gifted education. Our assumption is that curriculum is not high quality for any students, including gifted students, unless it first meets these standards.

# The Source and Organization of Curricular Content

What is the basis or source of curricular content? In other words, where should it "come from," and how should it be organized? Four general principles provide guidance.

## Principle 1: High-Quality Curriculum for All Students Is Rooted in the Disciplines

The starting point for selecting curricular content is not standards documents, textbooks, or district curriculum, but the disciplines themselves. Mathematics, science, history, the study of language and literature, technical subjects, and the arts form the foundation for most of what students learn in school. Well-crafted standards, textbooks, and national, state, or local curriculum frameworks and guides should *also* be discipline-oriented, but they are not the root source or foundation. Rather, the discipline itself should inform the emphasis, scope, and sequence of the curriculum.

When curriculum has a discipline-based orientation, it maintains fidelity to the essential content and ideas of the discipline, regardless of the age, grade level, or readiness of the students. Jerome Bruner (1960) asserted, "any subject can be taught effectively in some intellectually honest form to any child at any age of development" (p . 33). In other words, even young children should be learning some version of "real" biology, history, etc. A real botanist, for instance, shouldn't be shocked or dismayed by what the local kindergarten class is learning about plants and could recognize and defend it as true to the field of botany.

Curriculum designers, then, use the key concepts, organizing principles, and structure of the discipline as a framework for "seeing" the facts, theories, generalizations, laws, and skills that are most essential to an area of study and for selecting those most appropriate to a grade level or course. Because students are most likely to retain and transfer knowledge and skills when curriculum is focused on a few core ideas, it's critical that those ideas reside at the heart of the discipline, not tangentially to or alongside it. Perhaps not in the early grades, but over time students should be able to see where the discipline "fits" within the larger body of knowledge and whence it originates. The idea is for students to see knowledge as a whole rather than as discrete or disparate parts.

Even the most critical aspects of a discipline constitute a vast body of content. Therefore, designers must focus on that which is fundamental and enduring to the discipline. Given the constraints of time, curriculum can't afford to be distracted or waylaid by trivial topics, esoteric minutia, or laundry lists of facts. Bruner (1960) offered a simple test for sifting through the possibilities:

> We might ask, as a criterion for any subject taught in primary school, whether, when fully developed, it is worth an adult's knowing, and whether having known it makes a person a better adult. If the answer to both questions is negative or ambiguous, then the material is cluttering the curriculum (p. 52).

National science and mathematics standards documents (National Council of Teachers of Mathematics [NCTM], 2000; National Research Council [NRC], 1999) suggest that topics and content have importance and staying power if they are:

- useful in developing ideas and connecting areas across the discipline;
- representative of events or phenomena in the natural world;
- valuable for solving problems within or beyond the discipline;
- applicable to everyday situations and contexts;
- able to guide worthwhile investigations; and
- beneficial in deepening students' appreciation for the discipline.

Wiggins and McTighe (1998) take a similar view. According to their criteria, content that is enduring: (1) lies at the core of the discipline, (2) has lasting importance and meaning beyond the classroom, (3) reveals abstract or frequently misunderstood ideas, and (4) offers promise for engaging students.

Perhaps the telltale sign of a discipline-oriented curriculum is that the critical content, processes, and products and performances with which students engage are authentic to and mimic the work of practicing professionals. The curriculum is essentially a vehicle through which students develop the habits and skills of those who actually "do" the discipline. It brings the discipline to the student by approximating the conditions, problems, and questions faced by real writers, economists, geologists, statisticians, etc., as well as by everyday people.

## Principle 2: High-Quality Curriculum for All Students Is Relevant and Engaging

Curriculum that is discipline-based needn't be the educational equivalent of limp broccoli or a painful shot. On the contrary, high-quality curriculum should *invite* students into the study of a discipline by being relevant and engaging—two related, yet distinct attributes. Both relevance and engagement require meaningful connections between the student and what he or she is learning. Relevance refers to the *proximity* of the connection and engagement to the *duration* and *degree* of the connection.

For curriculum to be *relevant*, students must see and understand how it connects to their own lives—to what they have learned and experienced both in and outside of school—as well as to its importance for their futures in specific fields and as participating citizens. Relevance can likewise involve connections to daily life, real-world concerns, current events, and community interests that are significant to students and adults. A student's cultural background, gender, grade level, general interests, and out-of-school experiences are also factors to consider in ensuring that students "see themselves" in the curriculum.

Curriculum that is *engaging* sustains students cognitively and affectively by enticing them to invest time, energy, attention, and resources to grappling with worthy and challenging ideas and attaining pivotal knowledge and skills. Although engagement is also an instructional enterprise (i.e., teachers using instruction to engage students in the curriculum), the content, processes, and products that anchor the curriculum should be intuitively and predictably appealing to students in the target grade level.

It is crucial for curriculum designers to view relevance and engagement as *connected to* discipline-based content. There are numerous curricular topics that might be relevant and engaging to students but that are not authentic to a discipline or a wise use of instructional time. The challenge in curriculum design is to make prioritized disciplinary content and skills "come alive" to students by filtering it through the lenses of relevance and engagement.

## Principle 3: High-Quality Curriculum for All Students Is Integrative and Balances Breadth With Depth

Few experts, if any, condone teaching subjects as isolated entities. Likewise, few see curricular breadth and depth as an either/or proposition between which curriculum designers must choose. Some degree of integration and balance between breadth and depth is likely requisite to high-quality curriculum.

At its core, integration can allow students to see how ideas build on and relate to one another, how ideas form patterns and connections at a conceptual level, and how ideas form an integrated whole (Erickson, 2002; NCTM, 2000). Although the terms *integration* and *integrated* are widely and variably used in curriculum literature, most typically, integrative refers to connections within and across disciplines. Curriculum that is interdisciplinary will integrate topics, concepts, skills, and knowledge from different content standards, different school subjects (e.g., science and history), as well as different areas of intellectual and social life. Intradisciplinary connections in curriculum show relationships between or within different subject-matter area knowledge, principles, and skills. Integration should avoid the all-too-tempting trap of blurring lines between disciplines such that each is watered down or indistinguishable. When the disciplines are "lost" in the name of integration, the real casualty is student learning. Curricula that are planned around projects, activities, and topics that seem to be close to student experience or interests (e.g., pumpkins, medieval castles) are especially susceptible to such an "integration" defense.

Integrated or not, curriculum must maintain a balance between breadth and depth, lest it become bloated or myopic. Wiggins and McTighe (1998) defined depth as getting below a topic's surface, and breadth as "the extensions, variety, and connections needed to relate disparate facts and ideas" and bring power to learning (p. 101). American curriculum is notorious for including more topics than can be taught well (Schmidt, 1997). Many experts recommend curriculum address fewer topics and focus on powerful ideas in order to better illuminate concepts (e.g., Board on Science Education [BSE] & Center for Education [CFE], 2007; NCTM, 2006; NRC, 1996, 1999). Depth in at least some areas is necessary "so that the content has a better chance to be meaningful, organized, linked firmly to children's other ideas, and to produce insight and intuition rather than rote performance" (Schmidt, 1997, p. 140). Exploring content in depth might also involve students pursuing an area of special interest at a high level, studying important issues and problems related to a topic, or spending more time on learning a topic (Kaplan, 1974; VanTassel-Baska, 1989, 2005).

### Principle 4: High-Quality Curriculum for All Students Is Concept-Based

Typical curricula are often organized by topics or even skills. But the most powerful orientation is through *concepts*. Erickson (2002) defined a concept as "a mental construct, an organizing idea that categorizes a variety of examples" (p. 56). Usually represented in 1–2 words, a concept is timeless, universal, abstract, and broad. Concepts can be general or discipline-specific. General concepts can be used to organize content within and across disciplines. Examples include *conflict, change, perspective, systems*, and *patterns*. Discipline-specific concepts are used for classifying or categorizing topics and knowledge within a particular discipline, such as *function* (mathematics), *supply and demand* (social studies), *experiment* (science), *genre* (English), *composition* (art), or *offense/defense* (physical education).

Historically, experts in gifted education have championed concepts as critical to designing curriculum for highly able learners. Research on how people learn has revealed that concepts are beneficial for all learners, not just for high-level courses or for students after they have mastered "the basics" (Bransford, Brown, & Cocking, 2000; Hattie, 2012). First, concepts bring coherence to curriculum by uniting content, topics, and skills—in effect giving students mental organizers for connecting parts and making sense of the discipline. Because concepts come from the disciplines, they are vehicles for exploring the nature of the discipline, for thinking in disciplinary ways, and for developing expertise in the discipline (NCTM, 2006; NRC, 1998).

Ultimately, concepts give students (and teachers) a sense of the "bigger picture" or larger context for what they are studying. When students understand a subject on a conceptual level—not just on a factual level—they are equipped to see relationships and detect patterns within and between disciplines (Bruner, 1960; Erickson, 2002; NCTM, 2000). Conceptual lenses for curriculum also expedite learning by helping students connect new knowledge with old knowledge, transfer understanding to new situations, and retrieve previously learned knowledge quickly (Bransford et al., 2000; Hattie, 2012; Erickson, 2002; NCTM, 2000; NRC, 1998). Concepts shouldn't replace facts, but rather give facts places to "live and breathe."

Concepts can also be useful tests for the viability and substance of potential curricular topics and texts. Considering what the topic or text is "a study in" can help focus, refine, and weed out potential subject matter.

For example, *Charlotte's Web* could be a study in *relationships*. The Civil War could be a study in *unity* and *disunity*. Plants might be viewed as a study in *structure and function*, *systems*, or *interdependence*, and fractions as a study in *equivalence* or *proportionality*.

Concepts are most valuable when they are linked to important disciplinary content and skills. A concept-*only* approach (e.g., a unit on "change" divorced from content or focused on disparate content) is not likely to increase the transfer potential of the concept and may give students generalizations and ideas without substance. Rather, concepts are most powerfully and most appropriately leveraged tools for understanding and applying disciplines.

# The Goals and Outcomes of Curriculum

Even disciplinary, concept-based curriculum that is relevant and engaging must be prioritized into clear goals and outcomes that articulate what students should ultimately be able to do with what they learned by the end of a unit, a marking period, a grade level, or their school careers. The process should "begin" with the end in mind (Erickson, 2002; NRC, 1999; Wiggins & McTighe, 1998), recognizing that there are many possible ends. National and state standards provide a starting point for this task, but they are not by themselves sufficient sources of all desired goals and outcomes.

### Principle 5: High-Quality Curriculum for All Students Is Driven by Goals and Outcomes That Emphasize Deep Understanding and Transfer

In *Principles and Standards for School Mathematics*, the National Council of Teachers of Mathematics (2000) asserted, "Learning without understanding has been a persistent problem since the 1930s" (p. 20). Curriculum experts and professional organizations define understanding as a complex, multifaceted construct, and maintain that all learning outcomes should be centered on the goal of deep understanding. When students truly understand, they (1) grasp the underlying theories, principles, processes, attitudes and beliefs in an academic discipline; (2) can apply what they learn; (3) can transfer their understanding to familiar and unfamiliar contexts; and (4) integrate many types of knowledge (e.g., NRC, 1996, 1998). Wiggins and McTighe (1998) posited that understanding has six facets: explanation, interpretation, application, perspective, empathy, and self-knowledge. This is not a hierarchy, but six ways of viewing or thinking about understanding and what it might "look like" as students reveal it though their knowledge and skills. Each facet exists on a continuum from more novice to expert. Assessing student understanding should optimally involve pinpointing where students are on those continua.

If actually doing something with knowledge and skills beyond acquiring them is one of the real purposes of education, then curriculum should require that kind of transfer. This means that after students have had time to acquire and make sense of content and skills, they must apply their understanding to a circumstance they haven't seen or encountered previously—not simply regurgitate information on tests or in term papers.

It is too often the case that when a student is identified as being advanced or highly able in a subject, the student has mastered certain knowledge and skills at or beyond the grade level, but does not have deep understanding and is not able to transfer that knowledge and skills to new problems, situations, and tasks. A curriculum devoid of understanding and opportunities for transfer hurts these students as well as all students.

## Principle 6: High-Quality Curriculum for All Students Moves Learners Toward Expertise

The National Research Council (1998) asserted that the goal of schooling in general is "moving students in the direction of more formal training (or greater expertise)" (p. 13). Expertise is not a goal or outcome reserved for gifted students, but a desirable result for all students. The NRC's (1998) extensive synthesis of research on expertise concluded that, compared to novices, experts are better able to recognize patterns, approach problems in terms of core concepts or big ideas, use selective retrieval of information, spend more time defining a problem when solving one, and have stronger metacognitive skills. They also note that the development of expertise requires a deep store of knowledge as well as a conceptual framework for the subject matter.

Curriculum that is designed for nurturing expertise has several characteristics. First, it equips students with discipline-relevant knowledge and understanding (Erickson, 2002; NRC, 1999), employs authentic materials and methods to create products (BOSE & CFE, 2007), and integrates the teaching of metacognitive skills (NRC, 1999). There are also opportunities for students to reflect and self-evaluate through reading, thinking, discussing, and writing.

Because the development of expertise is an ongoing process, high-quality curriculum allows students to develop understanding, knowledge, and skills *progressively*. Therefore, the articulation of curricular scope and sequence across grades K–12 must provide consistency and continuity. Ideas and concepts are revisited, leading toward deeper, more complex, more refined, and increasingly sophisticated levels of understanding.

National standards documents support this approach by providing stepping-stones toward expertise. For example, the Common Core State Standards in English Language Arts (National Governors Association Center for Best Practices [NGA] & Council of Chief State School Officers [CCSSO], 2010a) are designed from the College and Career Readiness Anchor Standards—descriptions of what students should be able to do in Reading, Writing, Speaking & Listening, and Language by the end of 12th grade. Meeting or exceeding these standards doesn't make a student an "expert," but the standards are certainly things that experts in various related fields can do. Similarly, the companion Common Core State Standards in Mathematics (NGA & CCSSO, 2010b) characterize the Standards for Mathematical Practice, in particular, as descriptions of "varieties of expertise that mathematics educators at all levels should seek to develop in their students . . . [that] rest on important 'processes and proficiencies' with longstanding importance in mathematics education" (p. 6). Although grade-level expectations are articulated for kindergarten through high school, in many ways these standards are more useful viewed as a kind of continuum of expertise that provides guidance for promoting student growth without limiting it.

### Principle 7: High-Quality Curriculum for All Students Emphasizes Problems, Products, and Performances That Are True-to-Life

Because quality curriculum is ultimately preparation for life, it makes sense that goals and outcomes would emphasize generating, studying, and solving real problems and emulating, producing, or evaluating products and performances that are similar to those that experts, professionals, and everyday people face. Such work creates authentic transfer and relevance for students, as well as assessment opportunities for teachers.

In the real world, both experts and everyday people pursue problems that are important and interesting. These problems are not always well defined or structured, but they are significant in some way to individuals, communities, societies, or fields of study. They call for specific and broad-based knowledge, understanding, skills, and processes. At the same time, there isn't necessarily a formula for discovering their solutions, and personal traits and dispositions may be just as important to finding the "answer" as formal training.

High-quality curriculum should include such problems, products, and performances in the form of substantive tasks and assessments. Questions such as "Who does this in real life?" "What authentic situations require this kind of thinking?" and "What would bona fide expressions of this skill look like?" can help drive the design of curriculum that emphasizes this kind of work for students.

# Tailoring Curriculum

Even the highest quality curriculum is not optimally suited to all students "as is" and therefore must be tailored. Curriculum that adheres to the principles described thus far is primed for tailoring, while a rigid, lock-step curriculum with a strict pacing guide or sequencing, for example, is less likely to accommodate a range of student needs, preferences, and differences.

### Principle 8: High-Quality Curriculum for All Students Is Flexible to Accommodate Challenge and Support Differences in Learner Development, Strengths, Interests, and Preferences

All curriculum experts, professional organizations, and standards documents recognize that students differ from one another in many ways. Students vary in their readiness relative to goals and standards, concept and language acquisition, learning preferences, cultural background, talents, abilities, achievements, and interests. The reality of such differences requires that curriculum be flexible enough for teachers to tailor for individual needs and or patterns of needs among groups of students.

Curriculum that is flexible isn't "dumbed down"; rather, it promotes "teaching up" (Tomlinson, 2012). Regardless of individual differences, a high degree of challenge and high expectations should be in place for all learners. Tasks are achievable and give students satisfaction, even if they perceive them as difficult. Classroom-based pre- and formative assessments—not just standardized tests—are the tools through which teachers determine students' existing knowledge, beliefs, experiences, and preconceptions, and use this information to plan instruction.

Flexibility in curriculum allows students to simultaneously strengthen high skill areas and develop areas of weakness (Solomon, 1998). Supports for students with disabilities or who otherwise struggle with a certain aspect of school are in place, as are modifications for when students demonstrate unusual interest or exceptional talent in a subject.

A curriculum flexible enough to respond to student differences is also developmentally appropriate. Standards, curriculum, and assessment should reflect the most recent research findings about the thinking and capabilities of children. For example, because research has shown that children are more capable at a younger age than previously thought, curriculum in the primary grades may need to be more challenging (BOSE & CFE, 2007; National Association for the Education of Young Children [NAEYC], 2003).

Finally, a flexible curriculum should allow for some degree of student choice in learning. Research suggests that taking ownership of some aspect of learning can empower students, increase intrinsic motivation, and in some cases improve learning outcomes (cf., Assor, 2012; Patall, 2012). This means that choice should be an opportunity afforded to all students by design—not reserved as a privilege for higher achievers.

# Designing Advanced Curriculum

Thus far, our design principles have focused on high-quality curriculum for all students. These principles apply equally to the design of all curricula, regardless of school, program, course type, subject matter, or grade level. Although experts in gifted education have long advocated many of the principles in some form as especially or more appropriate to gifted students, there is little reason to believe that they are not requisite for all learners. Research does not suggest, for instance, that gifted students "need" or benefit from concept-based curriculum more than other students do—or that expertise is a worthy outcome for gifted students but not for everyone else.

Again, any curriculum intended for gifted students is not high quality unless it adheres to standards of high-quality curriculum in general. That said, even high-quality curriculum isn't inherently or naturally advanced. "Advanced" is a relative distinction; that is, curriculum can be advanced relative to the grade level or age of the students, advanced in that it represents content, processes, or products that are further down the continuum of expertise in the discipline, or (ideally) both.

So, what attributes characterize curriculum that is appropriate to the development of advanced knowledge, skills, and understanding? Put differently, were we evaluating curriculum for evidence of being more advanced, what would we look for?

At minimum, curriculum designated as more advanced should be aligned with above-grade-level content and/or process standards—not just with the *idea* of above-grade-level standards, but with actual above-grade-level standards. For example, an advanced writing curriculum for third graders in an Illinois school district would be aligned with at least grade 4 Common Core State Standards in opinion, informative/explanatory, and narrative writing.

Beyond standards, the content students study, processes and skills they employ, and the products they develop as evidence of their understanding should be distinguishable as qualitatively more advanced. Here, gifted education offers myriad guidelines for consideration. Sifted and synthesized, two principles emerge that can be viewed as a second set of lenses or filters through which to evaluate or adjust curriculum in gifted programs, advanced/honors courses, and special schools.

## Principle 9: High-Quality Advanced Curriculum Pursues Advanced Levels of Understanding Through Abstraction, Complexity, Depth, and/or Breadth

As previously explained in Principle 5, deep understanding is a desirable outcome of high-quality curriculum for all students. But, the deeper or more sophisticated the understanding, the more advanced the curricular goals will likely be. In designing an advanced curriculum, there are several ways to think about articulating and having students work toward advanced understanding: abstraction, complexity, depth, and breadth. Our descriptions of these concepts are drawn from the work of respected experts and seminal publications in gifted education (Kaplan, 1974, 1994; Maker & Nielson, 1996; National Association for Gifted Children [NAGC], 1994; Passow, 1982; Purcell, Burns, Tomlinson, Imbeau, & Martin, 2002; Renzulli & Reis, 2014; Rogers, 2002; Shore, Cornell, Robinson, & Ward, 1991; Tomlinson, 1997, 1999, 2005; U.S. Department of Education, 1993; VanTassel-Baska, 2005; Ward, 1980).

- ◆ **Abstraction** involves content, processes, and products that are more removed from or less familiar to students' experiences. This might mean that students focus on the implications and extensions of ideas rather than concrete examples and illustrations. Content might focus on symbolism or stress underlying meanings. Process-wise, students might formulate theories, examine the philosophical underpinnings of disciplines, or explore epistemological issues.

- ◆ **Complexity** is another way of modifying the curriculum to advance understanding. Content can be more complex when it is more intricately detailed, integrates knowledge and concepts from various disciplines, requires higher-level thinking processes, and incorporates different perspectives, theories, principles, and concepts associated with what professionals in the discipline know and do. Processes and products are more complex when they involve more steps or require more advanced resources, tasks, issues, problems, skills, or goals. For example, students might work with multiple abstractions, merge what they are learning with previous learning, or tackle problems that require more originality or elegance in their solutions.

- ◆ Advanced understanding can also be attained through examining curricular topics in more **breadth and/or with greater depth**. In gifted education, breadth refers to exposing students to wide variety within or across a content area or, more simply, to extending the core curriculum. Kaplan (1974, 1994) defined depth as ways of intensifying curriculum—some of which might include using the language of the discipline and examining details, trends, patterns, unanswered questions, rules, ethics, big ideas, and relationships to time.

A word of caution regarding the abstraction, complexity, and depth/breath as advanced curriculum design lenses: It's easy to *say* that program or course curricula ask students to "go deeper" or is "more complex." Such claims should be supported with well-reasoned, thorough explanations and justification of why or how the curriculum of interest is so-designed and is therefore more appropriate for some students than others. Figure 3.1 summarizes ways that designers can adjust the content, process, or products in curriculum to make it more advanced.

## Principle 10: High-Quality Advanced Curriculum More Closely Approximates the Work of an Expert, Disciplinarian, or Practicing Professional.

Principles 1 and 6 speak to designing curriculum for all students that is authentic to the discipline and to what experts and professionals understand, know, and do. The closer students are to doing "the real thing" or thinking "the real way," the more advanced it is. It makes sense, then, that an advanced curriculum would more closely approximate or directly mimic the work of experts, disciplinarians, and practicing professionals, with specific implications for *materials and resources* students access, *processes* students use, and problems they solve through *products or performances* they develop. Again, these descriptions reflect and synthesize the work of curriculum experts in gifted education.

**Advanced materials and resources.** The more "expert" someone is, the more "expert-like" the materials and resources that he or she accesses, studies, relies on, and synthesizes. Such materials for the design of advanced curriculum might include resources that are highly specialized, more abstract, require higher level reading or processing skills, or presume sophisticated background knowledge. Whether text-based or multimedia, such materials and resources might treat knowledge as tentative, be

- Addressing more authentic problems and audiences
- Working and producing in increasingly expert-like ways
- Delving into content in greater depth
- Exploring content in greater breadth
- Grappling with concepts, problems, issues, or outcomes that are more ambiguous or abstract
- Creating products or solving problems that are more transformational (i.e., that try to change people's minds, provoke change, reveal new or unusual insights)
- Examining ideas behind the ideas (e.g., philosophical underpinnings, conflicting or supporting theoretical/research support, epistemological issues)
- Detecting increasingly complex patterns or connections within and across disciplines
- Analyzing and formulating rules, ethics, or governing principles
- Pursuing "known" and "unknown" unanswered questions

**Figure 3.1.** Strategies for adjusting quality curriculum for advanced learning.

conceptually oriented, or illustrate interdisciplinary connections through concepts. The idea isn't that students are simply handed such materials to figure out on their own. On the contrary, if they are sufficiently challenging, students will likely need guidance or instruction in *how* to use them.

**Advanced processes.** The *process* of working in a more authentic or expert-/professional-like way could involve general or discipline-specific methods. In either case, such methods emphasize discovery, equip students to follow advanced research or inquiry-based procedures, and involve *learning how to learn* other necessary skills on-demand.

The process of working like an expert also involves *thinking* like one. Integrating higher level processing skills that an expert is likely to use in an advanced curriculum is therefore crucial. These might include processes for thinking critically, analytically, and creatively; making decisions; asking questions; generating new ideas; defending ideas; reconciling opposing viewpoints; reconceptualizing and transferring knowledge; and solving problems. Advanced curriculum also approximates expertise by developing increasingly sophisticated metacognitive abilities and self-understanding. Importantly, all thinking processes must be rooted in content and be a means to an end, rather than taught in isolation.

**Advanced problems, products, and performances.** Renzulli (1982) asserted that the catalyst for programs and curricula for gifted learners should be solving real problems and producing real solutions via authentic products and performances for actual audiences. Often, what is more "real" *is* more expert-like. A defining characteristic of these kinds of real problems is authenticity—they closely mirror problems or actually are problems in the real world with either no existing solution or a solution that is unknown to the student; are directed toward change or the production of new knowledge; and have a personal frame of reference for the student (Renzulli, 1982). Accordingly, advanced curriculum might compel solving problems by creating products or performances that are more transformational—that is, that try to change people's minds, provoke change, or reveal new or unusual insights (Tomlinson, 1997). Such products should emulate those developed by practicing professionals in a field or at least have a discipline-based foundation. The evaluation of these products can be more advanced if the products are assessed by qualified persons, such as expert judges or audiences who stand to benefit from the results, or according to advanced criteria or "goodness-of-fit" for a certain need.

In problem solving, product development, and performance, an advanced curriculum might also prompt students to take the knowledge they have learned and view it from another perspective through reinterpretation or extension, form new generalizations and ideas, or develop skills into creative forms for real audiences.

# What Advanced Curriculum Isn't

These aforementioned principles for designing high-quality advanced curriculum should replace faulty or questionable assumptions about what advanced curriculum really is. Program or course curriculum is not advanced because it's "more"—that is, because students have more homework, write more papers, read more pages, do more problems, etc. Neither are fun projects, memorizing Shakespeare, putting fairy tale characters on trial, building bridges, engaging in creativity exercises, or doing activities that have been planned with Bloom's taxonomy proof of advanced curriculum (or of high-quality curriculum for any student).

Similarly, curriculum is not advanced because it addresses or delves into topics that aren't part of the general curriculum. For instance, a senior seminar on battles of World War II should not be labeled "honors" because of the focus. Such a seminar could be low-level and superficial, or it could thoughtfully engage students in expert-like historical inquiry, but the topic itself matters little when it comes to classifying the curriculum as advanced.

Likewise, particular areas of study are not innately advanced by pronouncement. The study of Latin, for example, has been advocated as especially suitable for students who are talented with language. National standards now suggest that learning Latin (and Greek) roots should be part and parcel of language study for all students beginning in the elementary grades. And surely a Latin 1 course is not intrinsically advanced while Spanish 1, Chinese 1, and Hebrew 1 are rudimentary.

Faster pacing or going through curriculum more quickly is also often mentioned as an attribute of advanced curriculum. This most often means *increasing* the pace of learning by moving students more rapidly through basic skills (VanTassel-Baska, 1989) or an entire course of study (Shore et al., 1991). In reality, curriculum that lends itself well to faster pacing (or acceleration or compacting) rarely adheres to the principles for quality outlined in this chapter. In fact, it's the poor quality of curriculum that gifted education experts typically cite as a reason that gifted students should proceed through it more quickly or be liberated from it altogether.

It's true that when such curricula emphasize only topics, facts, and low-level skills rather than including conceptual lenses, a focus on deep understanding and transfer, and disciplinary skills, students might complete it more quickly, but they also may not have learned much, regardless of speed. At the very least, if faster pacing is an aspect of advanced curriculum design, the curriculum at issue should be of a defensible quality. Faster pacing can't make up for low-quality curriculum. Perhaps a more useful application of speed with regard to advanced curriculum is to think in terms of *decreasing* pacing to account for gaps in students' knowledge, skills, or understanding; to accommodate in-depth study; or to make sure a student can apply what he or she has learned (Tomlinson, 2005). In this way, one might say that an objective of advanced curriculum is to "slow students down" in order to encourage their growth.

Other often-cited attributes of curriculum for gifted students fail to hold water as criterion particular to advanced curriculum. These include more opportunities for self-directed and independent learning, choice in goal-setting, chances for in-depth and interest-driven investigations, development of agency and organizational skills, and variety in materials, learning activities, skills, and learning opportunities. If these things are desirable in curriculum—and they are—then they are desirable for all students. Passow's (1982) well-known three-question "test" is a simple and elegant way of measuring curricular equity in this regard. "Would other students of this age, if they knew the expectations, want to do it?" "Could other students of this age do it?" and "Should other students of this age benefit from doing it?" If the answer to any of these questions is "yes," then the curriculum should not be reserved for gifted learners.

# Conclusion

In summary, the three categories for considering curriculum include: (1) the source and organization of the curriculum, (2) the goals and priorities of the curriculum, and (3) the tailoring of curriculum. Using these categories, quality principles for curriculum design must be met for *all* students, not just those designated as advanced or gifted.

It is also important to understand what high-quality advanced curriculum is *not*. Offering students "more" is not sufficient evidence of advanced curriculum. Also insufficient is curriculum that is just different from what is offered in the general education sequence. Qualitatively more advanced curricula should pursue advanced levels of understanding of a discipline by exploring abstraction, complexity, breadth and/or greater depth, and to seek to emulate "experts" through use of advanced materials, more sophisticated problems, and authentic products and performances.

Without question, the first, best, and most efficient way to ensure that gifted students—and all students—receive an appropriate education is to design the highest quality general education curriculum possible. Gone are the days when low-quality general education curriculum made a defensible rationale for whisking the highest achieving students out of the classroom. Low-quality curriculum in a general education program is as problematic for *all* students as it is for students who might be identified as gifted. Likewise, advanced curricula that are used in gifted program settings and honors/advanced courses should, at minimum, manifest quality criteria advised for general education curriculum design *and* be distinguishable and defensible as more appropriate for students who are receiving it than for other students by applying the principles offered in this chapter.

# References

Assor, A. (2012). Allowing choice and nurturing an inner compass: Educational practices supporting students' need for autonomy. In S. L. Christenson, A. L. Reschly, & C. Wylie (Eds.), *The handbook of research on student engagement* (pp. 421–439). New York, NY: Springer.

Board on Science Education, & Center for Education. (2007). *Taking science to school: Learning and teaching science in grades K–8.* Washington, DC: National Academies Press.

Bransford, J. S., Brown, A. L., & Cocking, R. R. (Eds.). (2000). *How people learn: Brain, mind, experience, and school.* Washington, DC: National Academies Press.

Bruner, J. S. (1960). *The process of education.* New York, NY: Vintage.

Erickson, H. L. (2002). *Concept-based curriculum and instruction: Teaching beyond the facts.* Thousand Oaks, CA: Corwin.

Hattie, J. (2012). *Visible learning for teachers: Maximizing impact on learning.* New York, NY: Routledge.

Kaplan, S. N. (1974). *Providing programs for the gifted and talented: A handbook.* Ventura, CA: Office of the Ventura County Superintendent of Schools.

Kaplan, S. N. (1994). *Differentiating the core curriculum to provide advanced learning opportunities.* Sacramento, CA: California Association for the Gifted.

Maker, C. J., & Nielson, A. B. (1996). *Curriculum development and teaching strategies for gifted learners* (2nd ed.). Austin, TX: Pro-Ed.

National Association for Gifted Children. (1994). *Position paper: Differentiation of curriculum and instruction.* Washington, DC: Author.

National Association for the Education of Young Children. (2003). *Early childhood curriculum, assessment, and program evaluation: Building an effective, accountable system in programs for children birth through age 8.* Washington, DC: Author.

National Council of Teachers of Mathematics. (2000). *Principles and standards for school mathematics.* Reston, VA: Author.

National Council of Teachers of Mathematics. (2006). *Curricular focal points for prekindergarten through grade 8 mathematics: A quest for coherence.* Reston, VA: Author.

National Governors Association Center for Best Practices, & Council of Chief State School Officers. *Common Core State Standards for English Language Arts.* (2010a). Washington, DC: Authors.

National Governors Association Center for Best Practices, & Council of Chief State School Officers. *Common Core State Standards for Mathematics.* (2010b). Washington, DC: Authors.

National Research Council. (1996). *National science education standards.* Washington, DC: National Academies Press.

National Research Council. (1998). *How people learn: Brain, mind, experience, and school.* Washington, DC: National Academies Press.

National Research Council. (1999). *How people learn: Bridging research and practice.* Washington, DC: National Academies Press.

Passow, A. H. (1982). Differentiated curricula for the gifted/talented: A point of view. In S. Kaplan, A. H. Passow, P. H. Phenix, S. M. Reis, J. S. Renzulli, I. Sato, . . . V. S. Ward (Eds.) *Curricula for the gifted* (pp. 4–20). Ventura, CA: National/State Leadership Institute on the Gifted/Talented.

Patall, E. A. (2012). The motivational complexity of choosing: A review of theory and research. In R. M. Ryan (Ed.), *The Oxford handbook of human motivation* (pp. 248–279). New York, NY: Oxford University Press.

Purcell, J. H., Burns, D. E., Tomlinson, C. A., Imbeau, M. B., & Martin, J. L. (2002). Bridging the gap: A tool and technique to analyze and evaluate gifted education curricular units. *Gifted Child Quarterly, 46,* 306–321.

Renzulli, J. S. (1982). What makes a problem real: Stalking the illusive meaning of qualitative differences in gifted education. *Gifted Child Quarterly, 32,* 298–309.

Renzulli, J. S., & Reis, S. M. (2014). *The Schoolwide Enrichment Model: A how-to guide for talent development* (3rd ed.). Waco, TX: Prufrock Press.

Rogers, K. B. (2002). *Re-forming gifted education: How parents and teachers can match the program to the child.* Scottsdale, AZ: Great Potential Press.

Schmidt, W. H. (Ed.). (1997). *A splintered vision: An investigation of U.S. science and mathematics education.* Hingham, MA: Kluwer Academic Publishers.

Shore, B. M., Cornell, D. G., Robinson, A., & Ward, V. S. (1991). *Recommended practices in gifted education: A critical analysis.* New York, NY: Teachers College Press.

Solomon, P. G. (1998). *The curriculum bridge: From standards to actual classroom practice.* Thousand Oaks, CA: Corwin Press.

Tomlinson, C. (1997). Good teaching for one and all: Does gifted education have an instructional identity? *Journal for the Education of the Gifted, 20,* 155–174.

Tomlinson, C. A. (1999). *The differentiated classroom: Responding to the needs of all learners.* Alexandria, VA: Association for Supervision and Curriculum Development.

Tomlinson, C. A. (2005). Quality curriculum and instruction for highly able students. *Theory into Practice, 44,* 160–166.

Tomlinson, C. A. (2012). *How to differentiate instruction in mixed-ability classrooms* (2nd ed.). Alexandria, VA: Association for Supervision and Curriculum Development.

United States Department of Education, Office of Educational Research and Improvement. (1993). *National excellence: A case for developing America's talent.* Washington, DC: Author.

VanTassel-Baska, J. (1989). Appropriate curriculum for gifted learners. *Educational Leadership, 46*(6), 13–15.

VanTassel-Baska, J. (2005). Gifted programs and services: What are the non-negotiables? *Theory into Practice, 44,* 90–97.

Ward, V. S. (1980). *Differential education of the gifted.* Ventura, CA: National/State Leadership Training Institute for the Gifted and Talented.

Wiggins, G., & McTighe, J. (1998). *Understanding by design.* Alexandria, VA: Association for Supervision and Curriculum Development.

# CHAPTER 4

# Aligning Curriculum to Standards

**Susan K. Johnsen**

Standards are statements that define what all students need to know, understand, and be able to do. They form the foundation for the curriculum by stating the most important big ideas, concepts, and skills. Standards need to be rigorous so that all students acquire the cognitive and social skills that will enable them to succeed after high school and deal with the complex challenges of the 21st century.

In response to inconsistencies across state standards and concerns about U.S. students' mediocre performance on international tests, national content standards have been developed over the past 5 years (National Governors Association Center for Best Practices [NGA] & Council of Chief State School Officers [CCSSO], 2010a, 2010b; National Research Council [NRC], 2012). State agencies, schools, and professional associations have been busily reviewing these standards and aligning them to their curriculum, instruction, and assessments to ensure that students are mastering the core subject areas. This chapter will examine these national standards, including those that relate to gifted education, curriculum alignment models, and ways that schools can align their curriculum to these standards and differentiate them for gifted and talented students.

# National Content Standards

To succeed in college, career, and life in the 21st century will involve the alignment of the classroom with real-world environments (Partnership for 21st Century Skills, 2009). These skills will involve critical thinking and problem solving, communication, collaboration, and creativity and innovation. Beginning in 2009, the NGA and the CCSSO from 48 states, two territories, and the District of Columbia led the effort to develop a set of standards that would provide consistency and guidance to educators involved in curriculum development, its implementation, and the assessment of students' acquisition of knowledge and skills. Built on 21st-century skills, these Common Core State Standards (CCSS) address English language arts and mathematics and are internationally benchmarked. Currently, the CCSS have been adopted by 43 states, four territories, and the District of Columbia (NGA & CCSO, 2010a, 2010b); however, this number may change if additional states opt out in favor of state-developed standards.

Following the release of the CCSS, the NRC, the Science Teachers Association, the American Association for the Advancement of Science, and Achieve developed the Next Generation Science Standards (NGSS; NGSS Lead States, 2013). Since their release in 2013, states have joined together in forming a NGSS Network for adopting and implementing the standards. Similarly, the National Council for the Social Studies (NCSS; 2010) developed national curriculum standards. These standards have been disseminated to 110 affiliated state, local, and regional councils and associated groups.

The CCSS in math and English language arts, NGSS, and National Curriculum Standards for Social Studies are informed by research, reflective of the core knowledge and skills that students need to be college and career ready and are comparable to international expectations. Each of these sets of standards were built on previous standards, but they differ in some key areas:

1. *The English Language Arts Common Core State Standards* (CCSS-ELA). These standards emphasize the comprehension of more complex text and their academic language more than in previous standards (NGA & CCSSO, 2010a). Although the standards do not include a specific reading list, they do include certain types of content such as classic myths and stories from around the

world, foundational U.S. documents, seminal works of American literature, and the writings of Shakespeare. They emphasize the use of content-rich nonfiction in literature, history/social studies, sciences, technical studies, and the arts. They also ask students to develop the skills of not only recalling specific information but also effective argumentative and informative writing.

2. *The Mathematics Common Core State Standards* (CCSS-M). These standards ask educators to spend more time and focus on fewer topics than previous standards (NGA & CCSSO, 2010b). The topics are linked across grades and within and across domains. Some of the domains include numbers and operations, operations and algebraic thinking, geometry, and measurement and data. They emphasize rigor in conceptual understanding of key concepts, procedural skills and fluency in calculations, and application. Along with content domains, the CCSS-M also provides a set of process skills that educators need to develop in their students. Some of the eight process skills include reasoning abstractly and quantitatively, constructing viable arguments and critiquing the reasoning of others, modeling with mathematics, and expressing regularity in repeated reasoning.

3. *The Next Generation Science Standards.* Content and practices that require critical thinking and communication are intertwined within the NGSS as opposed to separating them into two distinct sets of standards. The standards are built around three major dimensions (NRC, 2012): scientific and engineering practices such as asking questions and defining problems; crosscutting concepts such as patterns and systems that unify the study of science and engineering through their common application across fields; and core ideas in the disciplinary areas of physical sciences, life sciences, Earth and space sciences, and engineering, technology, and the applications of science. Similar to the mathematics standards, the science standards focus on depth over breadth and authentic practices when solving problems in science.

4. *National Curriculum Standards for Social Studies.* These standards are structured around 10 themes: culture; time, continuity, and change; people, places, and environments; individual development and identity; individuals, groups, and institutions; power, authority, and governance; production, distribution, and consumption; science, technology, and society; global connections; and

civic ideals and practices. They focus on purposes, questions for exploration, knowledge, processes, and products. The standards also include description enhancements related to the 10 themes, standards-based classroom practices, a stronger focus on student products and their assessments, and an updated list of essential social studies skills and strategies (NCSS, 2010).

# National Curriculum Standards for Gifted and Talented Students

Although no specific gifted education standards have been developed for the core content domains, gifted educators have developed books for using the CCSS and the NGSS with gifted and advanced students (Adams, Cotabish, & Dailey, 2015; Adams, Cotabish, & Ricci, 2014; Hughes-Lynch, Kettler, Shaunessy-Dedrick, & VanTassel-Baska, 2014; Johnsen, Ryser, & Assouline, 2014; Johnsen & Sheffield, 2013; VanTassel-Baska, 2013). They have also developed program standards (Johnsen, 2012; National Association for Gifted Children [NAGC], 2010) that address curriculum differentiation (see NAGC Pre-K–Grade 12 Gifted Education Programming Standards). The programming standard in curriculum and instruction (see Standard 3) encourages, "educators [to] develop and use a comprehensive and sequenced core curriculum that is aligned with local, state, and national standards, then differentiate and expand it" (NAGC, 2010, p. 4). Within Standard 3, "educators apply theory and research-based models of curriculum and instruction related to students with gifts and talents and respond to their needs by planning, selecting, adapting, and creating culturally-relevant curriculum using a repertoire of evidence-based instructional strategies to ensure specific student outcomes" (NAGC, 2010, p. 4). Specific evidence-based practices ask educators to (a) develop comprehensive, cohesive programming based on standards; (b) incorporate differentiated curricula in all domains; (c) use balanced assessment systems; (d) pace instruction according to each student's rate of learning; (e) use specific strategies such as critical and creative thinking, metacognitive, problem solving, and inquiry models; (f) develop and use culturally responsive curriculum that integrates career exploration; and (g) use high-quality resources (Anderson & Krathwohl, 2001; Elder & Paul, 2004; Ford, 2006; Hartman, 2001; Kitano, Montgomery, VanTassel-Baska, & Johnsen, 2008; Siegle, 2004; Stiggins, 2008; Tomlinson, 2004; VanTassel-Baska, 2004).

In reviewing these standards and research-based practices, it's clear to see that overlap exists between the NAGC Programming Standards, the CCSS, and the NGSS. For example, all of the national standards focus on higher level thinking and problem solving. They also examine crosscutting themes within and across domains and fields, creating opportunities for interdisciplinary studies. However, the standards are not as clear about advanced students who might traverse the standards before the end of high school or who might need more enrichment and extensions. For these reasons, the standards are simply a starting point for the alignment process, particularly for gifted and talented students. States and local districts are left with the responsibility of identifying the key content and cognitive processes in the standards and providing the classroom teachers with ways for differentiating the standards for gifted and advanced students.

# Curriculum Alignment

Curriculum integrates standards within themes, concepts, or topics in an orderly progression and uses instructional methods that provide students with opportunities to show they have learned the content and skills (i.e., assessment). Curriculum alignment is therefore the extent to which there is an agreement or a match between standards and at least one of these three categories (i.e., curriculum, instruction, and assessment; Porter, 2002; Squires, 2012; Webb, 1997, 2002). The goal of alignment is to create a coherent system that informs the curriculum and supports student achievement.

It is important to align curriculum to standards. Alignment ensures that content is standards-driven and is coherent across grade levels and courses. It organizes the curriculum into a sequence of manageable units that eliminate gaps and duplications. Teachers know the important concepts and skills to emphasize, what content is taught at different grade levels and in different courses, and can eliminate excessive review and repetition. As a result of this knowledge, they can ensure a seamless progression for students from one level to the next. In turn, students experience the same opportunities to learn and receive the supports they need to achieve. Anderson (2002) suggested that curriculum alignment is central to the success of accountability and includes the taught curriculum, the tested curriculum, and the written curriculum. The written curriculum is usually the curriculum documents or frameworks produced by the school district, the taught curriculum is the written curriculum enacted by teachers in their classrooms, and the tested curriculum consists of formative, ongoing, and summative assessments such as curriculum-embedded tests, benchmark tests, and state standardized tests. When the written curriculum is taught, then educators can determine the differential effects of schooling on student achievement. Consequently, curriculum alignment has been cited as one of the most powerful strategies for improving student achievement (Center for Comprehensive School Reform and Improvement, 2009; Squires, 2012).

## Curriculum Alignment Models

In the past, most alignment models focused primarily on the content match between objectives and assessment items (Glaser, 1963; Hambleton, 1984; Tyler, 1949). They did not consider the level of cognitive complexity, which is emphasized in the new national standards, nor did they consider the alignment between various facets of the curriculum—the taught curriculum (enacted), the tested curriculum (assessed), and the written curriculum (intended); consequently, more comprehensive alignment methods have been developed. Three of these that examine the alignment with curriculum will be discussed in this section—The Surveys of Enacted Curriculum (SEC; Blank, Porter, & Smithson, 2001; Porter, 2002), the Webb Alignment Tool (Webb, 1997, 1999, 2002, 2007), and Achieve (Resnick, Rothman, Slattery, & Vranek, 2004; Rothman, Slattery, Vranek, & Resnick, 2002).

## The Surveys of Enacted Curriculum

The Council of Chief State School Officers developed the Surveys of Enacted Curriculum in conjunction with several partner districts and states (Vockley & Lang, 2009). The model can be used to analyze the content and alignment of curriculum and instruction to standards and assessments. The SEC model has been used to analyze the content and alignment of standards, curriculum, and assessments in mathematics, English language arts, and science in more than 30 states (Vockley & Lang, 2009). This survey addresses both content and cognitive demand in the intended, enacted, and assessed curricula. The content is defined by two features—instruction and instructional materials. The first feature focuses on the decisions that teachers make about what to teach, how much time to spend on a particular subject, what topics to cover, when and in what order, to what standards of achievement, and to which students. The second feature, instructional materials, includes the standards, textbooks, and achievement tests that influence teachers' content decisions. Five categories of thinking are used to determine cognitive demand: memorize, perform procedures, communicate understanding, solve nonroutine problems, and conjecture/generalize/prove (Porter, 2002). In using the survey, content analysts with a strong background in the domain either by teaching or supervision examine the content of their instruction and the instructional materials and code them along two dimensions: content and cognitive complexity. Next, content maps are developed that graphically display the curriculum content in relation to standards (intended curriculum), to assessments (assessed curriculum), and to instruction (enacted curriculum; see examples of content maps in the *Surveys of Enacted Curriculum* guide on the CCSSO website: http://www.ccsso.org/Resources/Programs/Surveys_of_Enacted_Curriculum_(SEC).html). Finally, the maps are visually compared to identify similarities and differences. Reviewers ask these questions when evaluating: Does the content fit the category of the standard in each type of curricula? Does the cognitive complexity match the standard in each type of curricula? What standards are emphasized? Do teachers devote the right amount of instructional time to the right content? Is there a balance of representation? What types of professional development do teachers need?

## Webb Alignment Tool

The Webb alignment process was developed for the National Institute for Science Education and the Council of Chief State School Officers in 1997 and has evolved over time (Webb, 2007). Webb's alignment model is based on four criteria: categorical concurrence, depth-of-knowledge consistency, range-of-knowledge correspondence, and balance of representation. These criteria are generally used when examining the tested curriculum.

♦ Categorical concurrence indicates how consistently the curriculum measures the same content areas and objectives for each of the standards. In examining the assessed curriculum, Webb (2002) suggested six questions as a minimum for an assessment attempting to measure content knowledge for each standard to make decisions about whether or not a student has met the learning goal for the standard.

♦ Depth-of-knowledge (DOK) consistency indicates the degree that the cognitive demands required from the student represent the complexity as stated in the standards. The DOK levels include: recall and reproduction, skills and concepts, strategic thinking, and extended thinking. Level 1, recall and reproduction, includes the recall of information such as a fact, definition, term, or a simple procedure, such as recalling details from a story or applying a formula. Level 2, skills and concepts, requires both comprehension and subsequent processing of text and some student decision making as to how to approach the problem or activity. Level 3, strategic thinking, requires reasoning, planning, using evidence, and a higher level of thinking than the previous two levels. Level 4, extended thinking, requires complex reasoning, planning, developing, and creating that connects ideas within the content area or among content areas over an extended period of time. For consistency, at least 50% of the questions on an assessment should be at or above the depth-of-knowledge level of the standard.

♦ Range-of-knowledge correspondence determines whether the breadth of knowledge expected of students on the basis of a standard corresponds to the breadth of knowledge that students need to correctly answer corresponding assessment items or perform in learning activities. This criterion is met if more than half of the objectives within a standard are targeted by the assessment items.

◆ Balance of representation measures whether objectives that fall under a specific standard are given relatively equal emphasis on the intended, enacted, and assessed curriculum. This criterion is met if 70% of the corresponding assessment items related to a learning goal are equally distributed among the objectives of a standard.

## Achieve

The Achieve model reflects concerns about specific subject areas and provides both a quantitative and qualitative alignment comparison between standards and assessments (Martone & Sireci, 2009). Evaluation dimensions in this model include content centrality, performance centrality, source of challenge, level of cognitive demand, balance, and range. With content centrality, the examiner rates the quality of the match between the standards and what students should know and be able to do at a particular grade level on a 5-point scale. With performance centrality, the quality of the match is between the verbs in the standards and the expectations for student performance. In determining the source of challenge, assessment items are reviewed to ensure reading level is appropriate, that items are fairly constructed, and that the writing prompts are accessible, use appropriate vocabulary, and have a clear purpose and audience. The level of cognitive demand describes the level of thinking required to respond to the assessed item. Similar to the DOK, there are four levels of cognitive demand: recall or basic comprehension, application of skill/concept, strategic thinking, and extended analysis. With the balance criterion, educators determine if the curriculum documents represent the depth and breadth of the content and performances of the standards. With the range criterion, the proportion of objectives within a standard is measured (e.g., if three objectives out of six are measured, then the proportion would be .50). In the first stage, an expert panel determines the content and performance centrality for each assessment item, considering how a set of items match the overarching standard (e.g., literary response or geometry). The panel then evaluates the source of challenge and determines the level of cognitive demand. Finally, the expert panel examines the overall level of challenge, the balance, and the range.

In summary, all of the models include both the content and the cognitive demand of the standards. The Achieve and Webb Alignment models tend to examine the assessments more closely than the Surveys of Enacted

Curriculum model. They include more attention to each item's reading level, construction, accessibility to different groups, vocabulary, purpose, and audience. On the other hand, the Surveys of Enacted Curriculum model focuses more on instruction and instructional materials. It examines standards, textbooks, and achievement tests as well as what to teach and how much time should be spent on what standards and in what order for which students. Given these differences, educators need to consider the purposes for the alignment documents (e.g., Does the district or agency want to examine how the standards are being implemented and assessed? Does the district or agency want to examine the quality of the assessments that are being used?). After establishing the purpose for the alignment, the school district or agency might select one or more models that will address its overall goals.

# Aligning Standards to the Written Curriculum

Using these and other models, state agencies and school districts have been aligning their curriculum to create frameworks that generally include some or all of these components: critical areas for each of the standard domains, key concepts and skills for each grade level or course, a scope and sequence or learning progression across grade levels and courses, and examples of learner outcomes and activities.

## Differentiation of Curriculum Documents

Throughout the alignment process, educators need to be aware of ways that the curriculum documents might be differentiated for gifted and talented students. Some of the following ways have been described in the *NAGC Pre-K–Grade 12 Gifted Programming Standards* (NAGC, 2010) and previous publications on adapting the Common Core and NGSS (Adams et al., 2015; Adams et al., 2014; Hughes-Lynch et al., 2014; Johnsen et al., 2014; Johnsen & Sheffield, 2013; VanTassel-Baska, 2013):

1. *Acceleration and pacing.* Some gifted and advanced students may already know the knowledge and skills in the standards or traverse the standards at a faster pace, so acceleration and pacing opportunities need to be addressed in the curriculum documents. For example, illustrations of how standards and clusters of standards might be compressed across grade levels might be presented within the scope and sequence document and integrated into interdisciplinary problems within example learner activities. In addition, knowledge about standards above the targeted grade levels needs to be included within vertical alignment documents to provide information to the instructor for designing preassessments and other types of assessments to advance students at a faster pace.

2. *Complexity.* More big ideas and connections within and across domains might be suggested in the documents to increase complexity. For example, sample learning activities on "symbols" might show how some advanced students might develop generalizations that connect symbols from the past to the future or how different perspectives influence identification of symbols.

3. *Creativity and innovation.* Open-ended problems might be provided as examples within learning activities to offer gifted and advanced learners opportunities to pose their own questions and problems. For example, high school students might examine issues related to global warming and identify major problems to solve using multiple domains (i.e., mathematics, science) whereas elementary students might conduct research and plan experiments on the effects of heat on plants and animals.

4. *Depth.* In adding depth, the scope and sequence and learning activity examples might include specialized vocabulary, details, patterns and trends, or rules (Kaplan, 2009). For example, important vocabulary might be included in the curriculum documents to show the progression so that teachers might use above-level vocabulary with advanced students.

5. *Interdisciplinary connections.* Because mathematics and English language arts are both tool subjects, they lend themselves to more interdisciplinary studies (Kaplan, 2009). Interdisciplinary examples can be presented in the key concepts or in the learner activities. Example units might describe how research projects could address the English language arts standard regarding research and

the mathematics data representation standard (VanTassel-Baska, 2013).

6. *Themes or concepts.* Major concepts and themes might be delineated in the essential questions or critical instructional areas of the curriculum documents. The critical areas might show not only important knowledge and skills at a particular grade level but also across grade levels and domains. For example, the themes of "patterns and relationships" in the mathematics standards within "Operations and Algebraic Thinking" might be connected to "patterns of events" in English and language arts within the reading standards for literature. Larger concepts might also be provided to show the connection between the themes: Patterns can be represented quantitatively and qualitatively.

7. *Higher order thinking.* Cognitive complexity is emphasized in the new national standards and is useful in differentiating the standards for gifted and advanced students. Along with other taxonomies such as Bloom's taxonomy (Bloom, Engelhart, Furst, Hill, & Krathwohl, 1956; Krathwohl, 2002) and Paul's Elements of Reasoning (Paul & Elder, 2004), Webb (1997) offers the depth-of-knowledge instrument to indicate the degree of cognitive demand when examining standards. When looking at standards, the expert panel needs to include not only the alignment with key concepts within each of the standards, but also the level of skill required of the students by analyzing the type of thinking skill.

8. *World applications.* Because students need to learn how to understand other nations and cultures, address global issues, and work collaboratively with individuals from diverse cultures, this differentiation principle should be incorporated within the curricular documents that include key content and skills for students (Partnership for 21st Century Skills, 2009). Many global problems require interdisciplinary perspectives from a variety of domains to arrive at innovative solutions and are ideal for the gifted and advanced student.

9. *Student interest.* To engage students in learning that is meaningful to them, student interest needs to be considered. Within the written documents, choice of content might be provided to show that flexibility exists in terms of research projects, problems, methods, and products or performances.

Using these differentiation principles, educators can create more differentiated curricular frameworks during the alignment process.

## The Alignment Process

**Identify critical areas.** The first step in the alignment process is to review the national and/or state standards, understand how they are organized, and decide what are the critical areas emphasized in a cluster of standards for each grade level or course. For example, the California Department of Education (CDE; 2013a, 2013b) has identified critical areas in mathematics and English language arts within its curriculum framework. Using the CCSS-M, the CDE identifies the critical areas for instruction at each grade level (e.g., fluency with addition and subtraction of fractions, developing multiplication of fractions and division of fractions, extending division to 2-digit divisors, integrating decimal fractions into the place value system, and developing understanding of volume). Similarly for CCSS-ELA, the curriculum framework identifies the important understandings for each strand (e.g., reading, writing, speaking and listening, and language) that students must demonstrate in each of the strand-specific set of College and Career Readiness Anchor Standards (e.g., key ideas and details, craft and structure, integration of knowledge and ideas, range of reading, and text complexity). Once these key areas are identified, then the next step is to examine if each of the standards measures the same content areas and objectives as the school or state's standard (i.e., categorical concurrence).

**Match content.** In comparing two sets of standards (e.g., national standards vs. school district standards), it's important to review them within a category (e.g., strand, domain, cluster, and/or standard). The content knowledge presented in each of the standards or cluster of standards needs to be compared to determine if is similar or the same. For example, within the CCSS-M domain of "Number and Operations in Base Ten," a cluster of standards identifies "place value" using "multi-digit whole numbers with decimals" as critical concepts. Within a similar domain and cluster within a school district, Table 4.1 shows some of the identified standards.

Looking at these five content standards, it's clear that standards 3, 4, and 5 are a closer match to the CCSS-M than the other two. A resulting content match table for each grade level might look like the one depicted in Table 4.2.

## Table 4.1

*Cluster of Standards for Number and Operations in Base 10*

1. Use a variety of methods and tools for computing with whole numbers.
2. Use inverse relationships between operations (e.g., addition and subtraction, etc.).
3. Add and subtract commonly used fractions with like denominators and decimals.
4. Compare, order and convert among fractions, decimals and percents.
5. Use place value structure to compare whole numbers and decimals.

## Table 4.2

*Content Map Table*

| Common Core State Standards in Mathematics for Grade 5 | | State or District Standards | Interdisciplinary Connections |
|---|---|---|---|
| *Domain* | *Cluster of Standards* | *Standard or Benchmark* | |
| Number and Operations in Base 10 | 1. Understand the place value system. | 1. Use place value structure to compare whole numbers and decimals. | "Structure"<br><br>In English language arts: Analyze the structure of texts, including how the parts relate to each other and the whole (Craft and Structure). |
| | 2. Perform operations with multi-digit whole numbers and with decimals to the hundredths. | 2. Add and subtract commonly used fractions with like denominators and decimals.<br><br>3. Compare, order and convert among fractions, decimals and percents. | |

**Table 4.3**

*Cognitive Demand Match Using Webb's
Depth-of-Knowledge Categories*

| Depth-of-Knowledge | CCSS-ELA Standard | District or State Standard |
|---|---|---|
| Level 1–Recall and Reproduction | Verify the preliminary determination of the meaning of a word or phrase by checking the inferred meaning in context or in a dictionary. | Use multiple resources to verify comprehension of vocabulary. |
| Level 2–Skills and Concepts | Use context as a clue to the meaning of a word or phrase. | Use context clues and text structures to determine the meaning of new vocabulary. |
| Level 3–Strategic Thinking | Interpret figures of speech in context and analyze their role in the text. | Infer word meaning through identification and analysis of analogies and other word relationships. |
| Level 4–Extended Thinking | Conduct short as well as more sustained research projects to answer a question or solve a problem. | Formulate open-ended research questions suitable for inquiry and investigation and develop a plan for gathering information. |

At this step, the expert panel might also identify themes and concepts that might be linked to other domains. In Table 4.2, the interdisciplinary theme of "structure" has been proposed as a possible connecting concept that might be used to develop units of study.

**Match cognitive demand.** Similar to examining content, the next step is to compare the cognitive complexity of the two sets of standards. Some examples are included in Table 4.3 using Webb's Depth-of-Knowledge (see Conley et al., 2011 for examples). The assigned level should reflect the level of complexity or cognitive demand of the work students might be required to perform, not its difficulty. The level is assigned based on the central performance described in the standard, not the verb alone. This step is particularly important for identifying standards that provide more higher order thinking for gifted and advanced student—more depth, complexity, and creativity. Level 4 standards can also be extended to engage students in their areas of interest such as sustained research projects.

**Match emphasis.** The next step is to review the content knowledge with the cognitive demand that is addressed in the curriculum. In this way, both the breadth of knowledge and the balance of representation can be examined and gaps can be identified.

In Table 4.4, the expert panel aligned specific standards at fifth grade by standard cluster and standard, noting that in some cases the school standard was at a lower level (e.g., 5KD1—Level 1 instead of Level 3) and in others it was at a different grade level (e.g., 6IKI3—6th grade). For CCSS-ELA 5.10, the school district didn't have a comparable standard. These gaps and differences help the school district align their standards more tightly to the Common Core State Standards in English Language Arts to ensure that the teachers know the important concepts and skill levels to emphasize.

The specificity of the alignment can vary along a continuum. Alignments can be made at the cluster level or at the specific standard level. Porter (2002) described the size of the match using "grain." A "coarse-grain" tends to be more global and general whereas a "fine-grain" tends to be more specific and targeted—a one-to-one correspondence.

**Develop scope and sequence.** Once the content, the cognitive demand, and the emphases have been determined for each standard, a common scope and sequence for both sets of standards can be developed that shows the learning progression from one grade level or course to the next level. The learning progression is designed to help teachers identify what is expected from students within and across grade levels or courses. Teachers are then able to compare how standards change and increase in content and cognitive demand and are able to accelerate gifted and advanced students as needed. For example, if a student has already acquired the expectations for one grade level, he or she can progress to the next level's expectations.

To create a seamless progression, it's important to understand how the standards are organized within and across domains, strands, and disciplines. For example, the CCSS-M are organized into domains (e.g., Measurement and Data in grades K–5 and Statistics and Probability in grades 6–high school), clusters (i.e., groups of related standards), and standards (i.e., specific statements that define what students should know and be able to do). The CCSS-ELA are organized into strands (e.g., Reading, Writing, Speaking and Listening), a strand-specific set of College and Career Readiness Anchor Standards that are common across all grade levels, and specific standards for each grade level. The NGSS are organized by cross-cutting concepts intended to provide a connective structure across disciplines (e.g., patterns, cause and effect, structure and function), disciplinary core ideas (physical, life, Earth and space, and engineering and

**Table 4.4**

*Emphasis Comparison Between School District and CCSS-ELA Standards*

| Anchor Standards | Reading Standards for Informational Text Grade 5 | | | | | | | |
| --- | --- | --- | --- | --- | --- | --- | --- | --- |
| | Key Ideas and Details | | Craft and Structure | | Integration of Knowledge and Ideas | | Range of Reading and Level of Text | |
| *Specific Standards* | CCSS-ELA | *School Standard* | CCSS-ELA | *School Standard* | CCSS-ELA | *School Standard* | CCSS-ELA | *School Standard* |
| DOK | | | | | | | | |
| Level 1 | | 5KD1 | | | | | | |
| Level 2 | | 5KD3 | | 4CS9 | | | | |
| Level 3 | 5.1 5.2 5.3 | 5KD2 | 5.4 5.5 5.6 | 5CS8 | | 5IKI5 | | |
| Level 4 | | | | | 5.7 5.9 | 6IKI3 7IKI1 | 5.10 | None |

technology), and grade-band endpoints in each of the disciplines at grades 2, 5, 8, and 12.

As an example, Table 4.5 shows the learning progression in the domain of "Operations and Algebraic Thinking" for clusters of related standards. Clearly illustrated is the development of the four basic operations in math, lending itself to acceleration. For example, students who had already gained fluency in adding and subtracting within 10 (see Grade 1) could progress to gaining fluency within 20 (see Grade 2), those who could solve problems with addition and subtraction (Grade 2) could progress to solving problems with multiplication and division (Grade 3), and so on.

Similar to the CCSS-ELA strands and the NGSS cross-cutting concepts, the CCSS-M domains are also connected to one another, as can be seen in Table 4.6. These relationships have clear implications for building complexity and depth within the standards for gifted and advanced students.

**Examples of learner activities.** The final component of the scope and sequence might include examples of learner activities to clarify the content, cognitive demand, and learner outcome for the standard in teacher-friendly language. For example, consider this "College and Career Anchor Standard for Reading": "Read and comprehend complex literary and informational texts independently and proficiently" (NGA & CCSSO, 2010a, p. 10). The related Grade 4 ELA standard reads, "By the end of the year, read and comprehend literature, including stories, dramas, and poetry, in the grades 4–5 text complexity band proficiently, with scaffolding as needed at the high end of the range" (NGA & CCSSO, 2010a, p. 12). In elaborating this standard, the curriculum document might describe how (a) equal emphasis is placed on the sophistication of what students read and the skills they might use when reading, (b) text complexity increases from kindergarten through college, (c) students need to make an increasing number of connections among ideas and between texts, and (d) evidence is considered when examining inconsistencies, ambiguities, and poor reasoning in texts (North Carolina Department of Public Instruction, 2012). More specific examples of differentiated learning activities might also be included for typical and advanced students (VanTassel-Baska, 2013). (See Table 4.7.)

## Table 4.5

*CCSS-M Standard Clusters for Domain of "Operations and Algebraic Thinking"*

| Grade K | Grade 1 | Grade 2 | Grade 3 | Grade 4 |
|---|---|---|---|---|
| Understand addition as putting together and adding to, and understand subtraction as taking apart and taking from. | Represent and solve problems involving addition and subtraction within 20. | Represent and solve problems involving addition and subtraction within 100. | Represent and solve problems involving multiplication and division. | Use the four operations with whole numbers to solve problems. |
| | Understand and apply properties of operations and the relationship between addition and subtraction. | Add and subtract within 20 fluently. | Understand properties of multiplication and the relationship between multiplication and division. | Gain familiarity with factors and multiples. |
| | Add and subtract within 20—fluency within 10. | Work with equal groups of objects to gain foundations for multiplication. | Multiply and divide within 100. | Generate and analyze patterns. |
| | Work with addition and subtraction equations. | | Solve problems involving the four operations, and identify and explain patterns in arithmetic. | |

**Table 4.6**

*Relationship Across Mathematical Domains for*
*"Operations and Algebraic Thinking" for Grade 4*

| Operations and Algebraic Thinking | Number and Operations in Base 10 | Number and Operations— Fractions | Measurement and Data |
|---|---|---|---|
| 4.OA Use the four operations with whole numbers to solve problems. | 4.NBT.4 Fluently add and subtract multi-digit whole numbers using the standard algorithm. | 4.NF.3c. Add and subtract mixed numbers with like denominators. | 4.MD2. Use the four operations to solve word problems involving distances, intervals of time, liquid volumes, masses of objects and money. |

# Steps for Getting Started

Key to developing all of the curriculum documents is the identification of a strong expert panel that is comprised of educators with content and teaching expertise. These educators should be carefully selected and will need to have the time and resources to complete the alignment process. The following checklist may be helpful to the expert panel in the alignment process:

1. Provide an orientation to those who may be involved in the process. Address questions about its purpose, the importance of the alignment process, and related research on the effects of alignment on learner outcomes.
2. Select panels at each grade level who are not only experts in their domain but also interested in the alignment process.
3. Review current state, school district, and/or CCSS, NGSS, and NCSS standards. Identify how each is organized into major strands, domains, concepts, clusters, and standards, noting similarities and differences.
4. Review current standards and curriculum maps to evaluate alignment to the CCSS, the NGSS, and/or other standards, matching content (major concepts and skills) for each grade level.

**Table 4.7**

*Examples of Differentiated Learning Activities*

**Strand: Writing**

**Anchor Standard for Reading: Text Type and Purposes**

| Specific Standard | Typical | Advanced |
|---|---|---|
| **Grade 3** Write opinion pieces on topics or texts, supporting a point of view with reasons. | Students will write an opinion piece stating three reasons why their parents should buy them a new game of their choosing. | After determining a self-selected local issue, advanced students will write an opinion piece, providing three reasons why they think their issue is important (e.g., razing a historic building to build a football stadium). Reasons should be logical and connected to the issue. |
| **Grade 5** Write opinion pieces on topics or texts, supporting a point of view with reasons and information. | Students will write a persuasive piece related to a local issue that states their own and opposing opinions, providing reasons and a logical concluding statement. | After determining a self-selected local issue, advanced students will identify multiple perspectives about the issue, and clearly state their opinion. They will provide reasons supporting their opinion and rebuttal reasons for alternative views. Students will present their opinions through their writing and orally via structured debates. |
| **Grade 8** Write arguments to support claims with clear reasons and relevant evidence. | Students will write an opinion piece related to a local issue in which opposing points of view are recognized, described and rebutted (e.g., euthanizing animals at the local SPCA). | After determining a significant historical or local issue, advanced students will write a newspaper editorial taking a definitive side on an issue. Each editorial will identify multiple perspectives about the issue, and clearly state the opinion. They will provide reasons supporting their opinion and provide rebuttal reasons for alternative views. Primary and secondary sources should be used to provide information (e.g., writing a pro and a con argument for the death penalty). Students will present their opinions formulated through their writing orally via structured debates with rebuttal opportunities. |
| **Grade 12** Write arguments to support claims in an analysis of substantive topics or texts, using valid reasoning and relevant and sufficient evidence. | Students will present arguments for a particular audience that has a different perspective than they do. They should formulate their argument to persuade and reflect the views and concepts of the opposing side (e.g., federal involvement in school lunches). | After determining a global issue of significance, advanced students will write two opinion pieces for two different audiences (e.g., presenting on global warming to Democrats and to Republicans). Assumptions about the audience should be evident in word choice, style, and rationale development. Students will present their opinions formulated through their writing orally via structured debates with rebuttal opportunities and implications for policy development. |

*Note.* Adapted from *Using the Common Core for English Language Arts With Gifted and Advanced Learners* (pp. 16–17) by J. VanTassel-Baska, 2013, Waco, TX: Prufrock Press.

5. Review current standards to evaluate alignment to the CCSS, the NGSS, and/or other standards, matching the cognitive demand using depth of understanding for each grade level.
6. Using the alignments, determine the emphases placed on particular standards and any gaps in the breadth of knowledge addressed for each grade level.
7. Evaluate all related curriculum documents such as scopes and sequences and align these to the CCSS, NGSS, and/or other standards across grade levels.
8. Determine if the units, learning activities, and other curriculum resources identify explicitly the main concepts of each of the standards.
9. Examine the curriculum documents to determine if differentiation is included for gifted and advanced learners—addressing acceleration, depth, complexity, and other dimensions.
10. Update and revise the curriculum so that it is aligned to the CCSS, the NGSS, and/or other standards.

Professional development will need to follow the alignment process so that teachers, administrators and others are aware of standards within and across grade levels and ways that they might move forward to field testing the standards, aligning the standards to instruction (i.e., the enacted curriculum) and to district assessments (i.e., the assessed curriculum).

# Issues

A number of issues have been raised by researchers regarding alignment and the process (Agostino et al., 2008; Beach, 2011; Blank et al., 2001; Martone & Sireci, 2009; Pickreign & Capps, 2000; Porter, 2002; Rothman et al., 2002; Webb, 1999). First, individuals conducting the alignment may pay attention more to the perceptual aspects of sets of standards (e.g., the concepts that are mentioned in the standard) rather than the cognitive demand (e.g., Depth-of-Knowledge Levels; Agostino et al., 2008). Moreover, differences between the standards developers and the review panel may exist in the meaning of the language used in the standard at both the conceptual and complexity levels (Beach, 2011; Pickreign & Capps, 2000). With either issue, what is more important—content, cognitive demand, or emphasis? According to the alignment models, a balance needs to occur among the content of the standards, level of cognitive demand, and the balance and range of content in the standards (Resnick et al., 2004; Webb, 2007).

Second, researchers raised the question of how fine the alignment needs to be (Martone & Sireci, 2009; Rothman et al., 2002). Is a broader alignment at the cluster or anchor standard level sufficient for developing instructional and assessments materials or does the alignment need to occur at the standard level? For example, in the Survey of Enacted Curriculum model, there is a list of specific topics across all grade levels where an educator can have a common view of all of the content from K–12. However, the number of topics can be difficult to manage, so often broad topic areas similar to strands in the Common Core or themes in the National Curriculum Standards for Social Studies are used. Studies have not yet examined the degree of alignment needed among the intended, enacted, and assessed curriculum to increase student achievement.

Third, some researchers are concerned about the standards and how they might reduce the breadth of the curriculum taught in the classroom (Martone & Sireci, 2009; Webb, 1999). This concern is particularly apparent as educators align the standards to the assessed curriculum. Not all of the standards can be assessed each year because of the time it takes to measure the complexity of the required performance. These constraints limit the content on the test and may therefore limit what teachers decide to teach in the classroom.

Fourth, in developing curriculum documents, some states and school districts are including rigid pacing guides, which influence the flexibility for attending to individual differences in students. Portions of the standards may need to be eliminated for students who already know the knowledge and skills. In addition, gifted and advanced students may need to be accelerated one or more grade levels in their areas of strength.

Fifth, implementation issues have been identified such as (a) identifying leaders who not only have the expertise but are also interested in the alignment process; (b) providing time to complete a thorough examination of the curriculum; (c) finding resources in times of budget challenges; (d) packaging the curriculum documents for clarity and utility; and (e) developing professional learning opportunities that are effective in influencing classroom instruction (Blank et al., 2001; CCSRI, 2009; Roseman & Koppal, 2008).

# Conclusion

Over the past 5 years, national standards have been developed to address students' mediocre performance on international tests and prepare them for higher education and future careers. These standards differ from previous standards in important ways: They emphasize more complex thinking and focus on depth rather than breadth. These changes and different emphases have led state agencies and schools to examine their current standards and align them to these new standards.

Although no specific gifted education standards have been developed for the core content domains, gifted educators have developed books for using the CCSS and the NGSS with gifted and advanced students and have programming standards that ask teachers to incorporate differentiated curricula in all domains.

The alignment process is the extent to which there is an agreement of match between standards and at least one of three categories: the taught curriculum, the tested curriculum, and the written curriculum. This chapter focused primarily on the process of aligning standards with the written or intended curriculum using three methods as a foundation: The Surveys of Enacted Curriculum, the Webb Alignment Tool, and Achieve. The alignment process included identifying critical areas for the standards; matching content, cognitive demand, and emphases between the standards; developing a scope and sequence; and providing examples of learner activities. Within each step of the alignment process, educators need to pay attention to differentiation principles.

Finally, the importance of identifying a strong expert panel that is comprised of educators with content and teaching expertise is essential to ensure a quality alignment and to avoid some of the issues raised by researchers. Strong curriculum documents that are aligned to rigorous standards and differentiated can benefit all students, particularly those who are gifted and advanced.

# References

Adams, C. M., Cotabish, A., & Dailey, D. (2015). *A teacher's guide to using the Next Generation Science Standards with gifted and advanced learners.* Waco, TX: Prufrock Press.

Adams, C. M., Cotabish, A., & Ricci, M. C. (2014). *Using the Next Generation Science Standards with gifted and advanced learners.* Waco, TX: Prufrock Press.

Agostino, J. V., Welsh, M. E., Cimetta, A. D., Falco, L. A., Smith, S., VanWinkle, W. H., & Powers, S. J. (2008). The rating and matching item-objective alignment methods. *Applied Measurement in Education, 21,* 1–21. doi:10.1080/08957340701580728

Anderson, L. W. (2002). Curricular alignment: A re-examination. *Theory Into Practice, 41,* 255–260.

Anderson, L. W., & Krathwohl, D. R. (Eds.). (2001). *A taxonomy for learning, teaching, and assessing: A revision of Bloom's taxonomy of educational objectives.* New York, NY: Longman.

Beach, R. W. (2011). Issues in analyzing alignment of language arts Common Core Standards with state standards. *Educational Researcher, 40,* 179–182. doi:10.3102/0013089X11310055

Blank, R. K., Porter, A., & Smithson, J. (2001). *New tools for analyzing teaching, curriculum, and standards in mathematics and science: Report from Survey of Enacted Curriculum project. Final report.* Washington, DC: Council of Chief State School Officers.

Bloom, B. S., Engelhart, M. D., Furst, E. J., Hill, W. H., & Krathwohl, D. R. (1956). *Taxonomy of educational objectives: The classification of educational goals. Handbook I: Cognitive domain.* New York, NY: David McKay Company.

California Department of Education. (2013a, November). *English language arts framework.* Retrieved from http://www.cde.ca.gov/ci/rl/cf

California Department of Education. (2013b, November). *Mathematics framework.* Retrieved from http://www.cde.ca.gov/ci/ma/cf/draft2 mathfwchapters.asp

Center for Comprehensive School Reform and Improvement. (2009, August). *Issue brief: Vertical alignment: Ensuring opportunity to learn in a standards-based system.* Washington, DC: Author.

Conley, D. T., Drummond, K. V., de Gonzalez, A., Seburn, M., Stout, O., & Rooseboom, J. (2011). *Lining up: The relationship between the common core state standards and five sets of comparison standards*. Eugene, OR: Educational Policy Improvement Center.

Elder, L., & Paul, R. (2004). *The art of asking essential questions*. Dillon Beach, CA: The Foundation for Critical Thinking.

Ford, D. Y. (2006). Creating culturally responsive classrooms for gifted students. *Understanding Our Gifted, 19*(1), 10–14.

Glaser, R. (1963). Instructional technology and the measurement of learning outcomes: Some questions. *American Psychologist, 18*, 519–521.

Hambleton, R. K. (1984). Validating the test scores. In R. A. Berk (Ed.). *A guide to criterion-referenced test construction* (pp. 199–230). Baltimore, MD: Johns Hopkins University Press.

Hartman, H. J. (2001). *Metacognition in learning and instruction: Theory, research and practice*. Dordrecht, The Netherlands: Kluwer Academic Publishers.

Hughes-Lynch, C. E., Kettler, T., Shaunessy-Dedrick, E., & VanTassel-Baska, J. (2014). *A teacher's guide to using the Common Core State Standards with gifted and advanced learners in the English Language Arts*. Waco, TX: Prufrock Press.

Johnsen, S. K. (Ed.). (2012). *NAGC pre-K–grade 12 gifted education programming standards: A guide to planning and implementing high-quality services*. Waco, TX: Prufrock Press.

Johnsen, S. K., Ryser, G. R., & Assouline, S. G. (2014). *A teachers' guide to using the Common Core State Standards with mathematically gifted and advanced learners*. Waco, TX: Prufrock Press.

Johnsen, S. K., & Sheffield, L. J. (Eds.) (2013). *Using the Common Core State Standards for Mathematics with gifted and advanced learners*. Waco, TX: Prufrock Press.

Kaplan, S. N. (2009). Layering differentiated curricula for the gifted and talented. In F. A. Karnes & S. M. Bean (Eds.), *Methods and materials for teaching the gifted* (3rd ed., pp. 107–135). Waco, TX: Prufrock Press.

Kitano, M., Montgomery, D., VanTassel-Baska, J., & Johnsen, S. (2008). *Using the national gifted education standards for Pre-K–12 professional development*. Thousand Oaks, CA: Corwin Press.

Krathwohl, D. R. (2002). A revision of Bloom's taxonomy: An overview. *Theory Into Practice, 41*, 212–218.

Martone, A., & Sireci, S. G. (2009). Evaluating alignment between curriculum, assessment, and instruction. *Review of Educational Research, 79,* 1332–1361.

National Association for Gifted Children. (2010, November). *NAGC pre-K–grade 12 gifted programming standards: A blueprint for quality gifted education programs.* Washington, DC: Author. Retrieved from http://www.nagc.org/uploadedFiles/Information_and_Resources/Gifted_Program_Standards/K-12%20programming%20standards.pdf.

National Council for the Social Studies. (2010). *National curriculum standards for social studies: A framework for teaching, learning, and assessment.* Retrieved from http://www.socialstudies.org/standards/curriculum

National Governors Association Center for Best Practices, & Council of Chief State School Officers. (2010a). *Common Core State Standards for English Language Arts.* Washington, DC: Authors.

National Governors Association Center for Best Practices, & Council of Chief State School Officers. (2010b). *Common Core State Standards for Mathematics.* Washington, DC: Authors.

National Research Council. (2012). *A framework for K–12 science education: Practices, crosscutting concepts, and core ideas.* Washington, DC: The National Academies Press.

NGSS Lead States. (2013). *Next Generation Science Standards: For states, by states.* Washington, DC: The National Academies Press.

North Carolina Department of Public Instruction. (2012). *Instructional support tools for achieving new standards.* Retrieved from http://www.ncpublicschools.org/acre/standards/support-tools/

Partnership for 21st Century Skills. (2009). *P21 Framework definitions.* Washington, DC: Author. Retrieved from http://www.p21.org/storage/documents/P21_Framework_Definitions.pdf

Paul, R., & Elder, L. (2004). *Critical and creative thinking.* Dillon Beach, CA: The Foundation for Critical Thinking.

Pickreign, J., & Capps, L. R. (2000). Alignment of elementary geometry curriculum with current standards. *Elementary Geometry Curriculum, 100,* 243–251.

Porter, A. C. (2002). Measuring the content of instruction: Uses in research and practice. *Educational Researcher, 31*(7), 3–14.

Resnick, L. B., Rothman, R., Slattery, J. B., & Vranek, J. L. (2004). Benchmarking and alignment of standards and testing. *Educational Assessment, 9*(1&2), 1–27.

Roseman, J. E., & Koppal, M. (2008). Using national standards to improve K–8 science curriculum materials. *The Elementary School Journal, 109,* 104–122.

Rothman, R., Slattery, J. B., Vranek, J. L., & Resnick, L. B. (2002). *Benchmarking and alignment of standards and testing. CSE technical report 566.* Los Angeles, CA: UCLA Center for the Study of Evaluation.

Siegle, D. (2004). *Using media and technology with gifted learners.* Waco, TX: Prufrock Press.

Squires, D. (2012). Curriculum alignment research suggests that alignment can improve student achievement. *The Clearing House, 85,* 129–135. doi:10.1080/00098655.2012.657723

Stiggins, R. (2008). *Assessment manifesto: A call for the development of balanced assessment systems.* Portland, OR: ETS Assessment Training Institute.

Tomlinson, C. A. (Ed.). (2004). *Differentiation for gifted and talented students.* Thousand Oaks, CA: Corwin Press.

Tyler, R. W. (1949). *Basic principles of curriculum and instruction.* Chicago, IL: University of Chicago Press.

VanTassel-Baska, J. (2004). *Curriculum for gifted and talented students.* Thousand Oaks, CA: Corwin Press.

VanTassel-Baska, J. (Ed.). (2013). *Using the Common Core State Standards for English Language Arts with gifted and advanced learners.* Waco, TX: Prufrock Press.

Vockley, M., & Lang, V. (2009). *Three approaches to aligning the National Assessment of Educational Progress with state assessments, other assessments, and standards.* Washington, DC: Council of Chief State School Officers.

Webb, N. L. (1997). *Criteria for alignment of expectations and assessments in mathematics and science education* (Research Monograph No. 8). Washington, DC: Council of Chief State School Officers.

Webb, N. L. (1999). *Alignment of science and mathematics standards and assessments in four states* (Research Monograph No. 18). Madison: University of Wisconsin-Madison, National Institute for Science Education.

Webb, N. L. (2002). *Alignment study in language arts, mathematics, science, and social studies of state standards and tests four states.* Technical

Issues in Large-Scale Assessment (TILSA) State Collaborative on Assessment & State Standards (SCASS). Madison: University of Wisconsin, Wisconsin Center for Education Research.

Webb, N. L. (2007). Issues related to judging the alignment of curriculum standards and assessments. *Applied Measurement in Education, 20*(1), 7–25.

# SECTION II

# Survey of Curriculum Models

# CHAPTER 5

# Survey of Curriculum Models in Gifted Education

## Frameworks for Developing and Implementing Differentiated Curricula

**Ann Robinson and Audrey Tabler**

## Introduction

Theorists, researchers, curriculum developers, and school practitioners have contributed to the development of and interest in a variety of curriculum models in gifted education. The primacy of curriculum developed or adapted to meet the cognitive and affective needs of gifted children and adolescents as a cornerstone of the field is a widely held tenet. Nevertheless, one of the challenges of a survey of curriculum models in gifted education is the blurred boundary between program models and curriculum models and their relationship to the instructional strategies that bring them to life.

The purposes of this chapter are to suggest a definition of curriculum models in gifted education, to survey descriptively the major models in current use, to describe selected examples of curriculum development and implementation projects guided by one or more of the models, and to summarize briefly the efficacy research supporting specific curricular models or projects, particularly those developed under the Jacob K. Javits Gifted and Talented Students Program. The practical criteria of models for which curricular products exist, the accessibility of demonstration projects and sites that document use and sustainability, and the availability of professional development for teachers who wish to implement specific curriculum guided the selection of models included in this chapter.

# Definitions of Curriculum Models in Gifted Education

VanTassel-Baska (1986), VanTassel-Baska and Brown (2001, 2007, 2009), and VanTassel-Baska and Wood (2010) grappled with the definitions of curricular models in gifted education and suggested criteria by which the models could be identified as emanating from within the field rather than from general education, be defined as curricular models, and be evaluated for their efficacy with talented learners.

The difficulty of discriminating between program and curriculum models in gifted education is severe and has been addressed previously by both VanTassel-Baska and Renzulli in different but complementary ways. For example, Renzulli (1986) edited a compendium of extant models under the inclusive title of *Systems and Models for Developing Programs for the Gifted and Talented*. The compendium included models as diverse as the Enrichment/Triad/Revolving Door Model (Renzulli & Reis, 1986) to the Structure of the Intellect (SOI) System for Gifted Education (Meeker & Meeker, 1986). The compendium was a snapshot of the multiplicity of approaches and the diverse levels at which model developers in the field during the 1970s and the 1980s targeted their efforts from interventions that focused on specific components of services to broad, systemic efforts that included curriculum as a part, but not the main focus of the model. The lens was refocused some 20 years later with a second compendium

(Renzulli, Gubbins, McMillen, Eckert, & Little, 2009). Some models from the first edition disappeared, and new models were added, but the diversity in focus and comprehensiveness of the models remains. Curriculum models are included in both editions, but they are elided with programs and with the even more expansive conceptualization of service delivery to talented students as a system.

Although VanTassel-Baska and Brown (2007) sought to draw a definitional boundary around curriculum models in gifted education in at least one report on their analysis of the efficacy of models, the authors identified them as amalgamated "program/curriculum models" (p. 344). They preceded their analysis of specific models with a conceptualization and description of two mega-models in gifted education which they noted represent the historically different approaches of acceleration and enrichment: Stanley's Talent Search Model and Renzulli's Schoolwide Enrichment Model.

In an initial report of the investigation, they established five criteria or components for the inclusion of a curriculum model in gifted education as a subject for their analysis (VanTassel-Baska & Brown, 2001). First, the model provides a framework for curriculum design and development. Second, the model must be transferable and usable in all content areas. Third, the model is applicable across the K–12 grade span. Fourth, the model is applicable across multiple school and grouping settings. And, finally, the model incorporates differentiated features for talented learners. Using these criteria, VanTassel-Baska and Brown (2001) reduced an initial pool of models under consideration from 20 to 11. The pool was further reduced when a rubric of 15 criteria based on important indicators of curriculum effectiveness was applied to the models. Among those criteria were key features important in teacher selection and development of curriculum that included research evidence regarding student outcomes, teacher receptivity, teacher training, the existence of curricular products based on the model, and evidence that the model had been used for teacher-developed curricula. In later reviews, VanTassel-Baska and Brown (2007, 2009) included curriculum models that did not meet their initial criteria for effectiveness, most notably the criterion of research on student learning impact. For the purposes of this chapter, some popular models without evidence of student or teacher learning impact are included in the review.

# Curriculum Models in Gifted Education

Curriculum models established for the purpose of meeting the unique needs of gifted and talented students have enabled practicing classroom teachers who serve these students to build appropriate and challenging instructional units, provide differentiated learning opportunities specific to students' abilities and interests, and stimulate the development of independent thinking and learning. In existence for more than four decades, currently applied curriculum models in gifted education are structured to challenge and to enrich the educational experiences of talented learners. The models continue to evolve as the diverse needs of talented learners change in the educational context.

A loosely chronological overview highlights aspects of selected models that serve as frameworks for curriculum development in gifted education and provides a brief description of each model, individuals credited with the design, key elements of the model, model development over time, target populations and delivery, and general support structure and resources.

## Stanley's Talent Search Model

An introduction in the late 1960s to a young boy whose mathematical ability was found to be well beyond what could be measured on grade-level tests was the beginning of the work that eventually led Julian Stanley to develop the Talent Search Model (Lee, Matthews, & Olszewski-Kubilius, 2008; Wai, 2015). His goal was to educate for individual development over an extended K–20 and postgraduate educational trajectory and included a method of identifying exceptional performance and appropriate instructional planning and programming to meet the individual needs of talented students. Stanley's model resulted in more than 40 years of research and practice in the field of gifted education with recent longitudinal reports of educational accomplishments related to the intensity and duration of student exposure to fast-paced curriculum and other accelerative experiences (Wai, Lubinski, Benbow, & Steiger, 2010).

The model features four key elements that include: (1) the use of an above-level, challenging testing instrument to identify students with exceptionally high mathematical, verbal, and more recently spatial reasoning ability; (2) a diagnostic testing-prescriptive instructional approach (DT-PI) that includes special classes for talented students to allow appropriate levels of instructional challenge; (3) the use of subject matter acceleration and fast-paced instruction in core subject areas; and (4) an endorsement for curricular flexibility in all schooling (VanTassel-Baska & Brown, 2009). Although Stanley's DT-PI approach to instructional and curricular planning can be implemented in a variety of settings, the Talent Search Model is widely associated with out-of-school programming offered by universities (Olszewski-Kubilius & Thomson, 2014).

Stanley's development of the model with colleagues at Johns Hopkins University began in 1971 with the establishment of the Study of Mathematically Precocious Youth (SMPY) to search for and serve students demonstrating advanced mathematical and scientific ability. From 1972 to 1979, SMPY pioneered the talent search concept (Brody & Mills, 2005; Swiatek, 2007; VanTassel-Baska & Brown, 2007). In 1980, the search was extended to identify students who demonstrated exceptionally high verbal reasoning ability (VanTassel-Baska & Brown, 2007, 2009).

In 1979, Stanley established the Center for Talented Youth at Johns Hopkins University to administer the program he developed, and in the early 1980s, replication talent searches were instituted at other sites across the country, the first being the Talent Identification Program (TIP), founded at Duke University in 1981. Duke TIP was followed shortly after by the Center for Talent Development at Northwestern University and the Rocky Mountain Talent Search at the University of Denver. In the late 1980s and early 1990s, state talent searches were founded at the University of Iowa and at Carnegie Mellon University in Pennsylvania (Lee et al., 2008). Stanley's approach also led to the development of national talent searches in countries beyond the United States (Swiatek, 2007).

Although the model initially focused on emerging adolescents, more recent applications have included younger students. Grades 3–12 now comprise the target population for the Talent Search Model. Students in grades 7 and 8 who demonstrate well-above-average performance on standardized assessments can take the ACT or SAT to qualify. Each year, approximately 200,000 gifted students participate in the talent search process (Olszewski-Kubilius & Thomson, 2014). As a result of participation in the Talent Search Model, students may be served through content-based acceleration in core subject areas, Pre-Advanced Placement and Advanced Placement (AP) courses, and afterschool settings for specialized instruction. Summer residential and day programs are offered at universities to provide fast-paced, specialized instructional programs that can be completed in 3 weeks (Assouline & Lupkowski-Shoplik, 2012; VanTassel-Baska & Brown, 2009).

The Stanley mega-model focuses more on program than curriculum development. Talented students are matched to a suite of articulated course offerings that can link to widely used offerings such as honors courses, Advanced Placement courses, and International Baccalaureate programs. Thus, the Talent Search Model informs the curricular issue of multiyear scope and sequence rather than the curricular building blocks of differentiated curriculum unit development.

## Renzulli's Schoolwide Enrichment Model

The Schoolwide Enrichment Model (SEM) provides enriched learning experiences and higher expectations for all children with a dual goal of developing academic and creative productive giftedness in young people (Reis & Renzulli, 2010). The model, coauthored by Joseph Renzulli and Sally Reis, emphasizes engagement in enjoyable and challenging learning experiences constructed around students' interests, learning styles, and product preferences and is manifested through three goals that include: (a) the arrangement of special services for students who demonstrate or show the potential for superior performance in school and extracurricular programs; (b) the infusion of high-end learning activities into the general education program that challenge all students to perform at advanced levels and allow teachers to determine students' needs for extended opportunities, resources, and encouragement in areas where superior interest and performance are demonstrated; and (c) the preservation and protection of the positions of individuals responsible for coordinating and implementing program goals (Reis & Renzulli, 2010).

Researched and field-tested over a period of 15 years by educators and researchers, the SEM is a product of the earlier Enrichment Triad and Revolving Door Identification Models (Renzulli & Reis, 1994). The Triad Model, developed in the mid-1970s and originally intended to serve as a gifted model, became the curriculum core of SEM and has been used by classroom, gifted education, and enrichment teachers to design and implement three types of enrichment opportunities: Type I general exploratory activities; Type II group training activities; and Type III individual and small-group investigation of real problems. Evaluation of research based on the Triad model prompted the development of the Revolving Door Identification Model, which broadened the talent pool to 10%–15% of the student population to allow academically able and creative students not selected for gifted programs but qualified by the use of multiple criteria in evaluative assessments to participate in enrichment and to revolve in and out of various levels of the three enrichment types, including Type III Enrichment opportunities (Reis & Renzulli, 2010). Although all students are encouraged to access Type I, II, and III Enrichment opportunities, Type III is usually more appropriate for those with higher level ability, interest, and task commitment (Reis, n.d.; Reis & Renzulli, 2010). Further application of the SEM model resulted in the Schoolwide Enrichment Model in Reading (SEM-R), designed to enrich instruction in a core curriculum area, and Renzulli Learning, an Internet-based program that develops personal profiles of students to allow teachers to differentiate instruction more efficiently and effectively, leading to increased student achievement (Reis, n.d.; Field, 2007, 2009).

The SEM mega-model focuses on various types of instructional strategies and activities, can be applied across content areas and grade levels, and includes creativity as an important student outcome. Instruction and curricular offerings based on student interest are a key feature of the model, but SEM can also be applied and implemented as a program structure.

## Talents Unlimited, Inc. and Talents Unlimited to the Secondary Power

The Talents Unlimited (TU) model was put into practice beginning in 1971 by Carol Schlichter to develop students' creative and critical thinking skills in the five "talent" areas of productive thinking, decision making, planning, forecasting, and communication in addition to basic academic talents (Newman, 2004; Schlichter, Hobbs, & Crump, 1988). According to the developer, TU is based on Guilford's multifactor conceptualization of intelligence (Guilford, 1956) and influenced by Taylor's multiple talent theory (Taylor, 1968). Talents Unlimited features four major components that include: (1) a description of the specific skill abilities, talents, and academic abilities that include the five talents; (2) model instructional materials; (3) in-service teacher training programs; and (4) an evaluation system to assess students' thinking skills (VanTassel-Baska & Brown, 2007, 2009).

The Talents Unlimited Model serves K–6 students through Talents Unlimited, Inc. and was extended later to include students in grades 7–12 at schools in Alabama, Arkansas, and New Mexico with a version of the model titled Talents Unlimited to the Secondary Power (TU²) (Schlichter et al., 1988; VanTassel-Baska & Brown, 2009). In both elementary and secondary settings, thinking skills lessons and activities are designed by teachers trained to implement model activities in various subject areas, to minimize the unproductive evaluation of creative ideas as right or wrong, to phrase questions in ways that elicit varied responses from students, to guide students in their thinking processes, and to extend concepts beyond the textbook for all students (Schlichter et al., 1988). Professional development and teacher training are components of the model that make provision for certifying teachers as TU trainers. According to VanTassel-Baska and Brown (2009), the focus on skill-based instruction for all students leads the TU model to be less differentiated for talented learners than other curricular models widely used in the field.

## The Purdue Three-Stage Model

The result of a course concept design for university students introduced in 1973 by John Feldhusen and his colleagues at Purdue University, the Purdue Three-Stage Model in gifted education was developed and initially explicated by Feldhusen and Kolloff at the elementary level (Feldhusen & Kolloff, 1978). It is an enrichment model with the objective of moving students from initial thinking process skills to complex independent activities. The stages of the model include: Stage I—teacher-led development of basic divergent and convergent thinking skills; Stage II—teacher-led and student-initiated opportunities for the development of more complex creative and problem-solving abilities; and Stage III—student-led and teacher-guided application of research skills to develop independent study skills. In the third stage of the Purdue model, talented students pursue more intensive investigations fueled by personal interests followed by communication of independent and group research results (Feldhusen & Kolloff, 1986).

Following the adaptation of the original Purdue Model into a Three-Stage Enrichment Model for Elementary Gifted Students articulated by Feldhusen and Kolloff (1978), the model was applied in the Program for Academic and Creative Enrichment, where effects on self-concept and creative thinking were investigated (Kolloff & Feldhusen, 1981, 1984). Perceptions of the students and their families on the positive long-term effects of the model on the thinking abilities and cognitive, affective, and social development attributable to the elementary intervention were documented in a qualitative study by Moon, Feldhusen, and Dillon (1994). The complementary companion to the Three-Stage Enrichment Model for Elementary Gifted Students is the Purdue Secondary Model for Gifted and Talented Youth, which features 11 components of programming to support enrichment and acceleration options: counseling services, seminars, Advanced Placement courses, honors classes, math-science acceleration, world languages, arts, cultural experiences, career education, vocational programs, and extra-school instruction (Feldhusen & Robinson, 1986). Taken together, the two companion models span K–12 grade levels and have been applied in both elementary and secondary settings (Moon, Kolloff, Robinson, Dixon, & Feldhusen, 2009).

## Sternberg's Triarchic Model

When applied to gifted education, the Triarchic Model designed by Robert Sternberg offers a unified structure for the integration of identification, instruction, and assessment procedures for talented students and corresponds to analytical, creative, and practical cognitive skills with a goal of improving students' ability to think for school and beyond (Sternberg & Clinkenbeard, 1995; Sternberg, Grigorenko, & Jarvin, 2001).

The model derives from Sternberg's triarchic theory of human intelligence (Sternberg, 1981, 1985), which includes memory-analytic, creative-synthetic, and practical-contextual abilities. Briefly, memory-analytic abilities, activated when one learns, compares, analyzes, evaluates, and judges, are those primarily measured in the identification, instruction, and assessment of the gifted, while creative-synthetic abilities are used to develop novel and high-quality ideas and products. Finally, practical-contextual abilities are used to succeed in everyday environments. The Triarchic Model considers these abilities, whether activated independently or in concert, as potentially significant in the development of curriculum to ensure appropriate matches are made to connect students' abilities with instruction (Sternberg & Clinkenbeard, 1995).

Initially, studies of the application of the Triarchic Model targeted gifted high school students learning psychology (Sternberg & Clinkenbeard,

1995), but were extended to include reading instruction with subsequent studies conducted on the use of triarchic instructional processes in elementary, middle, and high schools (Grigorenko, Jarvin, & Sternberg, 2002; Sternberg, Grigorenko & Jarvin, 2001). Examples of instructional adaptations across disciplines using the triarchic model as a guide to develop educational experiences that are analytic, creative, or practical are found in Sternberg and Clinkenbeard (1995) and Sternberg, Grigorenko, and Li-fang (2008).

### Gardner's Multiple Intelligences Model

Concerned with theoretical and practical factors related to human intelligence, Howard Gardner introduced the Multiple Intelligences Model (MI Theory; Gardner, 1983). The initial seven areas of intelligence defined by Gardner include verbal-linguistic, logical-mathematical, visual-spatial, musical-rhythmic, body-kinesthetic, interpersonal, and intrapersonal; naturalist was added later (Gardner, 1999).

Initially, the model theory was suggested as a way to develop assessments and monitor outcomes through the construction, administration, evaluation, and validation of assessment instruments to determine students' multiple intelligences and indicate students' strengths and weaknesses reliably. Gardner (1989) suggested that assessments, corresponding to MI Theory, be devised to test a student's ability to demonstrate problem-solving ability, as well as the propensity to create products, not measured in short-answer tests. Gardner and Hatch (1989) linked the theory and the assessments to the possibility of developing educational experiences. Two projects undertaken with colleagues, Arts Propel (Gardner, 1989) and Spectrum (Krechevsky, 1998) focused on assessments in specific domains. Gardner's interest in curricular application may have been shaped by his experience working with Jerome Bruner on the development of *Man, A Course of Study*, a popular humanities curriculum in the 1970s.

According to VanTassel-Baska and Brown (2009), Gardner conceptualized the model primarily to promote talent development for all learners, thereby making the model less differentiated for identified gifted learners. A plethora of commercially and freely available instructional and curricular materials are available for teachers to use should they wish to be guided by MI. Although he acknowledges the implementation of his ideas in schools, particularly the Key School in Indianapolis, Gardner (2011) stated that the curriculum development in schools using MI as a framework has "led a life of its own" (p. 303).

## The Autonomous Learner Model

The Autonomous Learner Model (ALM) was developed by Betts (1985) and Betts and Kercher (1999) as a framework for curriculum development to meet the cognitive, emotional, and social needs of gifted and talented students and to foster autonomy by helping them become independent, self-directed learners responsible for the development, implementation, and evaluation of their own learning (Betts & Kercher, 2009; Johnsen & Goree, 2005). Concerns among educators and researchers that the special affective needs of students related to their giftedness were often unmet led the developers to include experiences necessary for social and emotional growth of gifted individuals across multiple dimensions of the ALM (Betts, 1986).

The ALM features five major dimensions including: (1) orientation as students learn about self and their learning opportunities/responsibilities; (2) individual development as students learn about personal skills development, as well as concepts and attitudes important for autonomy in learning; (3) enrichment as students participate in exploratory and investigative studies, special programs and activities, and opportunities beyond the classroom that stimulate ideas for independent study topics; (4) seminars as students share in and facilitate discussions about their research findings from independent study with cohorts in small-group settings; and (5) in-depth study as students pursue topics for long-term independent or group research projects (Betts, 1985; Betts & Kercher, 1999; Betts & Kercher, 2009).

Originally designed to serve gifted students at the secondary level, the ALM can be adapted for use in elementary learning environments in all subject area domains (Johnsen & Goree, 2005; Uresti, Goertz, & Bernal, 2002), and as reported by the developer, it is one of the most widely used and recognized curriculum models in the United States (Betts, 1986; VanTassel-Baska & Brown, 2009). Materials, including planning forms and rubrics for instruction and for student projects, are available to support the ALM (Betts & Kercher, 2009).

## The Integrated Curriculum Model

The Integrated Curriculum Model (ICM) was developed by Joyce VanTassel-Baska (1986) to meet the needs of high-ability learners through exposure to advanced content, high-level process and product work, and intra- and interdisciplinary concept development and understanding (VanTassel-Baska, 2003; VanTassel-Baska & Brown, 2009).

The three dimensions of the model are employed to: (1) expose students to advanced content knowledge within the disciplines through accelerated coursework; (2) incorporate high-order thinking and processing by encouraging in-depth, independent learning habits; and (3) structure students' learning experiences centered around major issues, themes, and ideas with intra- and interdisciplinary applications to theoretical and real-world situations (Hockett, 2009; VanTassel-Baska & Wood, 2010).

VanTassel-Baska's model offers a comprehensive framework for curriculum design that addresses the characteristics of precocity, intensity, and complexity in the talented learner and reflects recent educational and psychological research on learning (VanTassel-Baska & Wood, 2010). With a decade and a half of Jacob K. Javits funding, VanTassel-Baska and her colleagues applied the ICM to develop curriculum units in the core content areas of language arts, science, social studies, and eventually, mathematics for talented learners (VanTassel-Baska & Brown, 2007, 2009). Recent ICM units include the arts, humanities, and Latin. Initially, the William & Mary ICM language arts units were developed for grades 2–10 and ultimately expanded to cover grades K–11, science units for grades K–8, and social studies units for grades 2–10 (VanTassel-Baska & Brown, 2009). An extensive suite of efficacy studies of the curricula in school settings has documented student learning impacts across multiple core content areas such as language arts (VanTassel-Baska, Zuo, Avery, & Little, 2002), reading (VanTassel-Baska, Bracken, Feng, & Brown, 2009), science (Kim et al., 2012; VanTassel-Baska, Bass, Ries, Poland, & Avery, 1998), and social studies (Little, Feng, VanTassel-Baska, Rogers, & Avery, 2007) and in a variety of administrative groupings (Feng, VanTassel-Baska, Quek, Bai, & O'Neill, 2004; VanTassel-Baska et al., 2008).

The developer reported that ICM has been used in Australia, Canada, Japan, Korea, New Zealand, Taiwan, and selected districts in the United States to plan and construct curriculum implemented in schools in 50 states, as well as international schools (Van Tassel-Baska & Brown, 2009). More than 25 William & Mary units, using national standards as a template and supported with discipline-related methods and materials, have been developed (Hockett, 2009) and are commercially available for teacher implementation or as guides for teachers developing their own ICM units.

Critical factors in the success of the ICM and its specific curriculum implementation include strong professional development, adequate resources, effective leadership, accountability, and the use of summative and formative assessments to evaluate progress. Teacher professional development is an integral component of the ICM and is offered through workshops and annual training opportunities at William & Mary (VanTassel-Baska & Brown, 2007, 2009).

## Kaplan's Grid: The Depth and Complexity Model

Sandra Kaplan designed the Grid, a framework for guiding the development of differentiated curricula by modifying standards-based curriculum for gifted and high-achieving students (Kaplan, 1986; VanTassel-Baska, 2003, VanTassel-Baska & Brown, 2009). Curriculum developers utilize Kaplan's Grid to organize the curriculum components of content, process, and product, with a focus on the dimensions of depth and complexity. In fact, the most recent iteration of the model identifies it as the Depth and Complexity Model of curriculum (Callahan, Moon, Oh, Azano, & Hailey, 2015).

According to the developer, depth and complexity have been referenced in the gifted education literature extensively, and in the early 1970s, the California Department of Education proposed that curriculum for gifted students "achieve depth, provide selective emphasis, and promote student interest in complex concepts beyond requirements of the standard curriculum" (California Department of Education, 1971, as cited in Kaplan, 2013). Funding through a Jacob K. Javits grant enabled the state department of education and experts in gifted education to refine the dimensions of depth and complexity and prepare a guide for educators (California Department of Education & California Association for the Gifted, 1994). To focus the learner, the Grid, or the Depth and Complexity Model, includes 11 prompts: language of the disciplines, details, patterns, unanswered questions, rules, trends, ethics, big ideas, across the disciplines, changes over time, and different perspectives. Each of the prompts is represented by a graphic image that serves as a visual cue to both teacher and student. For example, the prompt for unanswered questions is represented by large questions marks while the prompt for different perspectives is represented by a montage of lenses including eyeglasses, binoculars, and a magnifying glass (Kaplan, 2013).

Kaplan's approach has been implemented at the state and local levels, and teachers have developed their own curricula based on the model. The developer reports evidence from an unpublished 2009 study with gifted and nonidentified students in grades 2–4 in a Title I elementary school that implementation resulted in pre-post gains in social studies and language arts in student use of selected depth and complexity prompts (Kaplan, 2013). The model has also been integrated into an intervention project that resulted in student learning gains attributed to two language arts units (Callahan et al., 2015). Model support is available through published materials and teacher training, previously conducted throughout the country, and now offered independently by the developer (VanTassel-Baska & Brown, 2009).

## Maker's Matrix and the DISCOVER Assessment and Curriculum Model

The Maker Matrix Model was developed by C. June Maker (1982) to categorize the content, process, product, and environmental dimensions of an appropriate curriculum for the gifted (VanTassel-Baska & Brown, 2009). A later model, The Discovering Intellectual Strengths and Capabilities through Observation (DISCOVER), designed by C. June Maker and her colleagues, enhanced the problem-solving component of the Matrix Model (Sak & Maker, 2004), and added the role of the teacher and the role of the student as additional key elements of the curriculum. The DISCOVER model is reportedly influenced by the theories of Gardner's Multiple Intelligences and Sternberg's Triarchic Model with a focus on practical abilities, research in gifted education, and research related to creativity and its development (Sak & Maker, 2004). According to the developer, the DISCOVER Curriculum Model differs from other educational approaches built on the same theoretical works by the problem-solving continuum it presents. Schiever and Maker (1991) elaborated on the Getzels and Csikszentmihalyi (1976) model that used three problem types by extending it to include five types, forming a new matrix (the Problem Continuum Model) to develop and assess problem-solving abilities of students (Maker et al., 2006; Sak & Maker, 2004).

Because the DISCOVER Curriculum Model follows a constructivist perspective, its elements are reflective of those ideas dedicated to: constructing new knowledge founded on prior experiences, acquiring higher order thinking and problem-solving skills, integrating knowledge from one skill to learn another, presenting fewer topics with greater depth, and engaging students to become active participants in their own learning (Maker et al., 2006). A foundational purpose for the development of the model included the selection of problem-solving tasks that would engage individuals representing a wide range of ages, abilities, languages, ethnicities, and environmental backgrounds, as well as to identify students from at-risk populations whose abilities and potential often fail to be recognized (Sak & Maker, 2004).

Maker and her colleagues originally created the continuum to include five different problem types ranging from those requiring convergent thinking with single solutions (school-type, well-structured) to those that are more complex (real-world, ill-structured) in that they need to be defined and may have multiple methods and many possible solutions. Teachers use the DISCOVER Curriculum Model to develop units employing a matrix of the continuum of problem types and the multiple intelligences to guide planning and analyze plans for evidence of a variety of learning experiences and for student choice (Maker et al., 2006; VanTassel-Baska & Brown, 2009).

The model is supported with some teacher training. Research has taken place and is ongoing in a number of school districts in Arizona and in school systems in other states and countries using the matrix for curriculum development purposes (Maker et al., 2006; Sak & Maker, 2004).

## The Parallel Curriculum Model

The Parallel Curriculum Model (PCM), based on the collective work of Tomlinson, Kaplan, Renzulli, Purcell, Leppien, and Burns (2002), was developed for planning curriculum that appropriately challenges all learners, including those who are gifted (Hockett, 2009). It is a framework based on four dimensions, referred to as parallels, which can be used independently or in conjunction with one another. The parallels include the Core Curriculum, the Curriculum of Connections, the Curriculum of Practice, and the Curriculum of Identity.

Considered to be the foundation for the other parallels, the Core Curriculum is based on the standards, principles, key facts and skills, and conceptual knowledge of specific disciplines. Employing intra- and inter-disciplinary study practices, the curriculum of connections supports students' discovery of the interconnectedness between and among the concepts and principles of various fields of study. The curriculum of practice provides students with opportunities to develop a deeper understanding of a discipline through application, and in a sense, provides them with opportunities to become practicing professionals in the field. Finally, the curriculum of identity allows students to develop a deeper understanding of themselves and their place within given disciplines (Hockett, 2009; Tomlinson et al., 2002; VanTassel-Baska & Brown, 2009).

Significant features associated with the PCM include the identification of 10 curriculum components considered key factors in planning an effective curriculum. The factors are: content, assessment, introduction to the lesson or unit, teaching methods, learning activities, grouping strategies, resources, products, extension or enrichment activities, differentiation based on learner need (including ascending levels of intellectual demand), and lesson or unit closure. According to the developers, the feature that distinguishes PCM from other models is the concept of ascending intellectual demand or modifying the curriculum to match students' needs for increasing levels of knowledge, skills, and understanding (Purcell, Burns, & Leppien, 2002).

The model can be adapted for any learner, subject area, or grade level. Books that contain ready-to-use PCM units are available with additional units being developed by practitioners at various grade levels (Tomlinson et al., 2006). Teacher training is available on the implementation of the PCM through conferences and individual consultants (Hockett, 2009; VanTassel-Baska & Brown, 2009).

## Multiple Menu Model

According to the developer, Renzulli (2009), the rationale for the Multiple Menu Model was influenced by William James' theory of knowledge, Alfred North Whitehead's concept of romance, and the curricular theorists Bruner, Phenix, and Ward (Renzulli, 2009, 2013). Taken together, these influences resulted in a model that emphasizes disciplines and the methodology of the disciplines. The influence of James is seen in his explanation of the levels of knowing: knowledge-of (an acquaintance with a topic), knowledge-about (more in-depth knowledge of the content and methodology of a field), and knowledge-how (sufficient knowledge to generate new contributions to the field). In addition to the cognitive domain represented by James' theory of knowledge, the Multiple Menu Model incorporates Alfred North Whitehead's concept of romance, by which he meant interest. Individuals may move from an interest in an area through the acquisition of technical proficiency in the area to generalization, which is characterized as adding new knowledge to a field. Renzulli's interest in creative productivity may have been influenced by James and Whitehead. In the Multiple Menu Model, he has developed a "management plan" for developing curriculum that encourages students to reach for James' knowledge-how and Whitehead's generalization. Renzulli does so by specifying two families of menus that guide curriculum developers. First, the model specifies knowledge menus, which include the structure of a discipline, principles and concepts, knowledge about methodology, and specific topical knowledge with the greatest transfer. Second, the model specifies instructional techniques menus, which include instructional objectives and student activities, instructional strategies, instructional sequences, and instructional products. The Multiple Menu Model, thus, employs templates to assist educators in selecting and combining both knowledge and instructional techniques to create differentiated units of instruction (Renzulli, 2013). The Multiple Menu Model is one of several curriculum models in gifted education that have given rise to specific curricular applications implemented in schools.

The key features of the curriculum models reviewed in this chapter are summarized in Figure 5.1.

In the following section, examples of projects are shared that have adopted one or more of the previously discussed models. It is at this specific level of application that efficacy research is undertaken in schools.

| Model | Target Population | Subject Areas/ Focus | Teacher Training | Materials/ Programs | Locations | Resources |
|---|---|---|---|---|---|---|
| Talent Search Model | Elementary and secondary, grades 3–12 | Primarily designed to meet the needs of students with advanced mathematical and scientific ability; expanded to address exceptionality in high verbal reasoning ability | Facilitator training established by hosting universities | Above-level testing using ACT, SAT, or modified versions of EXPLORE and SCAT, Spatial Test Battery, etc.; university-based programs are offered in the summer, on weekends, after school, and through correspondence and online courses | U.S., Ireland, India | http://www.davidsongifted.org/db/Articles_id_10468.aspx  http://tip.duke.edu  http://cty.jhu.edu/talent  http://www.ctd.northwestern.edu |
| Schoolwide Enrichment Model (SEM) | All academically able and creative-productive children, expanded to reach a greater percentage of nonidentified students across grade levels | SEM can be applied across content areas; SEM-R targets reading comprehension, oral reading fluency, and attitudes toward reading | Annual, weeklong summer institute on the campus of the University of Connecticut | SEM-R (reading application to enrich instruction); Renzulli Learning (Internet-based program to differentiate instruction) | More than 2,500 schools across the country | http://www.gifted.uconn.edu/confratute  http://www.gifted.uconn.edu/sem/semres.html |
| Talents Unlimited, Inc. and Talents Unlimited to the Secondary Power (TU²) | Elementary and secondary, K-6 through Talents Unlimited Inc. and grades 7–12 through TU² | Thinking skills lessons and activities designed for various subject areas | Professional development and in-service teacher training programs are available | Model instructional materials with lessons and activities designed by teachers | Arkansas, Alabama, New Mexico, others in U.S. | http://talentsunlimitedonline.com |

**Figure 5.1.** Key features of curriculum models in gifted education.

| Model | Target Population | Subject Areas/ Focus | Teacher Training | Materials/ Programs | Locations | Resources |
|---|---|---|---|---|---|---|
| Purdue Three-Stage Model | Elementary and secondary talented students, K–12 | Promotes enrichment and acceleration options across multiple subject areas; focus on thinking skills | Available | Program for Academic and Creative Enrichment (PACE) for elementary students | Indiana | https://prezi.com/ hup-uthi0bwo/ the-purdue-three-stage-model |
| Sternberg's Triarchic Model | Elementary, middle, and high school | Designed to be used across disciplines | Availability from developer unknown | Published guides available for instructional adaptations | Used in the U.S. and other countries | http://www.gifted.uconn. edu/nrcgt/reports/ rm95126/rm95126.pdf |
| Gardner's Multiple Intelligences Model | Focus on talent development for all learners from preschool to grade 12 | Development of educational experiences through problem solving and product creation in both academic and nonacademic domains | Not available through model developer | Instructional materials developed by adopters available commercially through multiple publishers | Key School in Indianapolis; Arts Propel in Pittsburgh | http://multiple intelligencesoasis.org/ resources http://www.edutopia. org/key-learnin g-community-multipl e-intelligences-video http://www.pz.gse. harvard.edu/arts_propel. php |
| Autonomous Learner Model (ALM) | Designed to serve secondary gifted students, adapted for use in elementary schools | All subject areas; focus on affective development | Teacher training is available | Planning forms and rubrics | Used in the U.S. and other countries | http://nmgifted.org/ALM/ intro.html |

**Figure 5.1.** Continued.

| Model | Target Population | Subject Areas/ Focus | Teacher Training | Materials/ Programs | Locations | Resources |
|---|---|---|---|---|---|---|
| Integrated Curriculum Model (ICM) | High ability learners in grades K–11 | Core subject areas: language arts (K–11), sciences (K–8), social studies (2–10), and mathematics, the arts, and Latin | Professional development available through workshops or annual training opportunities | More than 25 discipline-specific William & Mary Units are available commercially for implementation or as guides for developing units | Australia, Canada, Japan, Korea, New Zealand, Taiwan, and selected districts in the U.S. | http://education.wm.edu/centers/cfge/curriculum/index.php |
| Kaplan's Grid: The Depth and Complexity Model | Promotes differentiated curricula for gifted and high achieving students at the elementary level | Social studies and language arts | Model support through published materials and independent teacher training offered by the developer | Teacher developed curricula based on the model | Used in the U.S. and in other countries. | http://www.byrdseed.com/introducing-depth-and-complexity<br><br>https://prezi.com/afjncleh3ygd/the-grid-the-depth-and-complexity-curriculum-model |
| Maker's Matrix and the DISCOVER Assessment and Curriculum Model | All students with a focus on underrepresented groups | Focus on problem types across a variety of disciplines | Independent teacher training offered by the developer | Curriculum materials may be teacher developed or existing curriculum may be reworked | Arizona, Kentucky, selected districts in the U.S. | http://Web.arizona.edu/~discover |
| Parallel Curriculum Model | All learners, including those who are gifted, at any grade level | Adaptable to any subject area | Required teacher training, trainer opportunities, and online professional development guides | Curriculum units are available and the model lends itself as a guide for teacher-created units | U.S. | http://www.corwin.com/upm-data/40655_lep1.pdf<br><br>http://www.sagepub.com/upm-data/32286_Strickland_Chapter_1.pdf |

**Figure 5.1.** Continued.

# Core Content Projects Incorporating Curriculum Models in Gifted Education

Certainly, research evidence of efficacy is the gold standard for a curriculum model in gifted education, but there are other factors that demonstrate the fruitfulness of a model. For example, one indicator of the practical influence of a curriculum model is the existence of curricular applications or projects that use the model to develop new curriculum products, implement commercially available curriculum developed from the model, or demonstrate teacher receptivity to the model in some way. Research funding and demonstration projects funded through the Jacob K. Javits Gifted and Talented Students Program have produced such curricular applications. The following selected projects representing core content areas are examples of curriculum models in action. In some cases, the application is built on a single model; in others, more than one curriculum model in gifted education was blended to deliver and field-test the intervention. These projects, organized in alphabetical rather than chronological order, demonstrate the influence of several of the models described previously in this chapter.

## CLEAR in the Language Arts

Two grade 3 language arts units were developed using a blended model incorporating elements from the Schoolwide Enrichment Model (SEM), the Depth and Complexity Model (Kaplan, 2013), and the Differentiated Instruction Model (Tomlinson, 2001). The units, *The Magic of Everyday Things* (poetry) and *Exploration and Communication* (research), were field-tested and found to increase achievement relative to a business-as-usual comparison classroom experience (Callahan et al., 2015). The units were recently published by Prufrock Press. See http://nrcgtuva.org/CLEARcurriculum.html for more information. The curricular units developed through an application of the Challenge Leading to Engagement, Achievement, and Results (CLEAR) model present an interesting conundrum, because the CLEAR model itself is a blend of three previously existing models (Azano, 2013). Thus, how educators determine which aspects of each model might guide their own curricular efforts presents a challenge. Implementing the existing curricular units developed through the CLEAR model would encourage fidelity to the model at this early stage of development.

## Project Mentoring Mathematical Minds

According to its developers, Mentoring Mathematical Minds (Project M³) is based on two curriculum models reviewed previously in this chapter: the Multiple Menu Model and components of the Parallel Curriculum Model (PCM). Curriculum units were based on the Core Curriculum and the Curriculum of Practice of the PCM. Mathematics is a foundational or core area of the curriculum, and both the Curriculum of Practice and the Multiple Menu Model are guided by the philosophy of students learning in a domain by thinking like expert practitioners of that domain. The M³ application of these curricular models resulted in efficacy studies, which documented gains in mathematics concepts and estimation for talented mathematics students in grades 3–5 (Gavin et al., 2007; Gavin, Casa, Adelson, Carroll, & Sheffield, 2009). Curriculum units developed for Project M³ are available for implementation by teachers and could be used as guides for teacher-developed curriculum. See http://www.gifted.uconn.edu/projectM3 for more information.

## Schoolwide Enrichment Model in Reading (SEM-R)

The Schoolwide Enrichment Model in Reading (SEM-R) developed by Reis and colleagues is a specific application of the Schoolwide Enrichment Model (SEM) and its predecessor, the Enrichment Triad, to the core subject area of reading (Reis & Fogarty, 2006). Focused on improving reading attitudes and fluency, SEM-R has been implemented and field-tested with students in grades 3–6 (Reis et al., 2007), in an afterschool program for grades 3–5 (Reis & Boeve, 2009), and in a comparison with basal reading programs (Reis, Eckert, McCoach, Jacobs, & Coyne, 2008; Reis, McCoach, Little, Muller, & Kaniskan, 2011). Results indicate positive outcomes with respect to this application of the SEM model as a framework for reading. A manual for implementing the SEM-R provides guidance to teachers wishing to adopt the strategies and develop curricular opportunities (Reis,

Fogarty, Eckert, & Muller, 2008). See http://www.gifted.uconn.edu/semr/index.html for more information.

### STEMStarters

STEMStarters is a science-focused project combining problem-based curriculum units developed through the Integrated Curriculum Model and biography study of eminent scientists, inventors, and engineers (Deitz, 2012; Robinson, 2006; Robinson, Dailey, Hughes, Hall, & Cotabish, 2014). Coupled with intensive peer coaching, STEM Starters demonstrated gains in science content, concepts, and process for a general cohort (Cotabish, Dailey, Robinson, & Hughes, 2013) and identified gifted students in grades 2–5 (Robinson, Dailey, Hughes, & Cotabish, 2014) and their elementary teachers (Dailey & Robinson, 2015; Robinson, Dailey, Hughes, Hall, & Cotabish, 2014). A scale-up, STEM Starters+, extends downward to grade 1 and incorporates engineering design (Robinson, 2015; Robinson, in press). The William & Mary Integrated Curriculum Model science units implemented in STEMStarters and STEMStarters+ are commercially available and the biography teaching guides, *Blueprints for Biography, STEM Series* are available from the developer (Robinson, 2006; Robinson, Kidd & Deitz, 2015). See http://ualr.edu/gifted/stemstartersplus and http://ualr.edu/gifted/curriculum/stemblueprints for more information.

# Conclusion

What conclusions can be drawn across curriculum models in gifted education that span decades, content areas, grade levels, and accessibility to teachers developing their own curricular units?

First, the models present a variety of perspectives and options to teachers seeking to implement existing curriculum or to develop their own. The models that focus on unit-level development are most likely to provide sufficient guidance and existing exemplars. Models that address more extensive blocks of curriculum present a greater challenge to the teacher-developer. Scope and sequence documents with individual course plans or activity "banks" that provide sufficient specificity for implementation are not as readily available as unit-level exemplars.

Second, the efficacy-based sifting of curriculum models now includes an infusion of programs and projects, largely funded through the Jacob K. Javits program, which include student outcomes. These projects, many of which incorporate curriculum models from the field, provide educators with evidence that they work. The field studies that form the evidence provide a more nuanced picture of what curricular interventions are possible in schools. The sample of such projects described in this chapter include the content areas of language arts, reading, mathematics, and science. They also include multiple curricular models demonstrating that positive effects are possible with multiple models in the field. Educators have choices.

Finally, the curricular models developed within the framework of gifted education continue to evolve. As general education curriculum theory and practice adopts many of the tenets of curriculum development for the more able learner, the distinctions between general curriculum models and specialized curriculum models continue to converge (Hockett, 2009). Conceptually based curriculum, problem-based and project-based learning models, and a variety of thinking skills models have been widely espoused by general education. What then, might a curriculum model developed for advanced learners bring to the table? To answer this question, it is helpful to differentiate between the curriculum as written and the curriculum as enacted. While the models, the concepts, and the principles of general and specialized curricula may share common ground, how advanced learners experience curriculum is the real test of appropriate differentiation. Are they engaged? Is the curriculum really adapted to accommodate individual differences? Is the depth of the curriculum available to advanced learners in a test-driven climate with curriculum pacing guides? Models must be enacted before teachers can determine if the structure on paper will support differentiated curriculum in action.

# References

Assouline, S. G., & Lupkowski-Shoplik, A. (2012). The talent search model of gifted identification. *Journal of Psychoeducational Assessment, 30*(1), 45–59.

Azano, A. (2013). The CLEAR curriculum model. In C. M. Callahan & H. Hertberg-Davis (Eds.), *Fundamentals of gifted education: Considering multiple perspectives* (pp. 301–314). New York, NY: Routledge.

Betts, G. T. (1985). *The Autonomous Learner Model for gifted and talented.* Greeley, CO: ALPS Publications.

Betts, G. T. (1986). The Autonomous Learner Model for the gifted and talented. In J. S. Renzulli (Ed.), *Systems and models for developing programs for the gifted and talented* (pp. 27–56). Mansfield Center, CT: Creative Learning Press.

Betts, G. T., & Kercher, J. K. (1999). *The Autonomous Learner Model: Optimizing ability.* Greeley, CO: ALPS Publications.

Betts, G. T., & Kercher, J. J. (2009). The Autonomous Learner Model for the gifted and talented. In J. S. Renzulli, E. J. Gubbins, K. S. McMillen, R. D. Eckert, & C. A. Little (Eds.), *Systems and models for development programs for the gifted and talented* (2nd ed., pp. 49–103). Mansfield Center, CT: Creative Learning Press.

Brody, L. E., & Mills, C. J. (2005). Talent search research: What have we learned? *High Ability Studies, 16*(1), 97–111.

California Department of Education, & California Association for the Gifted. (1994). *Differentiating the core curriculum and instruction to provide advanced learning opportunities.* Sacramento: California Department of Education.

Callahan, C. M., Moon, T. R., Oh, S., Azano, A. P., & Hailey, E. P. (2015). What works in gifted education: Documenting the effects of an integrated curricular/instructional model for gifted students. *American Educational Research Journal, 52,* 137–167. doi:10.3102/00002831214549448

Cotabish, A., Dailey, D., Robinson, A., & Hughes, G. (2013). The effects of a STEM intervention on elementary students' science knowledge and skills. *School Science and Mathematics, 113,* 215–226.

Dailey, D., & Robinson, A. (2015, April). *Improving and sustaining elementary teachers' science teaching perceptions: Results after a 2-year profes-*

*sional development intervention.* Paper presented at the annual meeting of the American Educational Research Association, Chicago, IL.

Deitz, M. C. (2012). *Gifted education teachers' perceptions on implementation of Blueprints for Biography: STEM Starters* (Unpublished doctoral dissertation). University of Arkansas at Little Rock.

Feldhusen, J. F., & Kolloff, M. B. (1978). A three-stage model for gifted education. *Gifted Child Today, 1*(4), 3–5, 53–57.

Feldhusen, J. F., & Kolloff, M. B. (1986). The Purdue three-stage model for gifted education. In J. S. Renzulli (Ed.), *Systems and models for developing programs for the gifted and talented* (pp. 126–152). Mansfield Center, CT: Creative Learning Press.

Feldhusen, J. F., & Robinson, A. (1986). The Purdue secondary model for gifted and talented youth. In J. S. Renzulli (Ed.), *Systems and models for developing programs for the gifted and talented* (pp. 153–179). Mansfield Center, CT: Creative Learning Press.

Feng, A. X., VanTassel-Baska, J., Quek, C., Bai, W., & O'Neill, B. (2004). A longitudinal assessment of gifted students' learning using the integrated curriculum model (ICM): Impacts and perceptions of the William and Mary language arts and science curriculum. *Roeper Review, 27,* 78–83.

Field, G. B. (2007). *The effect of using Renzulli Learning on student achievement: An investigation of Internet technology on reading fluency and comprehension* (Unpublished doctoral dissertation). University of Connecticut, Storrs.

Field, G. B. (2009). The effects of the use of Renzulli Learning on student achievement in reading comprehension, reading fluency, social studies, and science. *International Journal of Emerging Technologies in Learning, 4*(1), 29–39. doi:10.3991/ijet.v4i1.629

Gardner, H. (1983). *Frames of mind: The theory of multiple intelligences.* New York, NY: Basic Books.

Gardner, H. (1989). Zero-based arts education: An introduction to Arts PROPEL. *Studies in Art Education, 30,* 71–83.

Gardner, H. (1999). *Intelligence reframed: Multiple intelligences for the 21st century.* New York, NY: Basic Books.

Gardner, H. (2011). Intelligence, creativity, ethics: Reflections on my evolving research interests. *Gifted Child Quarterly, 55,* 302–304.

Gardner, H., & Hatch, T. (1989). Multiple intelligences go to school: Educational implications of the theory of multiple intelligences. *Educational Researcher, 18*(8), 4–10.

Gavin, M. K., Casa, T. M., Adelson, J. L., Carroll, S. R., & Sheffield, L. J. (2009). The impact of advanced curriculum on the achievement of mathematically promising elementary students. *Gifted Child Quarterly, 53,* 188–202.

Gavin, M. K., Casa, T. M., Adelson, J. L., Carroll, S. R., Sheffield, L. J., & Spinelli, A. M. (2007). Project M³: Mentoring mathematical minds—A research-based curriculum for talented elementary students. *Journal of Advanced Academics, 18,* 566–585.

Getzels, J., & Csikszentmihalyi, M. (1976). *The creative vision: A longitudinal study of problem finding in art.* New York, NY: Wiley & Sons.

Grigorenko, E. L., Jarvin, L., & Sternberg, R. J. (2002). School-based tests of the triarchic theory of intelligence: Three settings, three samples, three syllabi. *Contemporary Educational Psychology, 27,* 167–208.

Guilford, J. P. (1956). Structure of the intellect. *Psychological Bulletin, 53,* 267–293.

Hockett, J. A. (2009). Curriculum for highly able learners that conforms to general education and gifted education quality indicators. *Journal for the Education of the Gifted, 32,* 394–440.

Johnsen, S. K., & Goree, K. K. (2005). Teaching gifted students through independent study. In F. A. Karnes & S. M. Bean (Eds.), *Methods and materials for teaching the gifted and talented* (2nd ed., pp. 379–408). Waco, TX: Prufrock Press.

Kaplan, S. (1986). The Kaplan grid. In J. S. Renzulli (Ed.), *Systems and models for developing programs for the gifted and talented* (pp. 56–68). Mansfield Center, CT: Creative Learning Press.

Kaplan, S. (2013). Depth and complexity. In C. Callahan & H. Hertberg-Davis (Eds.), *Fundamentals of gifted education: Considering multiple perspectives* (pp. 277–286). New York, NY: Routledge.

Kim, K. H., VanTassel-Baska, J., Bracken, B. A., Feng, A., Stambaugh, T., & Bland, L. (2012). Project Clarion: Three years of science instruction in Title I schools among K-third grade students. *Research in Science Education, 42,* 813–829.

Krechevsky, M. (1998). *Project Spectrum: Preschool assessment handbook. Project Zero Frameworks for early childhood education, Volume 3.* Williston, VA: Teachers College Press.

Kolloff, M. B., & Feldhusen, J. F. (1981). PACE (Program for Academic and Creative Enrichment): An application of the Three-Stage Model. *Gifted Child Today, 4*(3), 47–50.

Kolloff, M. B., & Feldhusen, J. F. (1984). The effects of enrichment on self-concept and creative thinking. *Gifted Child Quarterly, 28,* 53–57.

Lee, S., Matthews, M., & Olszewski-Kubilius, P. (2008). A national picture of talent search and talent search educational programs. *Gifted Child Quarterly, 52*(1), 55–69. doi:10.1177/0016986207311152

Little, C. A., Feng, A. X., VanTassel-Baska, J., Rogers, K. B., & Avery, L. D. (2007). A study of curriculum effectiveness in social studies. *Gifted Child Quarterly, 51,* 272–284.

Maker, C. J. (1982). *Curriculum development for the gifted.* Austin, TX: Pro-Ed.

Maker, C. J., Muammar, O., Serino, L., Kuang, C. C., Mohamed, A., & Sak, U. (2006). The DISCOVER curriculum model: Nurturing and enhancing creativity in all children. *Journal of Educational Policy, 3,* 99–121.

Meeker, M., & Meeker, R. (1986). The SOI system for gifted education. In J. S. Renzulli (Ed.), *Systems and models for developing programs for the gifted and talented* (pp. 194–215). Mansfield Center, CT: Creative Learning Press.

Moon, S. M., Feldhusen, J. F., & Dillon, D. R. (1994). Long-term effects of an enrichment program based on the Purdue Three-Stage Model. *Gifted Child Quarterly, 38,* 38–48.

Moon, S. M., Kolloff, P., Robinson, A., Dixon, F., & Feldhusen, J. F. (2009). The Purdue Three-Stage Model. In J. S. Renzulli, E. J. Gubbins, K. S. McMillen, R. D. Eckert, & C. A. Little (Eds.), *Systems and models for development programs for the gifted and talented,* (2nd ed., pp. 289–321). Waco, TX: Prufrock Press.

Newman, J. L. (2004). Talents and type IIIs: The effects of the Talents Unlimited Model on creative productivity in gifted youngsters. *Roeper Review, 27,* 84–90.

Olszewski-Kubilius, P., & Thomson, D. (2014). Talent search. In J. A. Plucker & C. M. Callahan (Eds.), *Critical issues and practices in gifted education: What the research says* (2nd ed., pp. 633–643). Waco, TX: Prufrock Press.

Purcell, J. H., Burns, D. E., & Leppien, J. H. (2002). The parallel curriculum model (PCM): The whole story. *Teaching for High Potential, 4*(1), 1–4.

Reis, S. M. (n. d.). *Research that supports using the Schoolwide Enrichment Model and extensions of gifted education pedagogy to meet the needs of all students.* Retrieved from http://www.gifted.uconn.edu/sem/semresearch.html

Reis, S. M., & Boeve, H. (2009). How academically gifted elementary, urban students respond to challenge in an enriched, differentiated reading program. *Journal for the Education of the Gifted, 33*, 203–240.

Reis, S. M., & Fogarty, E. A. (2006). Savoring reading schoolwide. *Educational Leadership, 64*(2), 32–36.

Reis, S. M., & Renzulli, J. S. (2010). The Schoolwide Enrichment Model: A focus on student strengths and interests. *Gifted Education International, 26,* 140–156.

Reis, S. M., Eckert, R. D., McCoach, D. B., Jacobs, J. K., & Coyne, M. (2008). Using enrichment reading practices to increase reading fluency, comprehension, and attitudes. *Journal of Educational Research, 101,* 299–314.

Reis, S. M., Fogarty, E. A., Eckert, R. D., & Muller, L. M. (2008). *The Schoolwide Enrichment Reading Model reading framework.* Waco, TX: Prufrock Press.

Reis, S. M., McCoach, D., Coyne, M., Schreiber, F. J., Eckert, R. D., & Gubbins, E. (2007). Using planned enrichment strategies with direct instruction to improve reading fluency, comprehension, and attitude toward reading: An evidence-based study. *Elementary School Journal, 108,* 3–24.

Reis, S. M., McCoach, D. B., Little, C. A., Muller, L. M., & Kaniskan, R. B. (2011). The effects of differentiated instruction and enrichment pedagogy on reading achievement in five elementary schools. *American Educational Research Journal, 48,* 462–501.

Renzulli, J. S. (Ed). (1986). *Systems and models for developing programs for the gifted and talented.* Mansfield Center, CT: Creative Learning Press.

Renzulli, J. S. (2009). The Multiple Menu Model for developing differentiated curriculum. In J. S. Renzulli, E. J. Gubbins, K. S. McMillen, R. D. Eckert, & C. A. Little (Eds.), *Systems & models for developing programs for the gifted & talented* (pp. 353–381). Waco, TX: Prufrock Press.

Renzulli, J. S. (2013). Multiple Menu Model: A guide for developing differentiated curriculum. In C. M. Callahan & H. Hertberg-Davis (Eds.), *Fundamentals of gifted education: Considering multiple perspectives* (pp. 263–276). New York, NY: Routledge.

Renzulli, J. S., & Reis, S. M. (1986). The Enrichment Triad/Revolving Door Model: A schoolwide plan for the development of creative productivity. In J. S. Renzulli (Ed.), *Systems and models for developing programs for the gifted and talented* (pp. 216–266). Mansfield Center, CT: Creative Learning Press.

Renzulli, J. S., & Reis, S. M. (1994). Research related to the Schoolwide Enrichment Triad Model. *Gifted Child Quarterly, 38,* 7–20.

Renzulli, J. S., Gubbins, J. E., McMillen, K. S., Eckert, R. D., & Little, C. A. (Eds.). (2009). *Systems and models for developing programs for the gifted and talented* (2nd ed.). Waco, TX: Prufrock Press.

Robinson, A. (2006). Blueprints for biography: Differentiating the curriculum for talented readers. *Teaching for High Potential,* 7–8.

Robinson, A. (2015). STEM Starters+ ups the creative game for Arkansas! *AAGEAN Digest, 21* (1), 14.

Robinson, A. (in press). Developing STEM talent in the early school years: STEM Starters and its Next Generation scale up. In M. Sumida & K. S. Taber. (Eds.). *Teaching gifted learners in STEM subjects: Developing talent in science, technology, engineering, and mathematics.* New York, NY: Routledge.

Robinson, A., Kidd, K. A., & Deitz, M. C. (2015). Biography builds STEM understanding for talented learners. In B. D. MacFarlane (Ed.), *STEM education for high-ability learners: Designing and implementing programming* (pp. 173–189). Waco, TX: Prufrock Press.

Robinson, A., Dailey, D., Hughes, G., & Cotabish, A. (2014). The effects of a science-focused STEM intervention on gifted elementary students' science knowledge and skills. *Journal of Advanced Academics, 25,* 189–213.

Robinson, A., Dailey, D., Hughes, G., Hall, T. A., & Cotabish, A. (2014). STEM Starters: An effective model for elementary teachers and students. In R. E. Yager & H. Brunkhorst, (Eds.), *Exemplary STEM programs: Designs for success* (pp. 1–18). Arlington, VA: NSTA Press.

Sak, U., & Maker, C. J. (2004). DISCOVER assessment and curriculum model: The application of theories of multiple intelligences and successful intelligence in the education of gifted students. *Eurasian Journal of Educational Research, 5*(15), 1–15.

Schiever, S., & Maker, C. J. (1991). Enrichment and acceleration: An overview and new directions. In N. Colangelo & G. Davis (Eds.). *Handbook of gifted education* (pp. 99–110). Boston, MA: Allyn & Bacon.

Schlichter, C., Hobbs, D., & Crump, W. (1988, April). Extending Talents Unlimited to secondary schools. *Educational Leadership,* 36–40.

Sternberg, R. J. (1981). A componential theory of intellectual giftedness. *Gifted Child Quarterly, 25,* 86–93.

Sternberg, R. J. (1985). *Beyond IQ: A triarchic theory of human intelligence.* New York, NY: Cambridge University Press.

Sternberg, R. J., & Clinkenbeard, P. R. (1995). The triarchic model applied to identifying, teaching, and assessing gifted children. *Roeper Review, 17,* 255–260. doi:10.1080/02783199509553677

Sternberg, R. J., Grigorenko, E. L., & Jarvin, L. (2001). Improving reading instruction: The triarchic model. *Educational Leadership, 58*(6), 48–52.

Sternberg, R. J., Grigorenko, E. L. & Li-fang, Z. (2008). Styles of learning and thinking matter in instruction and assessment. *Perspectives on Psychological Science, 3,* 486–506.

Swiatek, M. A. (2007). The talent search model past, present, and future. *Gifted Child Quarterly, 51,* 320–329.

Taylor, C. W. (1968, December). Be talent developers—as well as knowledge dispensers. *Today's Education,* 67–70.

Tomlinson, C. A. (2001). *How to differentiate instruction in mixed-ability classrooms* (2nd ed.). Alexandria, VA: Association for Supervision and Curriculum Development.

Tomlinson, C. A., Kaplan, S. N., Renzulli, J. S., Purcell, J., Leppien, J., & Burns, D. (2002). *The parallel curriculum: A design to develop high potential and challenge high-ability learners.* Thousand Oaks, CA: Corwin Press.

Tomlinson, C. A., Kaplan, S. N., Purcell, J. H., Leppien, J. H., Burns, D. E., & Strickland, C. A. (2006). *The parallel curriculum in the classroom, Book 2: Units for application across the content areas, K–12.* Thousand Oaks, CA: Corwin.

Uresti, R., Goertz, J., & Bernal, E.M. (2002). Maximizing achievement for potentially gifted and talented and regular minority students in a primary classroom. *Roeper Review, 25,* 27–31.

VanTassel-Baska, J. (1986). Effective curriculum and instructional models for talented students. *Gifted Child Quarterly, 30,* 164–169.

VanTassel-Baska, J. (2003). Research on curriculum models in gifted education. In J. VanTassel-Baska (Ed.), *Curriculum planning & instructional design for gifted learners* (pp. 13–33). Denver, CO: Love Publishing.

VanTassel-Baska, J., & Brown, E. F. (2001). An analysis of curriculum models. In F. A. Karnes, & S. M. Bean (Eds.), *Methods and materials for teaching the gifted* (pp. 91–131). Waco, TX: Prufrock Press.

VanTassel-Baska, J., & Brown, E. F. (2007). Toward best practice: An analysis of the efficacy of curriculum models in gifted education. *Gifted Child Quarterly, 51,* 342–358.

VanTassel-Baska, J., & Brown, E. F. (2009). An analysis of gifted education curriculum models. In F. A. Karnes & S. M. Bean (Eds.), *Methods and materials for teaching the gifted* (3rd ed., pp. 75–106). Waco, TX: Prufrock Press.

VanTassel-Baska, J., & Wood, S. (2010). The integrated curriculum model (ICM). *Learning and Individual Differences, 20,* 345–357.

VanTassel-Baska, J., Bracken, B., Feng, A., & Brown, E. (2009). A longitudinal study of reading comprehension and reasoning ability of students in elementary Title I schools. *Journal for the Education of the Gifted, 33,* 7–37.

VanTassel-Baska, J., Zuo, L., Avery, L. D., & Little, C. A. (2002). A curriculum study of gifted-student learning in the language arts. *Gifted Child Quarterly, 46,* 30–44.

VanTassel-Baska, J., Bass, G., Ries, R., Poland, D., & Avery, L. (1998). A national study of science curriculum effectiveness with high ability students. *Gifted Child Quarterly, 42,* 200–211.

VanTassel-Baska, J., Feng, A., Brown, E., Bracken, B., Stambaugh, T., French, H., . . . Bail, W. (2008). A study of differentiated instructional change over three years. *Gifted Child Quarterly, 52,* 297–312.

Wai, J. (2015). Matching potential and passion leads to promise: A model for educating intellectually talented youth. In F. A. Dixon & S. M. Moon (Eds.), *The handbook of secondary gifted education* (2nd ed., pp. 237–259). Waco, TX: Prufrock Press.

Wai, J., Lubinski, D., Benbow, C. P., & Steiger, J. H. (2010). Accomplishment in science, technology, engineering, and mathematics (STEM) and its relation to STEM educational dose: A 25-year longitudinal study. *Journal of Educational Psychology, 102,* 860–871.

# Curriculum in the Core Subject Areas

# CHAPTER 6

# Language Arts Curriculum for Gifted Learners

### Elizabeth A. Fogarty

Showing up at school already able to read is like showing up at the undertaker's already embalmed; people start
worrying about being put out of their jobs.

—Florence King

## Introduction

Although alarming, the above quote is suitable for describing the situation of students who arrive in English language arts classrooms already
knowing the content.

I suppose she chose me because she knew my name; as I
read the alphabet a faint line appeared between her eye-

> brows, and after making me read most of *My First Reader* and the stock-market quotations from *The Mobile Register* aloud, she discovered that I was literate and looked at me with more than faint distaste. Miss Caroline told me to tell my father not to teach me any more, it would interfere with my reading. (Lee, 1960, p. 17)

> . . . I knew nothing except what I gathered from *Time* magazine and reading everything I could lay hands on at home, but as I inched sluggishly along the treadmill of the Maycomb County school system, I could not help receiving the impression that I was being cheated out of something. (Lee, 1960, pp. 32–33)

The words above belong to fictional character Jean Louise "Scout" Finch from Harper Lee's 1960 novel, *To Kill a Mockingbird,* as she recalls her first and subsequent days in first grade. Scout learned to crack the reading code at a very young age, becoming proficient at decoding and comprehending text well in advance of her 6-year-old classmates. Instead of celebrating the success of her young student, Miss Caroline tells Scout that she should forget everything she had learned and should no longer read at home with her father. Young Scout is not unlike today's talented readers who, like her, are also being cheated out of receiving challenging English language arts instruction.

This chapter looks at the importance of providing challenge to students gifted in the English language arts (ELA). The English language arts are described as three separate areas in this paper—literature, composition, and oral communication; the Common Core Standards delineate these as reading, writing, speaking and listening, and language. This chapter will briefly describe who gifted ELA students are, explain why their classroom experiences should look different from their nongifted peers, and provide suggestions for modifying curriculum to better meet the needs of these students.

# Who Is the Gifted Language Arts Learner?

There are several characteristics that signal learners who excel in the areas of reading, composition, and/or oral communication. Although some gifted ELA students might be facile in all three areas, the gifts of some might be more highly developed in one or two of the areas. Teachers may recognize these talents through formal means, such as standardized assessments, or through informal means, such as the recognition of student talent in writing after reading a student's outstanding essay or noticing a child's highly developed vocabulary. Detection of five or more of the behaviors from the right column of Table 6.1 can indicate advanced abilities in the English language arts, particularly when those behaviors exist across multiple categories.

Regular education classroom teachers might be unfamiliar with the characteristics of gifted ELA learners or instructional methods that will benefit them the most. A great deal of this unawareness is due to the lack of training provided for teachers about how to meet the needs of this population. In the third edition of *What Research Has to Say About Reading Instruction* (Farstrup & Samuels, 2002), several chapters are included on teaching students with different learning needs, including chapters on reading/learning disability interventions, instruction for students who are learning English, struggling readers, early intervention, and teaching culturally diverse learners. At no point in the text, however, is research shared on teaching students proficient in ELA. Even in the fourth edition published in 2011, there is no mention of how to provide instruction to students who are making reading progress ahead of their peers (Samuels & Farstrup, 2011). The National Council of Teachers of English (NCTE) provided position statements with guidance for teaching learners who are atypical in some way, including those who are on the autism spectrum, are English language learners, and are culturally and linguistically diverse (National Council of Teachers of English, 2014). In none of their statements, however, are there provisions for guidelines for teaching or the development of teachers trained to teach learners who are gifted in the language arts. With no mention of gifted students in the ELA research, teacher trainers may mistakenly ignore the unique learning needs of this population, instead utilizing strategies that leave gifted ELA students bored and their classroom experiences devoid of rigor. Therefore, although many

# Table 6.1

*Characteristics of Students Gifted in the English Language Arts*

| Characteristics | Behaviors |
|---|---|
| Enjoyment in the reading process | • Read avidly and with enjoyment<br>• Use reading differently for different reading purposes<br>• Demonstrate thirst for insight and knowledge satisfied through reading<br>• Pursue varied interests in and curiosity about texts<br>• View books and reading as a way to explore the richness of life<br>• Seek and enjoy depth and complexity in reading<br>• Develop a deeper understanding of particular topics through reading<br>• Demonstrate preferences for nonfiction<br>• Pursue interest-based reading opportunities |
| Read early and above level | • Read at least two grade levels above chronological grade placement<br>• May begin reading early and may be self-taught |
| Advanced processing | • Retain a large quantity of information for retrieval<br>• Automatically integrate prior knowledge and experience in reading<br>• Utilize higher order thinking skills such as analysis and synthesis<br>• Process information and thoughts at an accelerated pace<br>• Synthesize ideas in a comprehensive way<br>• Perceive unusual relationships and integrate ideas<br>• Grasp complex ideas and nuances |
| Advanced language skills | • Enjoy subtleties and complexities of language<br>• Demonstrate advanced understanding of language<br>• Use expansive vocabulary<br>• Use reading to acquire a large repertoire of language skills<br>• Use language for humor<br>• Display verbal ability in self-expression<br>• Use colorful and descriptive phrasing<br>• Demonstrate ease in use of language |

teachers excel and have been trained to teach struggling readers, there are many fewer with *explicit* training in teaching students advanced in the English language arts. Adding to this issue is the fact that classrooms are more crowded than in years past (Rich, 2013), an important consideration because studies have shown that students in smaller classes have teachers who are better able to track student learning and use data to create challenge through differentiation of the curriculum (National Council of Teachers of English, 2014).

In a 2013 study, Firmender, Reis, and Sweeny established that wide ranges of reading scores exist in elementary schools, even within gifted populations, indicating the need for differentiation in ELA classrooms. Acknowledging that vast differences exist among learners in the same classroom, teachers of English language arts must become familiar with strategies for modifying the curriculum for those in their classrooms who arrive proficient in their knowledge of content and their ability to apply that knowledge.

## Qualitatively Different

It is the responsibility of the ELA teacher to create program goals for gifted ELA learners that are appropriately distinct from those designed for their nongifted peers (Wood, 2008). In language arts classrooms, there are seldom opportunities for students who are proficient to be excused from material they already know (Reis, Burns, & Renzulli, 1992). Perhaps this is due to the fact that language arts skills are not established along a specific developmental continuum the way mathematical skills are developed. In math, for example, one learns the concept of place value before learning to add one-digit numbers, two-digit numbers, etc. Because they are sequential in nature, one can see the progression of the curriculum in a way that enables acceleration, compacting, etc. The progression in language arts is much more conceptually based, however, necessitating that teachers be able to accurately determine what students have already learned and understand what content is developmentally appropriate for them next.

In reading, there does exist, however, a set of stages through which readers progress. Originally conceptualized by Chall (1983, 1996) and later modified by Robinson, McKenna, and Conradi (2012), this list of stages begins with Emergent Literacy (Stage 0), and continues past the point at which students learn how to read into a stage in which they are Reading to Learn (Stage 3). At this point, readers are able to read to glean information from text and while students typically remain at this stage throughout upper elementary and middle school, gifted ELA students may be ready to progress into the final two stages before their age peers. Although typically encountered during high school, reaching Stage 4 means that readers are able to recognize multiple viewpoints found in text as they identify differences in authors' perspectives. Finally, readers move into a worldview in Stage 5 when they are better able to make comparisons between their own perspective and an author's, as well as to connect text within a global context. Although the work of Chall and Robinson and colleagues provides a continuum of stages spanning preschool through college, gifted ELA students will likely be able to move through these stages at a more rapid pace.

Accommodating the wide range of learner needs in the classroom can be difficult. The time consuming nature of the task may be the main reason that teachers often do not attempt to differentiate. Others cite the pressure to raise student achievement and recent increases in accountability for student achievement as reasons they do not differentiate. In all of the excitement generated about raising student achievement, some people forget the significance of both interest and motivation. So many educators revert to skill and drill and other uninteresting activities when pressured to raise student achievement, but this response is in direct conflict with the research base, which shows that engaged students perform better (Tomlinson & Callahan, 1992; VanTassel-Baska, Avery, Little, & Hughes, 2000) and differentiation has a positive effect on learning. Without motivation toward the content or the process, students will show little engagement in the learning. Additionally, student learning is directly related to motivation to learn (Pintrich, 1999). The antecedent to that motivation, then, is interest. Students must first find interest in what is happening in the classroom in order to engage and be motivated, with achievement as the culminating result. Figure 6.1 illustrates this cycle.

Considering the relationship among interest, motivation, and achievement can enable teachers to determine instructional methods that will reach each learner and create individual achievement growth. Doing so, however, requires a deep familiarity with the process of differentiating elements of classroom instruction.

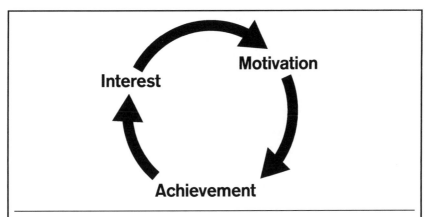

**Figure 6.1.** The achievement cycle must include both interest and motivation.

# Modifying Curriculum to Meet the Needs of Gifted ELA Students

This chapter will focus on a three-tiered process for modifying curriculum to meet the needs of gifted ELA students. Although the process can be used across any content area, examples will be provided illustrating the use with language arts. Initially, this process should begin with an examination of three main components of lessons or units in order to determine which areas to differentiate. Upon deciding what to differentiate, the five high leverage practices should be evaluated to decide which to utilize to create challenge or scaffolding for students. Finally, a set of questions can be used to assess whether sufficient rigor is present in the activities that have been developed.

## Step 1: What to Differentiate

There are three main aspects of the curriculum that should be considered during the process of differentiation: standard, area, and type. The first area, *standard (S)*, requires that all curriculum is based on the concepts to be learned or skills to be developed. The ability to identify the content and skills that are being taught is essential. Next, the *area (A)* is explored as teachers determine whether they will be differentiating the content that they teach, the processes used to teach something, or the products used to exemplify what is learned. Finally, teachers consider the *type (T)* of differentiation. This aspect addresses whether modifications will be made based on student readiness, learning profile, or interest. Additionally, teachers can differentiate more than one element in either *area* or *type*. As curriculum is created or modified, then, all three aspects are considered (S + A + T = Differentiation; see Figure 6.2) to yield differentiated curriculum to either increase or decrease the level of challenge in a given lesson or unit. Laying this foundation is an essential first step in the process because it establishes a purpose for the curricular modifications.

## Step 2: How to Differentiate

The next step is to determine which of the five high leverage practices to use. High leverage practices are critical in differentiation, allowing teachers to create extensions and enrichment, or to eliminate content when necessary. Although these practices are applicable in many types of classroom instruction, they can easily be applied to the instruction of literature, composition, and oral communication, and should form the basis of differentiation in the ELA classroom. See Table 6.2 for definitions of these practices.

## Step 3: Ensuring Rigor

Although it is important for all students to be able to comprehend the texts they read, advanced curriculum in the language arts classroom should prepare students to move beyond basic comprehension to analysis of literature. In thinking, once again, about the stages of reading development, everything after Stage 3 (Reading to Learn) requires readers to conduct textual analysis rather than to simply read for comprehension. Therefore, precocious readers must be exposed to reading instruction that develops their higher order thinking skills as the demands on their ability to decode and comprehend lessen. Understanding author's purpose and making textual connections will allow readers to move into more advanced stages of reading.

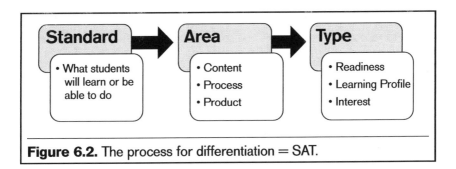

**Figure 6.2.** The process for differentiation = SAT.

## Table 6.2

*High Leverage Differentiation Practices*

| Curricular Essential | Research-Based Support of Practice | Definition |
|---|---|---|
| Preassessment | Maker, 2004; Reis et al., 1992; VanTassel-Baska, 2013 | Determine what students know before starting a unit and excuse them from content already mastered |
| Use of concepts, themes, big ideas | Kaplan, 2009; VanTassel-Baska, 2013 | Utilize themes and big ideas that allow students to see connections among content and disciplines |
| Pace of instruction | VanTassel-Baska, 2013; Wood, 2008 | Modify the pace of lessons to match student need, accelerating the pace with student proficiency |
| Creative productivity | Stephens & Karnes, 2009; VanTassel-Baska, 2013 | Encourage students to produce novel works |
| Interest-based choice | Maker, 2004; Renzulli & Reis, 2010 | Connect content to student interests or allow for choice whenever possible |

Teachers should consider that classroom activities should accentuate not only students' understanding of literature, but their appreciation as well. Planning activities that allow students to connect to texts in powerful and pleasurable ways increases the likelihood they will make reading part of their lifelong journey of learning. Faced with reading experiences that are unchallenging and overly repetitious, students may conclude that reading is boring—a chore to be endured. Swiatek and Lupkowski-Shoplik (2000) determined that failing to address the needs of gifted readers ultimately leads them to perceive reading negatively, thus causing them to lose interest. As illustrated in Figure 6.1, loss of interest can precipitate a decline in achievement.

One of the most important ways that teachers can combat deficits in motivation is by providing challenge in their classrooms. Essential for creating growth, adequate challenge (or rigor) must pervade all elements of students' classroom experience. Matusevich, O'Connor, and Hargett (2009) defined rigor as the following:

> Academic rigor is an essential characteristic of effective curriculum, instruction, and assessment. When they are challenged, students learn to use the full range of their talents and intellectual abilities to address authentic and complex academic tasks in professional and real-life events. All students should have the opportunity to participate in qualitatively different academic environments that build upon their interests, strengths, and personal goals. These environments should engage them actively and consistently in sophisticated investigations of materials, texts, interactive technologies, and learning activities, requiring students to understand and apply advanced critical and creative processes. Rigorous academic environments represent true communities of learning, encouraging both students and teachers to be risk-takers engaged in experimental, investigative, and open-ended learning processes. Together, members of inquiry-based learning communities can utilize effectively their existing knowledge while striving to create new knowledge. In these rigorous learning environments, students accept greater responsibility for developing and applying a deep understanding of significant concepts, generalizations, essential questions, and skills and procedures to problem finding and problem solving for which there are no predetermined limits. (pp. 46–47)

Beyond their definition of rigor, the authors also provide a set of guiding questions that can be used as criteria to determine whether curriculum is adequately challenging. Originally derived from a rubric created to determine whether programs for the gifted and talented were sufficiently rigorous, these questions can be used by teachers to evaluate curriculum for evidence of rigor. It is suggested that these questions be asked after using the SAT method and applying high leverage practices. Curriculum is not expected to meet every criterion present in the questions, but to hit several on the list.

In what ways does this lesson or unit:

1. have qualitatively different academic environments?
2. focus on more in-depth, complex concepts and ideas?
3. build upon students' interests, strengths, and personal goals?
4. engage students consistently in sophisticated investigations?
5. employ advanced critical processes? (Critical processes include finding, inventing, and sharing solutions to real-world problems as well as identifying problems [problem finding], determining accuracy, analyzing alternate solutions, making decisions, etc.)
6. employ advanced creative processes? (Creative processes include purposeful analysis, imaginative idea generation, and critical evaluation.)
7. employ investigative and open-ended learning processes? (These include exploration, experimentation, etc.)
8. encourage students to be risk takers?
9. utilize existing knowledge and require students to create new knowledge?
10. utilize and apply significant concepts and essential questions to problem finding and problem solving?
11. set no predetermined limits?
12. foster lifelong learning?
13. foster thinkers capable of independent reflection?
14. foster student self-evaluation? (Matusevich et al., 2009, p. 49)

# Differentiation of Literature Instruction

Although there are a myriad of possibilities for varying literature instruction, there are three hallmark principles of this instruction, which all ELA teachers should consider. These are:

- ◆ differentiating content based on readiness,
- ◆ differentiating levels of questions, and
- ◆ differentiating materials.

## Principle #1 for Literature Instruction: Differentiate Content Based on Readiness

Trying to deliver grade-level content to all learners in a classroom will likely yield great results for students who learn right on grade level, but terrible results for everyone else. To differentiate by ability, start with the first high leverage differentiation practice—preassessment. Evaluating students' content proficiency in reading can involve commercially available screening tools commonly used in today's classrooms or teacher-created instruments. Although the popularity of guided reading has prompted increased use of assessment for the creation of small-group instruction in elementary reading classrooms, these assessments are not typically used to allow teachers to determine which aspects of *upcoming content* students already know and how to compact them out of previously learned material. More typically, these assessments are used to determine group membership with peers at similar reading levels. However, preassessments should be administered so that students may demonstrate mastery and teachers can plan accordingly. Using preassessment to determine that gifted ELA students are able to identify the main idea of a grade-level text prior to a unit on finding main idea may allow the teacher to extend the skill into more complex texts, or move on to more advanced skills. Figure 6.3 shows how the SAT method is used to differentiate content by readiness for the above example.

## Principle #2 for Literature Instruction: Differentiate Levels of Questions

There are circumstances when it is preferable for all students in a group or class to read the same text. In these situations, a tiered discussion can be used as a high leverage practice to vary the pace of instruction. This strategy recognizes that some students will be ready to access the text at a more advanced point than others. Prior to the discussion, two or three discussion guides can be created and distributed to students based on their readiness levels. Guide A would include mainly questions accessible through text comprehension with 1–2 questions included requiring analysis or extrapolation from the text. For those reading on grade level, Guide B would include a mixture of questions accessible from the text and requiring extrapolation, while Guide C would include only questions requiring

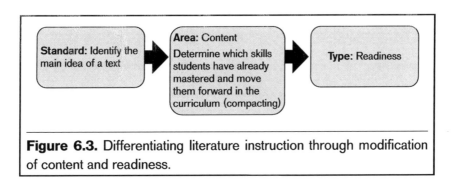

**Figure 6.3.** Differentiating literature instruction through modification of content and readiness.

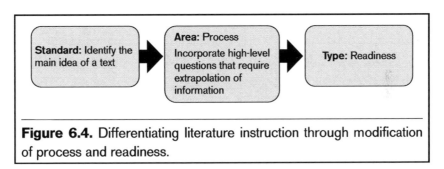

**Figure 6.4.** Differentiating literature instruction through modification of process and readiness.

students to extrapolate information. During the discussion, all students are able to contribute using the information from their respective guides with each group offering unique insight. Figure 6.4 shows how the SAT method is used to differentiate process by readiness for the above example.

## Principle #3 for Literature Instruction: Differentiate Materials

Teachers can also modify the materials used. Particularly when students' reading levels vary, teachers should choose texts that can reach different ability levels. In lieu of offering one grade-level text, which may restrict the complexity of themes that can be explored, multiple texts on the same theme should be matched to student readiness levels. One way to do this is to utilize concepts, themes, and big ideas to create rigorous experiences. If a teacher wishes to explore the theme of *change* for instance, he might choose the Newbery award-winning text *The Watsons Go to Birmingham: 1963* for on-level fifth-grade readers. Students reading this book would explore the theme of change as they see how outside incidences, such as the 16th Street Baptist Church bombing, can affect characters over the course of a text. Those students reading above grade level could be reading the text, *I Am Malala*, the memoir of Malala Yousafzai, who was shot by the Taliban. In this text, students could also be exploring the theme of *change*, but perhaps exploring why people don't change and the differences in genre of a memoir versus/as opposed to other types of texts. Additionally, those reading below grade level might read *Leaving Microsoft to Change the World*, a text that illustrates very concretely how moving from a job at Microsoft to founding the nonprofit organization Room to Read allowed John Wood to enact positive change. Choosing several books on the theme of *change* can enable all students in the classroom to access ideas that are adequately challenging to them. Figure 6.5 shows how the high leverage practice of using themes/big ideas can provide content and readiness differentiation.

# Differentiating Composition Instruction

Developing competency in writing is a multilayered process. Students must start with a foundational understanding of grammar that they will later incorporate into their writing. And although patterns certainly exist in the structures of writing, there is also a great deal of room for students to incorporate creativity. For all students, the goal should be that they become adept at writing about expository as well as persuasive topics. There are three hallmarks of differentiation in composition instruction:

- differentiate the topic,
- scaffold support skills, and
- differentiate content.

## Principle #1 for Composition Instruction: Differentiate the Topic

In a classroom of writers, several will be highly enthusiastic, several others will be completely disengaged, and everyone else will fall somewhere in between. Teachers recognize that leveraging best practices here

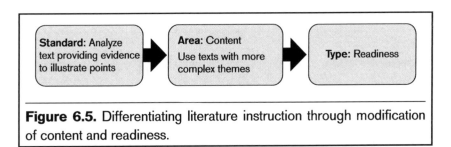

**Figure 6.5.** Differentiating literature instruction through modification of content and readiness.

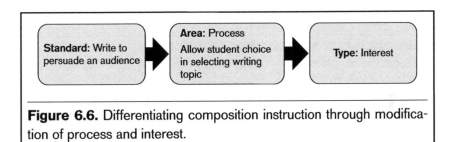

**Figure 6.6.** Differentiating composition instruction through modification of process and interest.

will ensure that all students, regardless of their ability level, will be able to make interest-based choices to determine what they'd like to write about. Or several choices of topics can be provided to students necessitating that they go in a new direction previously unexplored. Figure 6.6 illustrates how to differentiate process by interest for the above example.

### Principle #2 for Composition Instruction: Scaffold Support Skills

Before they can become capable writers, students must develop a working understanding of grammar. Even when students can develop creative ideas, their writing must be understandable. Grammar is one area of the curriculum where most students, including those gifted in ELA, do not have a lot of expertise. However, despite the fact that grammar lessons can include new content for all of the students in the class, gifted students are still likely to pick up on it quickly. Teachers are encouraged to utilize the high leverage practices of pace of instruction and preassessment as they work to determine what students already know and provide instruction in unfamiliar content (see Figure 6.7).

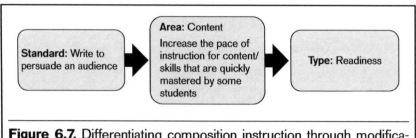

**Figure 6.7.** Differentiating composition instruction through modification of content and readiness.

## Principle #3 for Composition Instruction: Differentiate Content

Providing different content for students who enter the ELA classroom with advanced capabilities can accommodate for their previous knowledge and experiences.

In the case of capable writers, providing additional instruction in logic and reasoning can help them establish an underlying baseline for the thinking they will need to do in order to organize their writing. Without a baseline in thinking, they may be unable to construct arguments in their writing. Although it is important for students to learn to read critically so that they may analyze fiction texts to determine author's purpose, theme, etc., it is also essential that they learn to evaluate nonfiction texts. Doing so will allow them to determine the value of sources they read and later utilize to construct arguments in their expository writing. Although thinking logically is a goal for all learners, we might expect our advanced students to be able to do so earlier at a more complex level (see Figure 6.8).

Additionally, gifted students should be asked to justify the quality of their topic. An essential of good writing is the ability of the writer to convince the reader to continue in the text; without a compelling reason to do so, the reader is unlikely to persist.

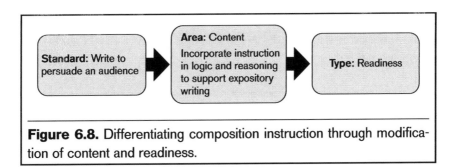

**Figure 6.8.** Differentiating composition instruction through modification of content and readiness.

# Differentiating Oral Communication Instruction

As the third area of language arts, oral communication allows for student self-expression. Students should develop their ability to speak fluently on both argument and expository topics. There are three hallmarks of differentiation in this area:

◆ increase level of abstraction,

◆ encourage creative productivity, and

◆ support debate.

## Principle #1 for Oral Communication Instruction: Increase Level of Abstraction

When asked to share their thoughts and opinions through oral communication, students should be able to do so using logical and rational arguments. As is true with written media, oral communication requires that sound reasoning undergird any message presented. As thinking moves from concrete to abstract, students become better able to hold multiple complex thoughts in their heads and therefore can speak extemporaneously. Differentiating the process for oral presentations to allow some to utilize notes and others to speak extemporaneously naturally provides a faster pace of instruction for gifted ELA students. Thus, varying the process by which the student communicates can provide opportunities for differentiation based on readiness (see Figure 6.9).

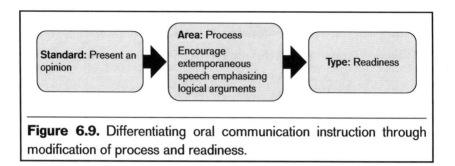

**Figure 6.9.** Differentiating oral communication instruction through modification of process and readiness.

## Principle #2 for Oral Communication Instruction: Encourage Creative Productivity

An essential component of oral communication instruction is the explicit teaching of group dynamics. Contributing to group discussions entails a basic understanding of the dynamics created in a group based upon the roles taken on by individual group members. Inexpert discussants might be interested only in seeing that their contributions are shared with the group, thus neglecting the importance of group process as an outcome of the experience. Those familiar with group dynamics, on the other hand, should be coached to recognize that a productive discussion should yield creative contributions from all members, and thus, creative productivity is a high leverage practice for this principle (see Figure 6.10).

## Principle #3 for Oral Communication Instruction: Support Debate

Some students mistake bickering for debate. The distinct difference between the two is that debate requires analytical and research skills, whereas arguing requires neither. Although some students may need to have debate formats that are more highly structured, such as delivering prewritten speeches on either the pro or con side of an argument, other students will be able to develop research-based arguments at a rapid fire pace during a timed debate. Differentiation can occur as students choose the topics of their debate (interest) and as teachers determine the degree of structure of the product, and can allow for differences in pace (high leverage practice) as some students progress more rapidly through the process (see Figure 6.11).

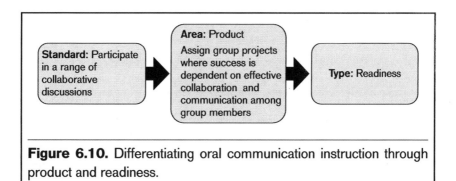

**Figure 6.10.** Differentiating oral communication instruction through product and readiness.

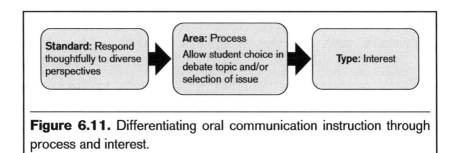

**Figure 6.11.** Differentiating oral communication instruction through process and interest.

# Conclusion

As teachers apply both the SAT method and utilize high leverage practices, they will begin to create lessons, which more adequately challenge the learners in their classrooms. Teachers can further check their progress in promoting rigorous lessons by conducting a self-assessment. Asking each of the questions derived from the rigor rubric (see Matusevich et al., 2009) encourages teachers to see whether gaps exist in their planning and whether students are being sufficiently challenged. It is through rigor and challenge that teachers can stave off boredom and foster both motivation and interest. The true importance of providing differentiated curriculum for gifted learners is to keep them connected to ELA principles that are increasingly challenging. As Florence King points out, the alternative is to leave them bored stiff!

# References

Chall, J. S. (1983). *Stages of reading development.* New York, NY: McGraw-Hill.

Chall, J. S. (1996). *Stages of reading development* (2nd ed.). Fort Worth, TX: Harcourt-Brace.

Farstrup, A. E., & Samuels, S. J. (2002). *What research has to say about reading instruction* (3rd Ed.). Newark, DE: International Reading Association.

Firmender, J. M., Reis, S. M., & Sweeny, S. M. (2013). Reading comprehension and fluency levels ranges across diverse classrooms: The need for differentiated reading instruction and content. *Gifted Child Quarterly, 57,* 3–14.

Kaplan, S. N. (2009). Layering differentiated curricula for the gifted and talented. In F. A. Karnes & S. M. Bean (Eds.), *Methods and materials for teaching the gifted* (pp. 107–136). Waco, TX: Prufrock Press.

Lee, H. (1960). *To kill a mockingbird.* Philadelphia, PA: Lippincott.

Maker, C. J. (2004). Developing scope and sequence in curriculum. In J. VanTassel-Baska & S. M. Reis (Eds.), *Introduction to curriculum for gifted students* (pp. 25–40). Thousand Oaks, CA: Corwin Press.

Matusevich, M. N., O'Connor, K. A., & Hargett, M. V. P. (2009). The non-negotiables of academic rigor. *Gifted Child Today, 32*(4), 44–52.

National Council of Teachers of English. (2014). *NCTE's position statements on key issues.* Retrieved from http://www.ncte.org/positions

Pintrich, P. R. (1999). The role of motivation in promoting and sustaining self-regulated learning. *International Journal of Educational Research, 31,* 459–470.

Reis, S. M., Burns, D. E., & Renzulli, J. S. (1992). *Curriculum compacting: The complete guide to modifying the regular curriculum for high-ability students.* Waco, TX: Prufrock Press.

Renzulli, J. S., & Reis, S. M. (2010). The Schoolwide Enrichment Model: A focus on student strengths and interests. *Gifted Education International, 26,* 140–156.

Rich, M. (2013, December 21). Subtract teachers, add pupils: Math of today's jammed schools. *The New York Times.* Retrieved from http://www.nytimes.com/2013/12/22/education/subtract-teachers-add-pupils-math-of-todays-jammed-schools.html

Robinson, R. D., McKenna, M. C., & Conradi, K. (Eds.). (2012). *Issues and trends in literacy education* (5th ed.). Boston, MA: Allyn & Bacon.

Samuels, S. J., & Farstrup, A. E. (2011). *What research has to say about reading instruction* (4th Ed.). Newark, DE: International Reading Association.

Stephens, K. R., & Karnes, F. A. (2009). Product development for gifted students. In F. A. Karnes & S. M. Bean (Eds.), *Methods and materials for teaching the gifted* (3rd ed., pp. 157–186). Waco, TX: Prufrock Press.

Swiatek, M. A., & Lupkowski-Shoplik, A. (2000). Gender differences in academic attitudes among gifted elementary education students. *Journal for the Education of the Gifted, 23,* 360–377.

Tomlinson, C., & Callahan, C. (1992). Contributions of gifted education to general education in a time of change. *Gifted Child Quarterly, 36,* 183–189.

VanTassel-Baska, J. (Ed.). (2013). *Using the Common Core State Standards for English Language Arts with gifted and advanced learners.* Waco, TX: Prufrock Press.

VanTassel-Baska, J., Avery, L. D., Little, C., & Hughes, C. (2000). An evaluation of the implementation of curriculum innovation: The impact of William & Mary units on schools. *Journal for the Education of the Gifted, 23,* 244–272.

Wood, P. F. (2008). Reading instruction with gifted and talented readers: A series of unfortunate events or a sequence of auspicious results? *Gifted Child Today, 31*(3), 16–25.

# CHAPTER 7

# Mathematics Curriculum for Gifted Learners

**M. Katherine Gavin**

Every student deserves and needs to learn something new
every day in mathematics class.

This is a simple mantra accepted by all teachers but one that is much
more difficult to live up to in practice, especially with regard to gifted mathematics students. The curriculum and how it is implemented is the key to
meeting students' needs. In this chapter, an in-depth look at essential components of an effective mathematics curriculum for gifted students will be
explored along with equally essential instructional strategies that create the
proper learning environment to help students explore the curriculum.

# Acceleration Versus Enrichment

The age-old debate to meet the needs of gifted mathematics students focused on whether to accelerate students through fast-paced texts in order to place them in higher grade-level curriculum or to provide more depth, breadth, and complexity to on-grade-level curriculum. Rather than continue this debate, gifted education experts and researchers agree that the right approach to designing effective curriculum for gifted students must be a combination of both approaches (Chamberlin, 2006; Gavin, 2011; Gavin & Sheffield, 2010; Hertberg-Davis & Callahan, 2008). As Schiever and Maker (2003) noted, "without both acceleration and enrichment, more is simply more" (p. 168). They emphasized that the curriculum must be *qualitatively* different from the regular curriculum. So adding puzzles and mazes or even interesting mathematics problems is not effective in meeting the needs of gifted students, nor is moving students quickly through the regular curriculum or even skipping a grade level in mathematics to enter the regular curriculum at a higher grade level. The first option may provide enjoyment for students but does not meet their needs in learning appropriate mathematics content in a coherent, focused manner. The second does not provide the appropriate high-level curriculum that these students need. Extra enrichment worksheets that are sometimes offered in the regular textbook curricula are generally just that . . . extra work for students without the extra rigor. What is needed is an advanced (above-grade-level) curriculum appropriate for the student that explores content in a deep and complex way. This curriculum needs to be coherently developed across the particular content area with interesting mathematical investigations to challenge gifted students. In addition, VanTassel-Baska and Brown (2007) recommended that gifted students receive instruction by subject area in an advanced curriculum that is flexibly organized and implemented based on students' learning levels that have been documented.

# Students as Practicing Mathematicians

A prime consideration for developing or evaluating effective curricula for gifted students is that the curriculum be based on best practices in teaching and learning outlined by experts in the gifted and talented field. Joseph Renzulli, Carol Tomlinson, Sandra Kaplan, and other leading experts in the field have found that curriculum designed to provide experiences where students actually apply the methods utilized by the professional to solve an interesting problem helps students understand the concepts of the respective discipline more deeply and make connections within and across disciplines more easily (Renzulli, Leppien, & Hays, 2000; Tomlinson et al., 2009).

Mathematicians and math educators also value the same type of experiences for students. In fact, the 2010 Common Core State Standards for Mathematical Practice (CCSS-M; National Governors Association Center for Best Practices & Council of Chief State School Officers, 2010) are in essence the principles of practicing mathematicians. These eight practices evolved from the National Council of Teachers of Mathematics (NCTM; 2000) process standards of problem solving, reasoning and proof, communication, representation, and connection. In addition, they rest on the five strands of mathematical proficiency specified in the National Research Council's report *Adding It Up* (2001): adaptive reasoning (the ability to think logically, provide explanations, and justify conclusions); strategic competence (the ability to create, represent, and solve problems); conceptual understanding (the ability to understand math concepts, operations, and relations); procedural fluency (the ability to carry out procedures flexibly, accurately, and efficiently); and productive disposition (the ability to see mathematics as sensible and useful and to believe in one's own self-efficacy).

The Standards for Mathematical Practice are, in fact, exactly what mathematicians do as they create and solve problems. Thus, all eight of the following Mathematical Practices should play a major role in the daily investigations in which students engage.

- Make sense of problems and persevere in solving them.
- Reason abstractly and quantitatively.
- Construct viable arguments and critique the reasoning of others.
- Model with mathematics.

◆ Use appropriate tools strategically.
◆ Attend to precision.
◆ Look for and make use of structure.
◆ Look for and express regularity in repeated reasoning.

In addition to these eight practices, in a recent publication edited by Johnsen and Sheffield (2013), the National Association for Gifted Children (NAGC) along with the National Council of Supervisors of Mathematics and NCTM have proposed a ninth practice: *Solve problems in novel ways and pose new mathematical questions of interest to investigate.* Gifted students, in particular, should have the opportunity to become creative problem solvers and problem posers.

The CCSS Mathematical Practices are what each student should be doing on a daily basis as they carry out the mathematical investigations in a given curriculum. Acting like the professional and working on simulated or real-life problems in the field also serve to motivate students. Hopefully this is the start of what Renzulli (2002) called "a romance with the discipline" (p. 36), a love and passion for mathematics that can direct students toward a career path in mathematics and math-related fields.

# Criteria for Effective Mathematics Curriculum for Gifted Students

Gavin and Sheffield (2010) have outlined four components that characterize an advanced, in-depth curriculum appropriate for gifted mathematics students:

1. Creative and complex problem-solving;
2. Connections within and access across mathematical and other content areas and across a wide range of contexts;
3. An inquiry-based approach that focuses on processes used by mathematicians; and
4. Appropriate pacing. (p. 58)

The model shown in Figure 7.1 reflects the fact that all four components are equally important and are the "legs" that support a curriculum

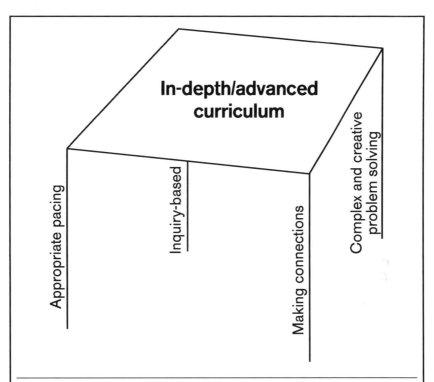

**Figure 7.1.** A model for curriculum for gifted mathematics students. *Note.* Reprinted from "Using Curriculum to Develop Mathematical Promise in the Middle Grades" (p. 58) by M. K. Gavin and L. J. Sheffiled, in *The Peak in the Middle: Developing Mathematically Gifted Students in the Middle Grades*, by M. E. Saul, S. G. Assouline, and L. J. Sheffield, 2010, Reston, VA: National Council of Teachers of Mathematics. Copyright 2010 NCTM. Reprinted with permission by NCTM and Copyright Clearance Center.

that is both advanced and in-depth. As Gavin (2011) pointed out, although the model was originally designed for gifted middle school students, it applies equally to all students across the K–12 grade span.

This model also inherently incorporates use of the CCSS Standards for Mathematical Practice. In order to create a rich, inquiry-based program with complex and creative problem solving and connections across content and contexts, students will use all of these practices as they investigate problems. Examining each "leg" will help illustrate the basic tenets of the model.

## An Inquiry-Based Approach

An inquiry-based approach should be the heart and soul of the curriculum investigations. NCTM (1989, 2000) has encouraged this approach in its two publications on curriculum standards that have revolutionized the way mathematics is taught for the general population. The CCSS Mathematical Practices actually require an inquiry-based approach in order to work. Students explore and discover when they are making sense of problems, reasoning, critiquing arguments, modeling, using tools, and looking for structure. Inquiry is the process that allows these practices to occur. And although these practices and inquiry are important for all students to engage in, Tomlinson (1994) indicated that it is the *level* at which and the *degree* to which students use them that are critical for gifted students. This must be the focus of the curriculum, not a once-in-a-while activity or even a once-a-week occurrence.

## Creative and Complex Problem Solving

Real problem solving deals with struggle. Mathematicians will be the first to agree with this and they love it . . . the harder, the better. If students already know how to solve the problem as soon as they read it, it is not a real problem. Mathematicians take hours, days, and even in some cases years to solve complex problems. Consider Fermat's Last Theorem that Pierre de Fermat scribbled onto a page in a math text in 1637 and was not proven until 1994! A curriculum that poses problems that require students to think at high levels, to test out ideas, to discuss their ideas with others, to change their minds, to start over, and finally to reach that "aha!" moment of discovery is what doing mathematics should be for gifted students. For this reason, there is not a linear progression to the solution process. In fact, Jensen (1980) created a model for this type of problem solving that shows how dynamic the process is (see Figure 7.2).

The model shows that this is a creative process of relating the problem to things you already know, investigating, talking to others, creating new questions and new solutions, and evaluating. Furthermore, there is no set order to the steps and problem solving does not end when you check your answer. Evaluation is part of the process and leads to more discussions, more explorations, and even new questions. It is quite an exciting and organic process.

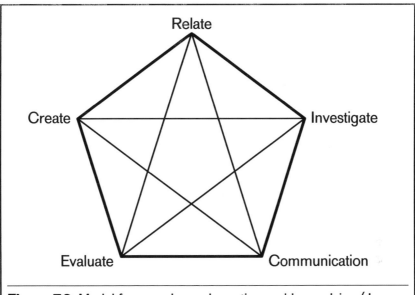

**Figure 7.2.** Model for complex and creative problem solving (Jensen, 1980).

## Connections Within and Across Mathematical and Other Content Areas and Contexts

Students who delve into this critical and creative problem-solving process will have built the support they need to easily connect their new mathematical knowledge to prior knowledge. They can recognize how mathematics content areas and the principles of mathematics connect to one another in a deeper way. Exploring real-world contexts helps to stimulate their interest and imagination and see how important mathematics is to the everyday operation of the world around them. Putting mathematics in context links this subject to other areas such as geography and science. The context can also provide links across math content areas from, for example, number to algebra or algebra to geometry.

## Appropriate Pacing

Pacing is an important component of any curriculum. For gifted students, repetition and practice is often not necessary or can be kept to a minimum even when learning new material. For example, some young gifted students can move very quickly to the abstract and may not even need the use of manipulatives. Pacing is a variable that teachers control. Therefore, it is important for teachers to assess the abilities of students. They can use observational data as students work on challenging tasks, interview students (especially very young students), and/or use unit, chapter, or end-of-year pretests to see if content has already been mastered. They can then use curriculum compacting to refrain from reteaching or repetition. This method has been proven effective especially for elementary students (Reis, Burns, & Renzulli, 1992). Once the grade-level mathematics content has been shown to be mastered, teachers can then provide the kind of inquiry-based, in-depth advanced curriculum that gifted students need.

However, there is a word of caution needed here. Once these rigorous and complex problem-solving investigations are under way, students may actually need to slow down. Going faster isn't always better. In fact, allowing students to discuss, struggle, and reflect takes time, but it is well worth it. It is the time taken to persevere in problem solving that yields the rewards of mathematical insight and solution to the problem. This is what instills a love and passion for mathematics in gifted students.

# Mathematical Discussions to Promote High-End Learning

Having an appropriately challenging curriculum for students is a great start in meeting the needs of gifted students. However, it needs to be implemented in a manner that is equally rigorous and encourages students to get involved in discussion while making use of the Mathematical Practices. We often think of mathematicians as loners, always working in isolation. In fact, although think time is a vital component of mathematical discovery, equally important is the time to brainstorm with peers and discuss ideas and problems. In this vein, discussion has been found to be very important in helping students come to deeper mathematical understandings and internalize complex knowledge (Biehler & Snowman, 1993; Vygotsky, 1978).

Students who have had practice discussing with fellow students and their teacher about how to solve problems have a tendency to persist for longer periods of time when working on new problems. They learn to explain their thinking to others, which is not an easy task, and also to revise their thinking based on others' comments. They realize that solving problems takes time and the process is enjoyable and enlightening. This helps them not give up so quickly. As students get better at communicating their mathematical ideas, they start to take more time thinking about a problem and structuring and clarifying their thoughts to better communicate them to their peers. As important, students learn to take into consideration a variety of different viewpoints and different methods in solving a problem. In effect, students become better mathematicians.

## Generating Productive Mathematics Discussions

Chapin, O'Connor, and Anderson (2013) have created *talk moves* to help teachers facilitate discussion. The five talk moves should be used in daily discussion around important mathematics to raise the classroom conversation to new levels and make good use of the Mathematical Practices.

1. *Revoicing*. The teacher restates a student's idea and then checks back with the student to see if it is accurate. This move helps students clarify their response or highlights an insightful idea.
2. *Repeat/rephrase*. The teacher asks other students to restate an idea another student has expressed. This move gives students an opportunity to discuss their peers' reasoning.
3. *Agree/disagree and why*. This move coincides with the Mathematical Practice to construct viable arguments and critique the reasoning of others. It is truly the heart of a high-level discussion. It is important for teachers to remain uncommitted to the validity of the idea at this point. They should allow students to struggle with their thoughts first before focusing on the correct concepts.
4. *Adding on*. This move allows students to expand upon ideas that have been expressed and allows more perspectives to be considered.
5. *Wait time*. This move enables all students to contribute to the discussion, not just the ones who process more quickly or are more vocal. The more complex the question, the more reason to allow wait time before engaging in conversation. Teachers should not

only wait to call on a student after posing a question, but also wait for a student who has been called on to share his or her idea.

Teachers in both Project M³ and Project M², research-based advanced curriculum programs for students in K–5, have used talk moves effectively with gifted students to promote high-end learning. In addition to the five moves listed, the Projects M³ and M² team added a sixth move that Chapin, O'Connor, and Anderson (2013) promoted but do not label as a talk move:

6. *Partner talk.* Using this talk move, teachers pose a mathematical question and then ask students to turn and talk to their partner about it. The class then comes together to discuss. This move is especially helpful for students who are reluctant to contribute their thoughts initially. Talking it out with a partner helps them organize their thoughts and gain confidence.

## Setting the Stage for Discourse

Teachers need to create a spirit of inquiry in the classroom where students are eager to take a risk and share an idea. The environment must encourage respect for one another and each other's ideas. Students need to be taught to listen carefully to what their classmates say and to carefully consider all ideas, as good mathematicians would do. This can be particularly difficult for gifted students who sometimes zero in on their own ideas and just want to tell the teacher about them. Therefore, the teacher is key to establishing the environment for respectful and engaging mathematical discussions. It is important to encourage students to voice all ideas, even incorrect ones, in order to assess their understanding and be able to move them forward in their thinking. In fact, misconceptions often provide interesting discussion that raises the mathematics to new levels and fosters a deeper conceptual understanding. To establish this environment, students must be alerted to their responsibility to contribute to a discussion, ask questions, listen to each other, and speak loudly so they can be heard. They need to be taught to respect each other's ideas and disagree with the idea but not the person, so it never reaches a personal level. In such an environment, students can be heard saying, "Now, I disagree with myself!" after hearing others' arguments for different viewpoints or answers.

# Assessment Considerations

The rule of thumb in creating assessments is that assessment must match instruction. Mathematics instruction for gifted students requires high-level discussion that encourages students to grapple with complex problems, justify their thinking, construct and critique arguments, and clearly explain their thinking. Thus assessment must require students to do the same. This cannot be accomplished solely with multiple-choice questions or fill-in-the-blank statements. Open-ended questions that are complex and require high-level thinking are in order. Students must be required to show their work and explain their thinking. They need to justify their reasoning and critique arguments. Teachers need to work with students, including gifted students, to develop this writing skill. This is not a skill that is innate, but rather honed carefully with guidance. Students need to understand what is expected of them in clearly explaining their thinking. Creating exemplary responses as a class, providing opportunities to critique and improve writing samples and using peer editing are some ways to develop students' abilities to write in this manner.

A sample written assessment question given to gifted fourth graders after they studied two-dimensional shapes is shown in Figure 7.3. To showcase what students are capable of doing, one gifted fourth grader's response is included.

# Curriculum Materials

### Differentiating Curriculum

It has been documented that the best way to provide appropriate mathematics instruction to gifted students is to have them grouped together by their ability in the subject area being presented. This has been proven true for mathematics instruction across a variety of grouping strategies including ability grouping (e.g., Gavin, Casa, Adelson, Carroll, & Sheffield, 2009; Kulik, 1992; Tieso, 2002), cluster grouping (Pierce et al., 2011), and in pull-out programs (Dimitriadis, 2012). It is much harder to determine

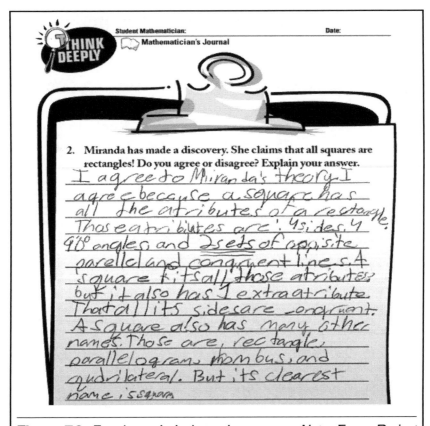

**Figure 7.3.** Fourth grader's journal response. *Note.* From *Project M³: Getting Into Shapes* (Teacher's Guide, p. 20) by M. K. Gavin, J. Dailey, S. Chapin, and L. J. Sheffield, 2007, Dubuque, IA: Kendall Hunt. Copyright 2007 by Kendall Hunt. Reprinted with permission.

what curriculum to use with gifted students once they are grouped together for instruction. It is important to remember that grouping without differentiating the curriculum provides no advantage to gifted students (Kulik, 1992).

Many gifted programs use commercial "enrichment" supplementary materials in their programs. Be aware that these usually are not research-based and thus do not have proven results in increasing mathematics achievement for gifted students. As stated earlier, to meet the needs of gifted students, a coherent, advanced, inquiry-based curriculum that develops the mathematics at high levels and encourages high-level discussions is needed. Existing curriculum created for all students can be modified for gifted students using the four criteria in the model (see Figure 7.1) for effective curriculum for talented students. It should also include instructional strategies to generate high-level discussions within the mathematics classroom as previously discussed. This takes time and effort and should be carried out by qualified personnel in gifted education *and* mathematics education.

The *content* must be differentiated qualitatively to meet the needs of gifted students. Gavin and Moylan (2012) have outlined seven research-based actions and practical steps to help in this process. They include:

1. selecting an appropriate concept-based investigation;
2. increasing expectations to require students to reach beyond their comfort zone;
3. facilitating class discussion about the important concepts;
4. encouraging students to communicate their thinking in writing;
5. offering additional support for students who may need background information;
6. providing extended challenges for students who need more; and
7. using formative assessment to inform instruction.

Some resources that highlight appropriate investigations for gifted students showing varying levels of difficulties across different math concepts include *Extending the Challenge in Mathematics: Developing Mathematical Promise in K–8 Students* (Sheffield, 2003) and *Using the Common Core Standards for Mathematics With Gifted and Advanced Learners* (Johnsen & Sheffield, 2013). Other investigations to consider include model-eliciting activities (Coxbill, Chamberlin, & Weatherford, 2013), Fermi Problems (problems that have quantitative answers and typically involve making rough approximations based upon certain assumptions and do not have unique solutions; see example in Gavin, Chapin, Dailey and Sheffield, 2015), advanced performance tasks similar in design to performance tasks in the Smarter Balanced Assessment for the Common Core State Standards but at higher levels (see http://sbac.portal.airast.org/practice-test/resources), and problem-based learning investigations (Gallagher & Gallagher, 2013). *However, in modifying the existing curriculum, beware of falling into the trap of putting together a series of unrelated, albeit interesting and challenging, explorations.* This does not constitute effective mathematics curriculum for gifted students. The mathematics concepts must be developed using a logical, mathematically sound progression that is coherent and in-depth and includes complex problem solving.

## Curriculum Designed for Gifted Mathematics Students

Although there is a paucity of research-based mathematics curriculum designed specifically for gifted students, two research-proven programs were created for that purpose. At the elementary level, *Project M³: Mentoring Mathematical Minds* (Gavin, Chapin, Dailey, & Sheffield, 2003–2007) is a series of curriculum units for gifted students in grades 3–5 that was developed under a U.S. Department of Education Javits Research Grant. This curriculum focuses on students thinking and acting like mathematicians within a classroom culture of verbal and written discussion. There is a strong focus on in-depth study of advanced math concepts. Research results have shown statistically significant gains on the Iowa Tests of Basic Skills. In addition, students have made significant gains on open-ended questions taken from released items on the Trends in International Mathematics and Science Study (TIMSS) and National Assessment of Educational Progress (NAEP) assessments. Project M³ students have outperformed a comparison group of like-ability peers from the same schools on these measures as well (Gavin et al., 2009). These units have won the Distinguished Curriculum Award from the National Association for Gifted Children for 6 consecutive years.

For younger students in grades K–2, *Project M²: Mentoring Young Mathematicians* (Gavin, Casa, Chapin, & Sheffield, 2007–2013) was developed under a National Science Foundation curriculum research grant. Research results showed similar gains and differences favoring the Project M² students (Gavin, Casa, Adelson, & Firmender, 2013; Gavin, Casa, Firmender, & Carroll, 2013). Firmender (2011) found that high-ability second-grade Project M² students had significantly higher mathematics scores on the Iowa Tests of Basic Skills and an open-ended assessment than their peers in the comparison group. These units have also won the Distinguished Curriculum Award from NAGC from 2010–2012.

# Sample Investigations for Gifted
# Students Across the Grades

The research-based activities described in this section focus on critical thinking and complex problem solving[1]. In addition, they pique student interest and creativity. All of them encourage students to grapple with challenging problems, discuss and write about their thinking, and justify their answers, just as mathematicians do. The focus on reflective writing (Think Deeply questions) is a critical piece in developing gifted students as strong mathematical thinkers. These questions focus on the big mathematical ideas of the investigation and are intended to have students think deeply about the mathematics. Writing about the mathematics and being asked to justify their reasoning advances students' understanding through reflection on their own ideas, a high-level metacognitive skill. It also helps students develop appropriate use of mathematical vocabulary.

## Grades K–2

In the advanced investigation from the Project M[2] unit, *Exploring Shape Games: Geometry With Imi and Zani* (Gavin, Casa, Chapin, & Sheffield, 2011), students help to create shape games for Imi and Zani, their bird friends from the Amazon. In this particular activity, students use a set of label cards and a set of attribute shapes. There are four shapes (circles, squares, triangles, and hexagons). Each type of shape comes in three different colors (white, black, and gray) and two different sizes (big and little). In playing the game, students take turns putting labels on intersecting loops and then filling the loops with the appropriate shapes. They are, in effect, sorting and classifying shapes, which requires not only understanding the properties of shapes but also seeing the relationships among two-dimensional shapes, a much higher level cognitive skill.

After playing the game, they are given the "Think Deeply" question in Figure 7.4 to write about. This question is intended to have students think

---

1  These activities also appear in *Identifying and Nurturing Math Talent* by M. K. Gavin (2011).

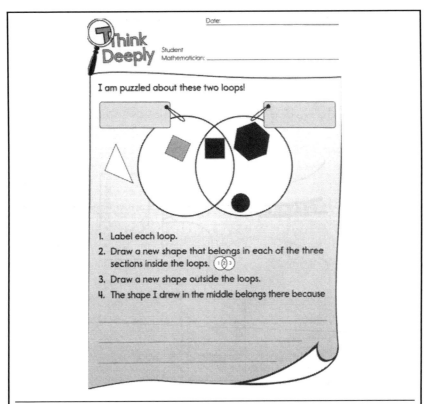

**Figure 7.4.** Think Deeply question. *Note.* From *Project M²: Exploring Shape Games: Geometry With Imi and Zani* (Student's Journal, p. 35) by M. K. Gavin, T. M. Casa, S. Chapin, and L. J. Sheffield, 2011, Dubuque, IA: Kendall Hunt. Copyright 2011 by Kendall Hunt. Reprinted with permission.

deeply about the mathematics, apply what they learned to a new situation and justify their reasoning.

For greater challenge requiring even greater skills in classifying and sorting, students can complete the activity on the Think Beyond Card as depicted in Figure 7.5.

## Grades 3–5

In the *Project M³: Mentoring Mathematical Minds* unit, *What Are Your Chances?* (Gavin, Chapin, Dailey, & Sheffield, 2008), students learn about

**Figure 7.5.** Think Beyond Card. *Note.* From *Project M²: Exploring Shape Games: Geometry With Imi and Zani* (Teacher's Guide, p. 183) by M. K. Gavin, T. M. Casa, S. Chapin, & L. J. Sheffield, 2011, Dubuque, IA: Kendall Hunt. Copyright 2011 by Kendall Hunt. Reprinted with permission.

the likelihood of events, the Law of Large Numbers, experimental and theoretical probability, and fair and unfair games based on probability. These topics are advanced topics for elementary students. The culminating project for their study of probability is to create a Carnival of Chance to raise money for a local charity. The carnival games that students create need to appear fair so the carnival-goers will want to play, but in reality must be unfair so that rather than giving away prizes, the students will be collecting money for their charity—an intriguing challenge for students! This project is an excellent example of the ninth Standard for Mathematical Practice, solving problems in novel ways and posing new mathematical questions of interest to investigate.

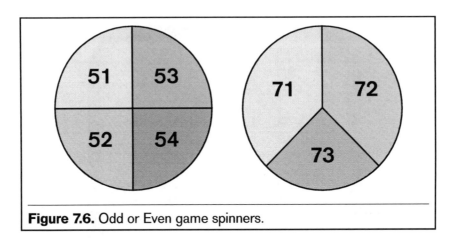

**Figure 7.6.** Odd or Even game spinners.

To help students get ready to create their own games, they analyze some games presented to them. In the Odd or Even game, two players must spin each of the spinners in Figure 7.6 and find the sum of the two numbers they land on. If the sum is odd, one player gets a point. The other player gets a point if the sum is even. First, students are asked to predict if the game is fair by just looking at spinners similar to the ones in Figure 7.6.

Students often think that the game is unfair. Some argue it is unfair because there are four numbers on one spinner and only three on the other. Still others think it might be unfair because there are four even numbers and only three odd numbers. In playing the game, results are mixed. Some teams find that there are more odd sums, other teams find more even sums, and still others end in a tie with equal even and odd sums. Students then determine the number of possible outcomes (i.e., the theoretical probability) and conclude that the game is fair.

The Think Deeply question that follows the investigation ("How could you change the rules of the game to make it an unfair game? Using probability, explain why the change makes the game unfair.") encourages critical analysis as well as a creative challenge. Students come up with a variety of novel solutions because there are many different ways to accomplish the task!

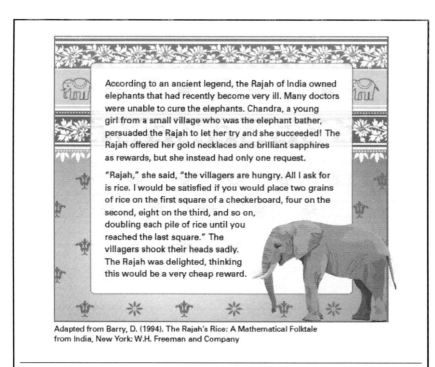

According to an ancient legend, the Rajah of India owned elephants that had recently become very ill. Many doctors were unable to cure the elephants. Chandra, a young girl from a small village who was the elephant bather, persuaded the Rajah to let her try and she succeeded! The Rajah offered her gold necklaces and brilliant sapphires as rewards, but she instead had only one request.

"Rajah," she said, "the villagers are hungry. All I ask for is rice. I would be satisfied if you would place two grains of rice on the first square of a checkerboard, four on the second, eight on the third, and so on, doubling each pile of rice until you reached the last square." The villagers shook their heads sadly. The Rajah was delighted, thinking this would be a very cheap reward.

Adapted from Barry, D. (1994). The Rajah's Rice: A Mathematical Folktale from India, New York: W.H. Freeman and Company

**Figure 7.7.** Legend of the Rajah's Rice. *Note.* From *Solve It: Focusing on Equations, Inequalities, and Exponents* by M. K. Gavin, L. J. Sheffield & S. H. Chapin, 2010, Dubuque, IA: Kendall Hunt. Copyright 2010 by Kendall Hunt. Reprinted with permission.

## Middle Grades

An interesting and challenging algebra problem in which students discover the power of exponential functions begins with the folk tale from India shared in Figure 7.7.

This investigation is taken from a prealgebra unit called *Solve It: Focusing on Equations, Inequalities and Exponents* (Gavin et al., 2010), part of *Math Innovations,* a middle grades math program for all students. This program has a strong focus on mathematical reasoning and Think Beyond challenges for gifted students in every lesson. After reading the story, students are asked to think, discuss, and write about the following questions.

What do you think? Was this a wise decision on Chandra's part? Defend your answer. In your answer, explain how this relates to exponential functions.

"Think Beyond" questions that extend student thinking about the function $y = 2^x$ include the following.

Predict the shape of the following graphs and how they each compare to the graph of $y = 2^x$.

a) $y = 2 \times 2^x$

b) $y = 2^{-x}$

c) $y = \left(\dfrac{1}{2}\right)^x$

d) Graph each equation on the same axes. Refine or add on to your predictions as needed.

# Conclusion

In conclusion, mathematics curriculum for gifted students must be qualitatively different from the regular curriculum in order to meet the needs of these students and develop their mathematical talent to its fullest. There are four components to consider when creating or searching for an appropriate curriculum: creative and complex problem solving, connections within and access across mathematical and other content areas and across a wide range of contexts, an inquiry-based approach that focuses on processes used by mathematicians akin to the Common Core State Standards for Mathematical Practice including the ninth standard on creativity, and appropriate pacing. The curriculum should be research-based, focused, coherent, and rigorous. Providing students with interesting and even challenging problems, puzzles, or investigations that are unrelated and do not lead to a deep and complex understanding of mathematical concepts is enriching, but does not provide the curriculum that these students deserve.

As important as rigorous content is the use of instructional strategies to develop students as mathematicians. In particular, high-level mathematical discussions should be the norm within the classroom in which students are comfortable and encouraged to agree and disagree with each other's thinking, take risks in finding solutions to problems, and create new questions to probe. These discussions, in turn, enable students to explain their thinking and defend their reasoning in writing, a necessary skill for mathematicians.

Our goal is to develop gifted mathematical thinkers who will become the leaders in the fields of education, business, science, and technology. In order to do so, we need to challenge students to think deeply about, discuss with others, and solve complex problems and then be able to share their insights verbally and in writing. Only then we will have the future leaders we need to support a global economy and make the world a better place in which to live.

# References

Biehler, R. F., & Snowman, J. (1993). *Psychology applied to teaching* (7th ed.). Boston, MA: Houghton Mifflin.

Chamberlin, S. (2006). Secondary mathematics for high-ability students. In F. A. Dixon & S. M. Moon (Eds.), *The handbook of secondary gifted education* (pp. 461–480). Waco, TX: Prufrock Press.

Chapin, S. H., O'Connor, C., & Anderson, N. C. (2013). *Classroom discussions: Using math talk to help students learn.* Sausalito, CA: Math Solutions Publications.

Coxbill, E., Chamberlin, S. A., & Weatherford, J. (2013). Using model-eliciting activities as a tool to identify creatively gifted elementary mathematics students. *Journal for the Education of the Gifted, 37,* 176–197.

Dimitriadis, C. (2012). Provision for mathematically gifted children in primary schools: An investigation of four different methods of organizational provision. *Educational Review, 64,* 241–260.

Firmender, J. M. (2011, April). *Advanced mathematics curriculum: The effect of Project M² on the achievement of mathematically talented students in grade 2.* Paper session at the annual meeting of the American Educational Research Association, New Orleans, LA.

Gallagher, S. A., & Gallagher, J. J. (2013). Using problem-based learning to explore unseen academic potential. *Interdisciplinary Journal of Problem-based Learning, 7*(1). Retrieved from http://dx.doi.org/10.7771/1541-5015.1322

Gavin, M. K. (2011). *Identifying and nurturing math talent.* Waco, TX: Prufrock Press.

Gavin, M. K., Casa, T. M., Adelson, J. L., Carroll, S. R., & Sheffield, L. J. (2009). The impact of advanced curriculum on the achievement of mathematically promising elementary students. *Gifted Child Quarterly, 53,* 188–202.

Gavin, M. K., Casa, T. M., Adelson, J. L., & Firmender, J. M. (2013). The impact of advanced geometry and measurement units on the achievement of grade 2 students. *Journal for Research in Mathematics Education, 44,* 478–510.

Gavin, M. K., Casa, T. M., Chapin, S. H., & Sheffield, L. J. (2007–2013). *Project $M^2$: Mentoring young mathematicians* (series). Dubuque, IA: Kendall Hunt.

Gavin, M. K., Casa, T. M., Chapin, S. H., & Sheffield, L. J. (2011). *Project $M^2$: Exploring shape games: Geometry with Imi and Zani.* Dubuque, IA: Kendall Hunt.

Gavin, M. K., Casa, T. M., Firmender, J. M., & Carroll, S. R. (2013). The impact of advanced geometry and measurement units on the mathematics achievement of first-grade students. *Gifted Child Quarterly, 57,* 71–84.

Gavin M. K., Chapin, S. H., Dailey, J., & Sheffield, L. J. (2003–2007). *Project $M^3$:Mentoring mathematical minds* (series). Dubuque, IA: Kendall Hunt.

Gavin, M. K., Chapin, S. H., Dailey, J., & Sheffield, L. J. (2008). *Project $M^3$: What are your chances?* Dubuque, IA: Kendall Hunt.

Gavin, M. K., Chapin, S. H., Dailey, J., & Sheffield, L. J. (2015). *Project $M^3$: How big is big?: Understanding and using large numbers.* Dubuque, IA: Kendall Hunt.

Gavin, M. K., Dailey, J., Chapin, S. H., & Sheffield, L. J. (2008). *Project $M^3$: Getting into shapes.* Dubuque, IA: Kendall Hunt.

Gavin, M. K., & Moylan, K. G. (2012). 7 steps to high-end learning. *Teaching Children Mathematics, 19,* 184–192.

Gavin, M. K. & Sheffield, L. J. (2010). Using curriculum to develop mathematical promise in the middle grades. In M. Saul, S. Assouline, & L. J. Sheffield (Eds.), *The peak in the middle: Developing mathematically gifted students in the middle grades* (pp. 51–76). Reston, VA: National Council of Teachers of Mathematics.

Gavin, M. K., Sheffield, L. J., & Chapin, S. H. (2010). *Math innovations course 3: Solve it: Focusing on equations, inequalities, and exponents* (Student ed.). Dubuque, IA: Kendall/Hunt Publishing Company.

Hertberg-Davis, H., & Callahan, C. M. (2008). A narrow escape: Gifted students' perceptions of Advanced Placement and International Baccalaureate programs. *Gifted Child Quarterly, 52,* 199–216.

Jensen, L. R. (1980, August). *A five-point program for gifted education.* Paper presented at the International Congress on Mathematical Education, Berkeley, CA.

Johnsen, S. K., & Sheffield, L. J. (2013). *Using the Common Core State Standards for Mathematics with gifted and advanced learners.* Waco, TX: Prufrock Press.

Kulik, J. A. (1992). *An analysis of the research on ability grouping: Historical and contemporary perspectives* (RM9204). Storrs: University of Connecticut, The National Research Center on the Gifted and Talented.

National Council of Teachers of Mathematics. (1989). *Curriculum and evaluation standards for school mathematics.* Reston, VA: Author.

National Council of Teachers of Mathematics. (2000). *Principles and standards for school mathematics.* Reston, VA: Author.

National Governors Association Center for Best Practices, & Council of Chief State School Officers. (2010). *Common Core State Standards for Mathematics.* Washington, DC: Author.

National Research Council. (2001). *Adding it up: Helping children learn mathematics.* Washington, DC: The National Academies Press.

Pierce, R. L., Cassady, J. C., Adams, C. M., Speirs Neumeister, K. L., Dixon, F. A., & Cross, T. L. (2011). The effects of clustering and curriculum on the development of gifted learners' math achievement. *Journal for the Education of the Gifted, 34,* 569–594.

Reis, S. M., Burns, D. E., & Renzulli, J. S. (1992). *Curriculum compacting: The complete guide to modifying the curriculum for high-ability students.* Mansfield Center, CT: Creative Learning Press.

Renzulli, J. S. (2002). Expanding the conception of giftedness to include co-cognitive traits and to promote social capital. *Phi Delta Kappan, 84*(1), 33–58.

Renzulli, J. S., Leppien, J. H., & Hays, T. S. (2000). *The Multiple Menu Model: A practical guide for developing differentiated curriculum.* Waco, TX: Prufrock Press.

Schiever, S. W., & Maker, C. J. (2003). New directions in acceleration and enrichment. In N. Colangelo & G. A. Davis (Eds.), *Handbook of gifted education* (3rd ed., pp. 163–173). Boston, MA: Allyn & Bacon.

Sheffield, L. J. (2003). *Extending the challenge in mathematics: Developing mathematical promise in K–8 students.* Thousand Oaks, CA: Corwin Press.

Tieso, C. L. (2002). *The effects of grouping and curricular practices on intermediate students' math achievement* (RM02154). Storrs: University of Connecticut, The National Research Center on the Gifted and Talented.

Tomlinson, C. A. (1994). Gifted learners: The boomerang kids of middle school. *Roeper Review 16,* 177–182.

Tomlinson, C. A., Kaplan, S. N., Renzulli, J. S., Purcell, J. H., Leppien, J. H., Burns, D. E., . . . Imbeau, M. B. (2009). *The parallel curriculum: A design to develop learner potential and challenge advanced learners* (2nd ed.). Thousand Oaks, CA: Corwin Press.

VanTassel-Baska, J., & Brown, E. (2007). Toward best practice: An analysis of the efficacy of curriculum models in education. *Gifted Child Quarterly, 51,* 342–358.

Vygotsky, L. S. (1978). *Mind in society.* Cambridge, MA: Harvard University Press.

# CHAPTER 8

# Science Curriculum for Gifted Learners

## Michael S. Matthews

## Introduction

What should educators be looking for in an effective science curriculum for students identified as talented, academically advanced, or gifted learners? Although there are a few prepackaged curricula that have been demonstrated to be effective (see for example the selections detailed by Matthews, 2012), there simply are not enough of these offerings available to construct an entire curriculum sequence spanning K–12 education. In addition, commercially published curricula are becoming ever-more expensive, while funding allotted to purchase textbooks is not growing at the same rate. In some locations, textbook funds even have been the target of substantial budget cuts; in North Carolina, for example, one state budget proposal allocated just $0.60 per student per year for this purpose. Finally, some commercially available science curricula simply are not very good, whether for typical or advanced learners—poorly designed laboratory exercises or factual errors don't help anyone learn!

Sixty cents per child does not go very far, and of course money alone cannot make up for poorly developed commercial materials. Rather than point the reader toward something to purchase, this chapter suggests some considerations for developing science curriculum for the gifted or academically advanced learner and offers some suggestions for how one might think about the goals of existing science curricula and how these might be modified to better address the needs of gifted and advanced learners. Some readers may find this frustrating to some degree, but philosophically, it is in line with the view that teaching is a profession—the teacher is the expert in the room, and should therefore be the person making the important decisions about what and how students will learn (Matthews, 2012). In addition, the space constraints of this chapter would not be sufficient to lay a foundation for instruction in even a single grade level and discipline, much less for all of K–12 science. With these considerations and this philosophy in mind, this chapter provides the reader with suggestions that will be helpful in both developing relevant curricular modifications and in evaluating and selecting instructional materials developed by others. General considerations that are relevant for anyone working with students identified as gifted or academically advanced will be presented, as well as a brief theoretical overview of the role of argumentation in the science classroom. Specific recommendations for the classroom that are based on the author's experience working with a very bright and motivated team of middle school students engaged in preparing for the Science Olympiad competition are also included.

# Contextual Considerations in Developing Science Curriculum for the Gifted

## Understanding the Educational Context

Science occupies an interesting niche in the ecology of contemporary education. Although it is considered a core academic content area, it is rarely the subject of standardized testing, and so in comparison to reading, language arts, or mathematics, it often receives relatively little instructional time. At the elementary level, most teachers have had little if any specialized training in teaching science, and only a few bring the same passion to the subject that is evident in their work in other content areas such as reading instruction. At the secondary level, teachers more commonly are able to specialize in teaching within their content expertise, and the subject of science begins to receive a more equitable amount of instructional time. Still, despite the more specialized training, teacher effectiveness in science classrooms (as in most educational settings) ranges from incredibly strong all the way down to mediocre and below. Although there certainly are some pockets of excellence, international comparisons continue to convey the unwelcome finding that mediocrity is characteristic of learner outcomes in the sciences in U.S. schools as a whole. For example, Fleischman, Hopstock, Pelczar, and Shelley (2010) summarized results from the 2009 Program for International Student Assessment, and found that U.S. students' performance in science literacy "was not measurably different from the OECD average" (p. iv).

When basic instruction is limited by a lack of curricular emphasis and limited teacher preparation, it may seem out of order to consider what great science instruction looks like. In fact, however, this makes it all the more vital to encourage classrooms of excellence; these provide models to show other students, parents, and teachers what is possible. In addition, one of the central tenets of gifted education, whether we call it talent development, gifted education, advanced academics, or something else, is taking a strengths-based approach rather than one focused solely on remediation of what learners cannot do. Given this context and perspective, what should science curriculum and instruction for the gifted look like?

**The science classroom should attend to individual differences.** Although there has been some disagreement about this in the literature, some students identified as gifted display multipotentiality, or the aptitude to excel in multiple content domains. Other students, also identified as gifted, may have a narrower range of interests or a more uneven profile of abilities that favors learning in the sciences over other content areas. Still other students may be characterized as twice-exceptional, in that they display advanced academic ability in the sciences or another academic domain, yet suffer concurrently from a learning disability or other difficulty in specific areas or even across content areas.

Even within the sciences, a given learner may show a very narrow preference, as for paleontology, or a broader scope of interests and aptitudes such as in the life sciences in general. These differences, and others, mean that really there is no such thing as "the" student gifted in science. Individual differences in motivation, determination, or persistence also contribute to further differences in what a given student can (or will) achieve. However, through a combination of appropriate grouping, differentiated instruction, and attention to each student as an individual, the recommendations in this chapter can be of use in meeting the learning needs of all students who show advanced academic potential in the sciences.

**The science classroom should use effective instructional grouping practices.** Although it has been said by many others, it bears repeating here that instructional grouping should be flexible; talent is best viewed as being domain-specific, meaning that a student who is an excellent reader may not necessarily also demonstrate excellence in math, or in science, even though both areas can benefit from advanced reading abilities. In addition, other nonintellectual factors—and motivation is key among them—contribute to variation in students' engagement and achievement across content units and even in different types of learning tasks within a content area of interest. The presence of these differences suggests that effective instructional grouping must be both flexible and responsive to individual differences in interest, ability, and motivation in order to be most successful.

One very effective way to provide for different levels of prior knowledge about a topic is to use a pretest before each instructional unit. By considering the pretest scores from a given classroom, students can then be given different learning opportunities based on their demonstrated level of mastery. For example, students who already know 90% or more of the unit's content probably should not be expected to sit through the same lecture as students whose scores show they currently know only around 10% of the unit's content. Instead, the students who have demonstrated mastery of the basic content of the unit can be given individualized opportunities to learn about more specialized aspects, through individualized means such as developing a report to present later to their classmates. If a third group demonstrates mastery of around half the unit's content, these students might be engaged in targeted learning activities related to the content they did not yet know, with other extension activities to fill the place of the content they already have mastered. Students in the 10% pretest mastery group also may need additional development in the unit's vocabulary, in addition to completing a wider selection (in comparison to students in the 50% group) of the activities geared toward learning the unit's conceptual content.

One important practice in this type of differentiated learning environment is to inform students ahead of time about the pretest and grouping process. Having a fully transparent system to assign students to instructional groups allows all students to be aware that with greater effort, or interest leading to such effort, they can move up to a different instructional group for the next unit if they desire to do so. This flexibility of grouping from one unit to the next is a key feature distinguishing effective ability grouping from the often-permanent instructional tracking practices that were widespread (and widely criticized as inequitable) during the 20th century. Effective instructional grouping goes hand in hand with the strengths-based approach described next.

**The science classroom should focus on strengths.** As already mentioned, one of the most difficult tendencies to overcome in providing education to highly able students in any content area is the desire to focus instruction on remediation of perceived or actual weaknesses. No adult looks for a college major or a career in a field he or she cannot do, or does not enjoy—so, why do we focus on deficits so frequently in K–12 education? Instead, effective instruction should be focused on what students already can do well—or what they have shown an extraordinary aptitude for—and on how to develop these abilities from the level of an above-average aptitude or strength toward a level recognized by student, parent, and teacher alike as excellence. To consider what this might look like, some ideas learned from a track record of success in Science Olympiad, an extracurricular science competition, will be examined later in this chapter. First, however, one additional area of promising practices in science learning—teaching about the nature of scientific knowledge, and specifically the role of argumentation in conveying this nature to students—will be considered.

# Argumentation in the Science Classroom

## What Is Argumentation, and Why Should It Be Used in Science Learning?

The skill of argumentation, also called *argumentative competence* or *reasoning*, has been noted in the education literature over the past couple of decades. As described in an integrative review by Rapanta and her colleagues (2013), "argumentation seems to provide opportunities for students to refine their understanding of the content, prompting them to sort relevant from irrelevant information, make connections across contexts, and increase the explanatory power of their knowledge" (p. 484). These higher-order skills and critical thinking outcomes are broadly consistent with the stated goals of gifted education practice; this consistency suggests that it would be helpful for those teaching in gifted education settings to look more deeply at this body of work.

Although argumentation is conceived as a general skill that occurs across educational contexts and is not specific to the content of science, Rapanta and her colleagues noted that argumentation is included as part of the inquiry content in the U.S. National Science Education Standards (National Research Council, 2000) for grades 5–12. Specifically, these authors attributed the rise of argumentation in science curricula to a developing contextual understanding of scientific knowledge as provisional, evidence-based, and subject to change as new data are gathered. However, this is the perspective of a content expert, and most K–12 students (as well as many adults who may not have studied science beyond their high school or introductory college coursework) have not yet developed this understanding.

Students at the K–12 level tend to view scientific explanations as facts, rather than as provisional interpretations that are consistent with currently available data. Engaging in argumentation requires students to use facts to support a point of view, and there is now good evidence that engaging in such argumentation helps the learner develop a more nuanced understanding of the nature of science. There is also some suggestion (e.g., Osborne, Simon, Christodoulou, Howell-Richardson, & Richardson, 2013) that refocusing science instruction on *how* we know something, as opposed to *what* we know, also may increase the level of engagement that students feel toward learning science.

Argumentation is a form of practice that leads to learning, but it also is an expression of learning and a demonstration of what one can say about one's own learning. Thus, although argumentation clearly relates closely to science learning, it also holds promise as a skill that students can transfer to what they learn in other fields of study, and that also can be applied to understanding interdisciplinary problems and curricula.

## What Does Argumentation Look Like in the Science Classroom?

Numerous articles on argumentation have been published in recent years in venues like *Science Education, Journal of Research in Science Teaching, The Science Teacher*, and others. However, despite these resources, it is difficult to provide a general enough example to be relevant to all readers. Interested teachers are encouraged to search these venues for articles relevant to the specific age range and content area of interest.

Sampson, Enderle, and Grooms (2013) provided a useful framework illustrating the components of a scientific argument. These include a claim or claims, evidence relevant to the claim, and a justification that conveys the assumptions and concepts upon which the interpretation of the evidence is based. These authors also offer an example, based on excerpts from Watson and Crick's seminal paper about the structure of DNA, to illustrate what an effective argument might look like.

It is a somewhat easier task to explain some of the roadblocks that a teacher might expect to encounter in adopting an argumentation-based framework in the classroom. Teachers participating in a study of the use of argumentation as a teaching strategy (Osborne et al., 2013) identified a number of obstacles to its use. These are listed in Table 8.1, along with some suggestions for how to overcome each.

Sampson and colleagues (2013) additionally related some difficulties that students may encounter in beginning to apply argumentation skills in the science classroom. They noted that students initially may not understand the difference between data and evidence: Evidence must include both the data and the students' analysis and proposed interpretation based on it, but beginning learners may believe that the data alone are sufficient. The authors noted that inexperienced learners sometimes may be too quick to generalize from limited information, or may rely upon only data that confirm their ideas, whereas an effective argument must also explain any contradictory observations that may have been made. The greatest challenge, they reported, is in the area of justification; here students must explain their underlying assumptions in terms of the theories or concepts that have guided their analysis and interpretation.

A final useful suggestion from these authors (Sampson et al., 2013) is in criteria for evaluating students' use of argumentation following their collection of data. The authors suggested both empirical and theoretical criteria are relevant. Empirical criteria include the fit between the claim

**Table 8.1**

*Obstacles to Implementation of Argumentation in the Science Classroom and Recommendations for Addressing Them*

| Obstacle | Explanation of Obstacle | Recommendation | Comments |
|---|---|---|---|
| Varied student ability | Less able learners found it difficult to express arguments; teachers ascribed this to lack of vocabulary or conceptual understanding. Some teachers felt students might be confused by the presence of both factual content and claims about the content in the same lesson. | Use flexible ability grouping; pretest students on concepts and offer additional vocabulary development opportunities as needed; place argumentation later in the curricular sequence. | Additional scaffolding may also be necessary for students who are English learners or who have had limited opportunities for prior science learning. |
| Classroom management | Teachers felt it was more difficult to manage student behavior and classroom noise levels during argumentation activities. | Adjust and communicate effectively the expectations for classroom behavior prior to argumentation activities; practice additional management strategies if necessary. | Changing expectations may also need to be communicated to administrators or others who may be involved in the teacher evaluation process. |
| Organization of instructional time | Difficulty determining the balance between argumentation and more traditional instructional activities; uncertainty about evaluation of oral versus written expression of student thinking. | Try different approaches to figure out what balance you are most comfortable with using. Keep in mind that Osborne and colleagues (2013) stated that it may require 18 months to 2 years or more to become comfortable with new instructional practices. | It may be helpful also to involve colleagues or students in the discussion of evaluation methods and the balance of activities. |

**Table 8.1,** *continued*

| Obstacle | Explanation of Obstacle | Recommendation | Comments |
|---|---|---|---|
| Difficulty stimulating student discussion | Students may tend to agree with one another, rather than taking sides on a topic. | Use varied strategies to assign students to opposing perspectives, and provide scaffolding for how to develop an effective argument. | Resources on formal debate strategies may be usefully applied to argumentation in the science classroom. Consider also drawing upon historical debates to foster argumentation. |
| Lack of scripted curricula | Appropriate opportunities for incorporating argumentation into science learning will vary by grade level and content area, so few commercially available curricula are likely to be available. | Start small; develop one or two opportunities to apply argumentation skills per semester, then add more as needed once these initial units have been thoroughly developed. | This also may be viewed as a strength, because of the professional autonomy it allows the teacher to develop the most appropriate curriculum and instruction for meeting her or his students' learning needs. |

*Note.* Obstacles are based on Osborne et al. (2013).

and evidence; the sufficiency of the amount of evidence; the appropriateness and rigor of the data collection procedure; and the appropriateness of the chosen method of analysis. Suggested theoretical criteria include the ability of the claim to contribute to an understanding of the natural world, and the consistency of both the claim and its associated data analysis with the current understanding of the phenomenon. The professional educator will be capable of adapting these criteria into a rubric, or using them to evaluate and modify as needed a rubric developed by someone else, to yield evaluation benchmarks that can be applied to any science content amenable to argumentation.

## Argumentation and Considerations for Curriculum Development

Based on the findings by Sampson and colleagues (2013), an introductory activity would seem reasonable to help students learn the difference between data and evidence. Again, evidence involves both data and its interpretation, which may be preliminary or tentative during the learning process. Before trying to develop examples with specific science content, the teacher probably should begin with a general discussion of logic in argumentation and of different sorts of fallacies. This can help students learn to reason by example and to develop their understanding of effective argumentation, and hence of evidence. One clever guide that could be used for this purpose is Ali Almossawi's very accessible 2014 book, *An Illustrated Book of Bad Arguments*. To follow this, the teacher can select specific examples of current or historical scientific theories or perspectives whose adoption has been contentious and that are relevant to the content of specific science coursework.

It may be a good idea to begin with historical controversies as a model of the process of argumentation, before moving to complex current issues such as climate change that will require students to develop a more nuanced understanding. For example, Lamarck's ideas about the inheritance of acquired characteristics might be appropriate to introduce ideas about scientific evidence in a biology class, while continental drift could be a relevant starting point in a geology or Earth science course. The teacher's professional knowledge about different possible events can also be applied to group students for instruction, based on readiness, interest, or other appropriate instructional considerations.

# Learning From the Science Olympiad[2] Competition Experience

## What Is Science Olympiad?

Science Olympiad is a U.S. nonprofit organization that runs science competitions for teams of students in grades 3–12. At the middle and high school levels, 15-student teams from different schools compete in a series of 23 themed events, which are drawn from all areas of the sciences as well as engineering and technology. The mix of events changes somewhat from year to year, but there are always some components that require pencil-and-paper or test-based learning and others that require hands-on expertise (see, for example, North Carolina Science Olympiad, 2014; Science Olympiad, 2014). The slate of events is developed such that a wide variety of student competencies will be required to form a successful team. Currently nearly 7,000 teams from all 50 U.S. states compete in Science Olympiad (SO) tournaments at the regional, state, and national levels. In addition to official tournaments, some schools and universities sponsor invitational tournaments that teams may attend to practice the year's SO events prior to the official tournaments; these also are excellent learning opportunities.

Although every school would benefit from fielding one or more Science Olympiad teams, the time commitment required to put together a successful team can be enormous. In addition, not every school may have sufficient interest to field a team, and even in schools with one or more SO teams, the majority of students will have their learning needs met in the classroom setting—making SO involvement less necessary. Following are some of the lessons learned from the experiences of volunteer coaches working with a successful SO team. Successful, as defined here, means that the school's team placed highly at the regional and state tournaments, and that the team advanced to the national tournament 3 years in a row in the middle school division. A number of parent and teacher coaches working together were responsible for elaborating these principles for the team's

---

2 Note that Science Olympiad (http://soinc.org/) should not be confused with the similarly-named International Science Olympiads, which usually have only one 4–6 person high school-aged team representing each country, and a narrow focus that consists of different, loosely affiliated tournaments within each scientific discipline.

development, but these ideas also can be applied to developing science curriculum for the gifted in the classroom setting. Of course these are not new ideas, but they do not appear to have been presented together elsewhere in the literature.

## Lessons of Science Olympiad for the Science Classroom

**Set higher goals for student achievement.** Science Olympiad competitions include both "build" events and "lab/test" events. The lab/test events are very similar to what students usually do in the science classroom; they require laboratory analyses and procedures to be carried out, or require students to study for written tests of knowledge about a given subject. One key difference, however, is that SO events tend to have a much higher ceiling than typical science classroom assessments do. In other words, even very well-prepared teams seldom are able to score 100% on a SO event test, whereas it is not unusual for several students in a classroom to achieve a perfect score on the typical middle or high school science test.

The drawback to tests on which a score of 100% correct is routinely achievable is that these can lead students to develop unhealthy attitudes toward achievement. Specifically, high-ability or gifted students who become accustomed to always making a perfect score may simply give up later in life, when they eventually encounter content that suddenly has become difficult. They may feel traumatized the first time they encounter such difficulty. Providing students with loftier learning goals earlier in their education, with appropriate support when one's learning or achievement goals are not achieved on the first try, leads to the development of a more realistic sense of self-efficacy and self-esteem, as well as helping the learner to develop a more resilient attitude toward difficult content.

**Broaden content connections.** Another way that SO lab and test events differ is in the breadth of content students will encounter in a given event. Although assessments of classroom curricula tend to have a relatively narrow focus, SO assessments often require students to demonstrate a far broader understanding. This breadth might include interdisciplinary connections such as the intellectual history of the field, cross-curricular content within the sciences (such as the chemistry that underlies a biological process), or drawing upon skills in diverse areas such as art to convey an understanding of scientific content.

In the typical science classroom, students learn a narrowly prescribed slice of the curriculum and then are tested on this content. Outside of Advanced Placement courses, which draw upon content from the full course in a single high-stakes exam at the end of the school year, students only rarely are expected to recall information from earlier units when they take tests for later units. Although some later content does build upon earlier learning—such as the way in which knowledge of different models of the atom informs one's later understanding of chemical reactions—all too often students come to understand each unit in isolation, rather than building a comprehensive mental model of an entire field of study and its many interrelated parts.

Although framed in various terms, there has been some suggestion in the literature that students identified as gifted may be global (or holistic) thinkers (e.g., Young & Fouts, 1993), although other studies did not find this pattern (Grigorenko & Sternberg, 1997). Current thought tends to favor giftedness as being primarily a domain-specific construct, but as Dai (2009) noted, domains may be defined in a variety of ways and some definitions are broader than others. Depending on the degree to which science instruction is framed within specific narrow domains, providing high-ability learners with the opportunity to develop a broad understanding of scientific fields may be more appropriate than the typical narrow approach of many science textbooks and curricula. In addition, having a global understanding of a discipline is characteristic of expert thinking in a domain. This suggests that students who demonstrate the potential for advanced achievement in the sciences may benefit from curriculum and instruction designed to foster a broad-based understanding.

Specific steps teachers can take to foster these outcomes could include, for example, Socratic discussion at the conceptual level, increasing the focus on the intellectual history of a concept, or argumentation, as described in the previous section of this chapter.

**Focus instruction on being wider, deeper, and faster.** In successful SO coaching for lab and test events, we have found three key words to be *wider*, *deeper*, and *faster*. Because the first- and second-place teams sometimes are separated by only fractions of a point, developing a wider knowledge base is the key to being able to achieve every possible point during the competition. Careful attention to nuances in grading can mimic the competition experience in the classroom, while also helping to avoid the 100% performance issues discussed earlier.

Classroom teachers can accomplish the goal of a wider curriculum by reading broadly on their subject (and having students do the same), in order to gain as much related knowledge as possible. In SO events, tests used in previous years are often available as study guides, and these may suggest additional directions in which to develop questioning with students. For example, in an event about forensic science, fingerprinting was one of the topics. Most schools' teams had studied enough to know the parts of the fingerprint and the basics of how fingerprints are collected at a crime scene. To develop a wider knowledge base, the winning team also had considered the history of fingerprinting (who came up with the concept and when); the term for the science of studying fingerprints; what compounds secreted by the skin were responsible for leaving fingerprints, and how each component responded to the different methods of developing a print; the mathematical reliability of fingerprint-based identification; and the effectiveness of fingerprints compared to other biometric identifiers that might be used at a crime scene.

Deeper knowledge also is relevant. In one of the lab-based events, one step in an identification protocol for an unknown substance required students to use Benedict's reagent to test for the presence of reducing sugars. Through practice, most teams in the competition knew how to use the materials provided to perform this test. However, at the more advanced levels of competition, this was not enough. Students on the winning teams also had studied the chemical makeup of the reagent, and the chemical reaction that produces its characteristic color change. Furthermore, they could apply this knowledge to explain why table sugar (which normally tests negative) would test positive when heated in the presence of an acid.

Working faster is the third component necessary for success in Science Olympiad competitions. Many of the events feature either an overall time limit or a limited amount of time to perform each station within the competition. Some SO events allow the use of reference materials, analogous to an open book examination in school. In either case, time is at a premium. For example, one team competing at the national level was not able to complete one of its events in the allotted time, and they placed poorly as a result, even though the students knew the content very well in the practice sessions. In another case, the entomology exam given to high school students was taken directly from a graduate-level university course on the topic; the winning team managed to achieve a score of 80% correct, but the less-prepared teams had very few correct answers due to the time limit and their somewhat slower speed in using their reference materials. At the higher levels of the SO competition, test designers often use speed as one means of separating strong, well-prepared teams from their competitors who are strong, well-prepared, and also fast.

In gifted education, we know that processing speed is one of the subtest areas measured in comprehensive individually administered IQ testing. Not every student identified as gifted excels in this area, but many do. Speed as a component of academic achievement is rarely emphasized in K–12 programming, but it does play a part in Advanced Placement exams, to name one relevant example. Speed used to be heavily emphasized in learning the multiplication tables, although today this type of practicing for automaticity is given far less emphasis in the classroom than it used to receive. Ultimately, students may find that their college courses, especially large first-year courses in the STEM fields, will use speed as a means of reducing the number of students who achieve high enough grades to declare a major in the field.

Later in life, working in a career, the speed with which one can accomplish tasks also is closely related to overall productivity; for example, this author recalls a titration that had to be done every day to calibrate lab instruments before the actual (paying) work of the lab could be started. The first few times it took an hour and a half each day to complete the process, even though plenty of titrations had been conducted previously in high school and college. After 6 months of daily practice, the whole process was shortened to around 20 minutes, leaving a lot more time to accomplish the actual analyses. The same is true for everything from lab activities to writing to statistical analysis to keyboarding skills; developing speed as well as accuracy in one's work is vital to successful performance.

**Other differences between Science Olympiad and the classroom.** Events in Science Olympiad competitions are norm-referenced; that is, each team aims to perform better than their opponents do, and the team with the best score wins the event whether or not anyone gets all of the answers correct. In fact, due to the breadth of content and the advanced level of difficulty of competition events, it is unlikely that any team will achieve a perfect score. This is a very different experience for the student than in the K–12 classroom, where gifted students (and their often-vocal parents) work with the expectation that top performance is equivalent to a top grade. Thus, while modifying classroom instruction to be wider, deeper, and faster is appropriate from a learning point of view, it is likely that the teacher who does so will also need to modify his or her grading practices so that an A still can be obtainable by less-than-perfect (yet still demonstrably high) performance on these types of extremely rigorous tasks.

Another key area of difference between laboratory exercises in the typical science classroom and those in a Science Olympiad competition is in the nature of the expected outcomes. Most SO events require repeated practice of a given measurement or other applied technique, resulting in the accurate estimation of an unknown quantity. But rather than measuring something new, the school science lab experience often is geared toward the observation of some prespecified outcome. For the gifted science learner, outcomes of these lab activities may be glaringly obvious well before the activity actually begins, either due to the learner's prior knowledge or to his or her having read ahead in the textbook out of general interest. This makes class boring! It may not be until a student begins Advanced Placement coursework, often in the latter years of high school, that he or she encounters laboratory exercises designed around unknown outcomes, whether in the classic sense (determining which of several possible substances is present) or in the inquiry sense (figuring out an answer without knowing the possibilities ahead of time).

Even at the Advanced Placement level, it is rare for learners to engage in sustained practice of any single method or technique. Yet, in upper level college or graduate coursework or in laboratory work, efficiency depends heavily on one's technical expertise and ability to work almost automatically on common procedures or techniques while concentrating attention on the more complex aspects of the task. We see this ideal expressed clearly in athletic training in the schools, but it also should become a part of how we teach for excellence in the sciences.

## Implications for Curriculum Development

To summarize, there are several implications that observations of Science Olympiad competition suggest for science curriculum and instruction for gifted and academically advanced learners. First, the content of science instruction should have both greater depth and greater breadth than it usually does. This requires more from the teacher, but also requires more of the students. Although grades of A may still be common in the gifted science classroom, scores of 100% should be less achievable. Second, speed of task completion—although not at the expense of accuracy—should be emphasized more heavily. Repeated practice in specific, routine, but relevant tasks is one way to achieve greater efficiency in this area. Contests between student teams, or possibly even between students and teachers or other adults, can be used to make such practice more engaging. Finally, at least some learning tasks should be designed to have outcomes that are not predetermined. For example, regular measurements to monitor water quality in a local waterway would allow repeated practice, would help develop speed and accuracy (particularly if an analysis is repeated on the same sample by different teams of students, and graded based on agreement to others' results), and would have outcomes that are not predetermined yet also are valued by stakeholders beyond the classroom environment. Thus, such an activity would meet most of the characteristics that experience with students in Science Olympiad suggests are valuable to the development of scientific expertise.

# Conclusion

This chapter opened with some thoughts on the context of science teaching and learning, and some philosophical and research-based recommendations staked out the author's position relative to this context and argued that others also should hold these views. This proceeded to another rather theoretical discussion about the role of argumentation in science instruction. The chapter concluded with some more concrete suggestions for specific ways that science curriculum and instruction should be modified, based on experiences working with highly able (and high-achieving) science students in the Science Olympiad competition. These concrete ideas were contextualized with regard to the chapter's earlier points about the expectations of teachers, students, and parents.

This approach may have raised more questions than it answered. If so, this is good—reflective practice is vital to developing one's teaching abilities! By thinking about the issues and ideas raised here, educators are engaging in what Torrance and other creativity theorists have called *incubation*. This represents a necessary pause in one's conscious thought processes after learning new material, while the subconscious mind continues to work out the details of how all this fits into existing conceptualizations and practice.

# References

Dai, D. Y. (2009). Essential tensions surrounding the concept of giftedness. In L. V. Shavinina (Ed.), *International handbook on giftedness* (pp. 39–80). New York, NY: Springer Science.

Fleischman, H. L., Hopstock, P. J., Pelczar, M. P., & Shelley, B. E. (2010). *Highlights from PISA 2009: Performance of U.S. 15-year-old students in reading, mathematics, and science literacy in an international context* (NCES 2011-004). Washington, DC: U.S. Department of Education, National Center for Education Statistics.

Grigorenko, E. L., & Sternberg, R. J. (1997). Styles of thinking, abilities, and academic performance. *Exceptional Children, 63,* 295–312.

Matthews, M. S. (2012). *Science strategies for students with gifts and talents.* Waco, TX: Prufrock Press.

National Research Council. (2000). *Inquiry and the National Science Education Standards.* Washington DC: National Academy Press. Retrieved from http://www.nap.edu/openbook.php?isbn=0309064767

North Carolina Science Olympiad. (2014). *About North Carolina Science Olympiad.* Retrieved from http://www.sciencenc.com/team-help/about.php

Osborne, J., Simon, S., Christodoulou, A., Howell-Richardson, C., & Richardson, K. (2013). Learning to argue: A study of four schools and their attempt to develop the use of argumentation as a common instructional practice and its impact on students. *Journal of Research in Science Teaching, 50,* 315–347. doi:10.1002/tea.21073

Rapanta, C., Garcia-Mila, M., & Gilabert, S. (2013). What is meant by argumentative competence? An integrative review of methods of analysis and assessment in education. *Review of Educational Research, 83,* 483–520. doi:10.3102/0034654313487606

Sampson, V., Enderle, P., & Grooms, J. (2013). Argumentation in science education: Helping students understand the nature of scientific argumentation so they can meet the new science standards. *The Science Teacher, 80*(5), 30–33.

Science Olympiad. (2014). *Science Olympiad: The nation's most exciting K–12 science competition.* Retrieved from http://www.soinc.org

Young, E. R., & Fouts, J. T. (1993). Field dependence/independence and the identification of gifted students. *Journal for the Education of the Gifted, 16,* 299–310. doi:10.1177/016235329301600306

# CHAPTER 9

# Social Studies Curriculum for Gifted Learners

## Shelagh A. Gallagher

The cornerstone of democracy is the informed citizen. Solutions to social problems require the insights that emerge from diverse perspectives and experiences. . . . When citizens of a democracy are deprived of an effective social studies education it places both the citizen and the democracy at risk. . . . One of the most important factors in the fall of republics great and small throughout history has been when citizens no longer felt connected to their government and became disinterested in what that government was doing. (Maryland Council for Social Studies, 2010)

What could be a more fascinating topic of study than the human condition, delving into questions of who we are collectively and as individuals, how we came to live where we live, in the manner in which we live? What could be more important than teaching students how human strengths and frailties have shaped the course of life on our planet, or to cultivate in them the skills and attitudes that will sustain our future growth as a nation and a world? These questions unite the collection of fields joined under the umbrella term *social studies*. Social studies is

> the study of the social sciences and humanities to promote civic competence. . . . drawing upon such disciplines as anthropology, archeology, economics, geography, history, law, philosophy, political science, psychology, religion, sociology, as well as . . . the humanities, mathematics, and natural sciences. The primary purpose of social studies is to help young people develop the ability to make informed, and reasoned decisions for the public good as citizens of a culturally diverse, democratic society in an interdependent world. (National Council for Social Studies, 2010, p. 3)

This is a sizeable agenda and an essential one; yet ironically, requirements for education in social studies have declined significantly over the past 20 years. Only 21 states require students to pass a social studies test in order to graduate from high school, compared to 34 states in 2001. Only 9 of those 21 require a state test in civics (see http://www.civicyouth.org/maps/state-civic-ed/index.html). The Center for Education Policy (2007) reported that 36% of surveyed school districts decreased instruction in social studies since the passage of No Child Left Behind (NCLB). An average of 176 minutes per week is currently spent on social studies instruction in the United States compared to 503 and 383 minutes in language arts and mathematics, respectively. Ironically, decreases have been greatest in low-performing schools, arguably schools with the students in greatest need of civic empowerment.

Figure 9.1 is the backdrop for a discussion of social studies education and gifted students. Justifications for gifted programs often included exhortations about our desire for gifted students to become the leaders of their generation. In an era when the study of history, citizenship, and global connections are at an all time low, how can we ensure civic leadership among the nation's most talented students?

| Social Studies Imperative | Description of Imperative |
|---|---|
| Social studies teaching and learning are powerful when they are meaningful. | Meaningful social studies builds curriculum networks of knowledge, skills, beliefs, and attitudes that are structured around enduring understandings, essential questions, important ideas, and goals (NCSS, n.d., para. 8). |
| Social studies teaching and learning are powerful when they are integrative. | The subjects that comprise social studies—i.e., history, economics, geography, political science, sociology, anthropology, archaeology and psychology—are rich, interrelated disciplines, each critical to the background of thoughtful citizens. The social studies curriculum is integrative, addressing the totality of human experience over time and space, connecting with the past, linked to the present, and looking ahead to the future. Focusing on the core social studies disciplines, it includes materials drawn from the arts, sciences, and humanities, from current events, from local examples and from students' own lives (NCSS, n.d., para. 10). |
| Social studies teaching and learning are powerful when they are value-based. | Social studies teachers recognize that students do not become responsible, participating citizens automatically. The values embodied in our democratic form of government, with its commitment to justice, equality, and freedom of thought and speech, are reflected in social studies classroom practice (NCSS, n.d., para. 12). |
| Social studies teaching and learning are powerful when they are challenging. | Student work should reflect a balance between retrieval and recitation of content and a thoughtful examination of concepts in order to provide intellectual challenges. The teacher must explain and model intellectual standards expected of students. These include, but are not limited to: clarity, precision, completeness, depth, relevance, and fairness (NCSS, n.d., para. 15). |
| Social studies teaching and learning are powerful when they are active. | Active lessons require students to process and think about what they are learning. There is a profound difference between learning about the actions and conclusions of others and reasoning one's way toward those conclusions. Active learning is not just "hands-on," it is "minds-on" (NCSS, n.d., para. 17). |

**Figure 9.1.** Qualities of powerful and authentic social studies.

# Components of Differentiation in Social Studies: Duration, Intensity, and Authenticity

Differentiation of any lesson or curriculum should be guided by the unique needs presented by a particular group of students. As a group, gifted students tend to absorb knowledge faster than typically developing students. They also tend to acquire the ability to reason conceptually earlier. These advanced skills obviously give gifted students a learning advantage; however, they also come with some pitfalls. Because gifted students learn facts more easily, they can learn to rely on low-level thinking skills and avoid using higher order thinking skills unless they are presented with information or reasoning they find challenging (Gallagher, 2009b). On the whole, gifted students are more inclined than typically developing students to ask open questions and to prefer inquiry-based learning environments (Gallagher, 2012a). These are characteristics that compel adjustments to a gifted student's learning experience.

Fortunately, social studies provides a helpful foothold for differentiation. It is a field filled with intradisciplinary connections and natural interdisciplinary connections: Economics naturally bridges social studies with mathematics just as anthropology connects history and science. Psychology incorporates social science, biology, chemistry, and more. Art and literature are also natural companions to the study of history. In fact, everything that happens in any field of study is inherently an element of history. Concept-centered teaching is supported in social studies. The National Council for Social Studies (NCSS; 2010) has identified a set of 10 concepts that undergird and connect the different branches of the field: (1) culture; (2) time, continuity, and change; (3) people, places, and environments; (4) individual development and identity; (5) individuals, groups, and institutions; (6) power, authority, and governance; (7) production, distribution, and consumption; (8) science, technology, and society; (9) global connections; and, (10) civic ideals and practices. The aims of social studies instruction described in Figure 9.1, which orient instruction toward meaningful engagement with academic material, also undergird differentiated instruction. What remains is to ensure that the curriculum is altered in ways that increase the level of challenge without decreasing engagement or interest.

Kirk, J. Gallagher, and Coleman (2014) identified two essential components of effective differentiation: *duration* and *intensity*. *Duration* refers to the amount of time spent in differentiated study. The duration of differentiated experiences should vary according to the extent of a student's needs. Short duration differentiation is achieved through modification of individual lessons; longer duration differentiation is actualized through curriculum alterations that allow students to skip an already-mastered topic, that integrate independent study, or that increase the length of a differentiated unit of study. *Intensity* refers the level of challenge, depth, abstractness, or complexity built into differentiated study. Intensity is partially dependent on duration, because the cultivation of advanced thinking requires sustained effort over time.

A third component of differentiated activity is *authenticity*. All students should have authentic educational experiences to bring social studies alive; however, authenticity has added dimensions for gifted students, including exposure to the ways expert practitioners think and opportunities to see and participate firsthand in social leadership. Authentic social studies experiences should include a balance of (a) activities that *immerse students in social studies*, cultivating fascination with specific individuals, events, and epochs, and (b) activities that teach students *forms of expert reasoning in the social sciences*, introducing them to methods of research and discipline-specific frameworks for thinking about information.

**Increasing duration of differentiated activity.** One means of creating short duration differentiation is through tiered classroom lessons (Tomlinson, 2004). As the term suggests, *tiering* an assignment accordingly involves transforming a learning objective or set of objectives into a set of activities, each at a different level of challenge. All three levels occur simultaneously but students select or are assigned to the level that will provide an intellectual stretch. An example of a tiered assignment for an independent research project is included in Figure 9.2. In this example, Tier 3—the most challenging level—is distinguished from the others by its requirement of additional primary resource documents (content modification), the use of persuasive essay (process modification), and the use of a speech to the Nobel committee (product modification). The use of the Nobel committee as the target audience also adds a layer of complexity to the content, because it will require students to read about the Nobel prizes and their different criteria in order to prepare a convincing speech.

Tier 1: Select a famous historical person of interest to you. Read about that person in at least two encyclopedia or online articles. Write a two-page summary of the key information about that person's life and why they were influential.

Tier 2: Select a famous historical person of interest to you. Read about that person first in an encyclopedia or online article, then in a brief biography about that person. Identify a job for which you think she or he would be best suited in the present day. Develop a two-page resume about that person's life as if he or she were applying for that job.

Tier 3: Select a famous historical person of interest to you. Read about that person first in an encyclopedia or online article, then through at least four primary documents related to that person. Develop a persuasive speech and presentation using any medium to convince one of the Nobel Prize committees that this individual should be a Nobel Prize recipient.

**Figure 9.2.** Example of a tiered assignment about a famous historical person, grades 4–5. *Note.* From *Tiering to Avoid Tears* by L. Robinson, 2011, retrieved from http://www.learnnc.org/lp/editions/every-learner/6680. Copyright 2011 by L. Robinson. Reprinted with permission.

A similar approach is presented by Nunley (2001), who uses a method called *layered curriculum*. In this approach, students are offered a number of different activities designed around Bloom's taxonomy. All students are required to complete a set of lower-order C assignments, then students who are motivated or able can progress to more analytical or abstract B- or A-level assignments. Students who complete the C-level activities with time to spare choose activities at higher levels and complete the appropriate assignments. This approach responds to the fact that gifted students often learn basic information more quickly; it also allows all students a clear path to higher level learning.

An example of layered curriculum is provided in Figure 9.3. Students might spend as much as a week on this series of activities. Notice that the activities at each level are varied to accommodate different learning styles, and all students are allowed choice. The C-level assignments are designed to ensure students meet required learning standards. Some students might select options that allow them to move on relatively quickly to B and then A-level activities. Completing an option does not guarantee full points, each assignment must meet acceptable standards. This approach takes longer to set up, and it is best to create materials with a team of colleagues so

| C Level (40 Points Needed) | B Level (30 Points Needed) | A Level (20 Points Needed) |
|---|---|---|
| 1. Timeline of events of journey from England to America. (10 points) | 1. With a partner or in a small group, create a secret handshake Separatists might use to pass on information, and the information they might need to pass. Show it to the class. (5 points) | 1. Write a letter to the King giving three reasons, with support, why you don't agree with the Church of England. (10 points) |
| 2. Listen to three teacher lectures. (5 points) | 2. Create a Venn diagram comparing the similarities and differences between the Church of England the Separatists' religion. (10 points) | 2. Be the King and explain (with at least 3 reasons) to your subjects (the class) how Separatists are nonconformists and why you cannot allow nonconformists in your country. (10 points) |
| 3. Listen to three teacher lectures and take notes. (10 points) | 3. Create a list of questions (3–5) you would ask the King about his religion and create a list of questions (3–5) you might have for the Separatists. (10 points) | 3. Write an essay explaining why being "separate" is sometimes necessary, using the Separatists in England as an example. (10 points) |
| 4. Read section in book on pilgrims (could be on tape, group read, or alone). (5 points) | 4. Write a personal account (a page) of what happened to you as a Separatist the night the English ship captain betrayed you and your people. (20 points) | 4. As a Separatist, write a letter to a relative explaining why the New World will be a good place for you and your religious community. (10 points) |
| 5. Write a prayer the Separatists might say before escaping England. (5 points) | 5. With a partner or small group, create a short skit of the night the Dutch ship helped most of the Separatists escape. (5 points) | 5. Create a two-page essay describing how the Separatist movement is both positive and negative change, with a specific example of each. (20 points) |
| 6. Make a poster giving four reasons why the Separatists decided to leave. (10 points) | | |
| 7. Write three diary entries—one as a rich nobleman living in England, one as a farmer, and one as a poor beggar or thief. (15 points) | | |
| 8. Make a schedule of the typical Sunday for a Separatist. (5 points) | | |

**Figure 9.3.** Example of layered curriculum on the topic of Separatist flight from England (grades 3–4). Adapted from *Layered Curriculum for Separatist Flight From England* by Paul Moellering, n.d., retrieved from http://help4teachers.com/PaulSeparatistsInEngland.htm.

| C Level (40 Points Needed) | B Level (30 Points Needed) | A Level (20 Points Needed) |
|---|---|---|
| 9. Make a poster telling Separatists what they could do in church and what they could not. (10 points) | 6. Create a conversation between two or three Separatists arguing why or why they should not go to America. (10 points) | 6. Write an essay in which you consider the criteria the Separatists used to make their decision to leave. Were the criteria reasonable or not? Why do you think so? (20 points) |
| 10. Create a poster or pamphlet made by Bradford attacking the King of England. (10 points) | 7. You are a Separatist's child, write a letter to a Dutch friend explaining why you are thinking of giving up the Separatist way of life. (10 points) | |
| 11. Make a list why the King allowed the Separatists to go to America. (5 points) | 8. Using a Venn diagram, compare and contrast the Pilgrims and the Strangers. (10 points) | |
| 12. Make a list of different things a Separatist brought on the Mayflower or Speedwell to take to the New World. (5 points) | | |

**Figure 9.3.** Continued.

that everyone can share in the creative process and benefit from the resulting collection of learning experiences. Fortunately, Nunley provided many examples in different subject areas and grade levels on her website: http:// help4teachers.com/samples.htm.

Another, relatively easy way to increase *duration* of differentiation in social studies is to integrate social studies with other subjects. Opportunities for this kind of integration increased with the passage of the new Common Core State Standards (CCSS; National Governors Association Center for Best Practices & Council of Chief State School Officers, 2010). The CCSS language arts standards include a section with recommendations to integrate reading, writing, and listening into social studies and science, but equally important, the language arts standards introduce an increased emphasis on nonfiction reading. Nonfiction literature, including current events, biography, and primary resources, form an inherent crossover from language arts into social studies, making interdisciplinary study natural.

An example of this blend of language arts and social studies is Michael Clay Thompson's series of activity books focusing on literary analysis of famous American documents. In *Free at Last* (2004), Thompson helps students arrive at a new appreciation for Martin Luther King's "I Have a Dream" speech. Thompson blends historical background with an in-depth analysis of the structure of the speech, including anaphora, poetics, vocabulary, and grammatical structure. Through this analysis, students come to appreciate the structure and beauty of effective communication, as well as how careful structure of a seminal speech can change the course of history. An excerpt from the book is presented in Figure 9.4.

Duration can also be achieved through curriculum compacting, where students have an opportunity to demonstrate they have already achieved mastery on a given topic, for example, ancient Greek civilization. Students who achieve mastery on a pretest comprised of required content standards on ancient Greece could then either accelerate to the next topic of study, or work with their teacher to create an independent social studies project, for instance, creating a special presentation on the Elgin marbles from the Parthenon.

**Increasing the intensity of social studies.** Increased intensity can be achieved by altering content, process, product, and learning environment. Changes to content and process are the most crucial; changes in product and learning environment tend to follow naturally once content and process have been altered. Content modifications can take one of four forms: (1) *accelerated* content—moving students through the core curriculum

Martin Luther King's emphasis on the future tense is the inevitable consequence of his visionary emphasis on the future. If we look at the language of the speech, we see that he not only used the future tense abundantly, he also filled his speech with words that all pointed to one meaning: Now is the time for the future to begin. Now is the time for freedom. Now is the time for the United States to rise up and live out the full meaning of its creed, that all men are created equal.

*I have a dream that **one day** the state of Alabama, whose governor's lips are **presently** dripping with the words of interposition and nullification, **will be** transformed into a situation where the little black boys and black girls **will be** able to join hands with little white boys and white girls and walk together as sisters and brothers. I have a dream today. I have a dream that **one day** every valley **shall be** exalted, every hill and mountain **shall be** made low, the rough places **will be** made plain and the crooked places **will be** made straight, and the glory of the Lord **shall be** revealed, and all flesh **shall see** it together. ...*

**Figure 9.4.** Excerpt of speech analysis (grades 5–8). *Note.* From *Free at Last* (pp. 44–45) by M. Thompson, 2004, Unionville, NY: Royal Fireworks Press. Copyright 2004 by Royal Fireworks Press. Reprinted with permission.

more quickly; (2) *enriched* content—providing additional information associated with the topic being studied; (3) *sophisticated* content—adding depth, complexity, and abstractness to an area of study; or (4) *novel* content—introducing topics that students would not usually encounter until much later in their schooling (Gallagher & Gallagher, 1995). An example of each of these forms of differentiation in relation to the study of the American Revolution is included in Figure 9.5.

One of the most fundamental content modifications for gifted students is enhancing the conceptual level of instruction. Learning to reason using broad-based, abstract ideas not only adds sophistication, it helps students organize and remember larger chunks of information.

Teachers who wish to increase the level of sophistication of their curriculum must first become familiar with the concepts undergirding social studies and their application across cultures and eras. One example of such preparation was the exercise engaged in by the social studies faculty of the Illinois Mathematics and Science Academy. Each faculty member wrote a position paper describing a core concept in social studies and its application to their content. The faculty then shared these papers, creating a "conceptual repository" that could be used to create differentiated activities. An excerpt from an essay on scarcity is included as Figure 9.6. Note how scarcity is connected to the NCSS theme of production, consumption, and

| Form of Content Differentiation | Example Based on Content From the American Revolution |
|---|---|
| Acceleration | Compact or telescope the study of the American Revolution content so students who have achieved mastery of content standards can move more rapidly to the French and Indian War. |
| Enrichment | While studying the American Revolution, students complete a project that extends their understanding. Examples include: (a) a research project on the impact of the printing press on the Revolution, (b) an in-depth analysis of a portion of the *Federalist Papers*, or (c) a report on a biography of Thomas Jefferson. |
| Sophistication | Students determine the criteria that make a historical event a "revolution," and then determine if the American Revolution was a revolution or something else. Students could compare the American and French Revolutions to see which best matches the criteria. |
| Novelty | Students study different content from American history that they would not usually see, for instance, the Chinese exclusion laws. |

**Figure 9.5.** Examples of content differentiation.

distribution, and how the discussion moves from a description of scarcity to its application across many different social studies fields.

Students' understanding is enhanced when they learn how to use concepts as tools for interpreting historical events. Gallagher (2012b) used shapes to give concrete form to the NCSS theme of individuals, groups, and institutions. Figure 9.7 shows how the concepts are introduced to students with highly accessible examples. Students can then use the symbols to represent the shifting relationships among different individuals, groups, and institutions throughout history. They could depict how a group might rise in an institution, which individuals are "in" or "out" of a group and why, how the status of different groups changes over time, what happens when the "base" of institution grows or shrinks, and more.

**Process modifications.** Process modifications increase the amount of critical and creative thinking that is embedded in social studies curricula. The most effective process modifications do more than introduce single strategies to students; they provide students with ways to structure their thinking. There are many different ways this can be accomplished. Kaplan and Gould (2005) identified *content imperatives* that encourage students to

---

**Scarcity**

Scarcity is a universal situation experienced by everyone, every nation, every society and every institution. The concept is usually encountered and discussed in the economic sense, such as, "every economics system must answer the question of how to provide for the production and distribution of goods and services from a country's limited resources for the unlimited wants of its citizens."

The argument by Senesh (1989), that economic events always produce other events might help us better understand why the French national assembly was concerned with making property a "natural, inalienable and sacred" right of man in 1789, why Columbus sailed west in 1942, and one might even argue that the scarcity of time allotted to humankind, according to the first century apostles, helped make the 10 Commandments "law" instead of "philosophy." . . .

Scarcity is a political, psychological, and sociological concept as well as an economic axiom. Scarcity helps explain why someone in our society always seems to be dissatisfied. This condition then triggers another set of connections. Angry people demand political solutions as well as economic ones for their scarcity problems. Politicians become involved with the allocation of productive resources and the distribution of wealth in response to angry people who are responding to scarcity. We struggle to find the solutions to problems which (sic) fit our society's values, norms, and beliefs. And when the gap between our "actual" satisfaction of needs and our "expected" need satisfaction becomes too great, society goes through the trauma of revolutionary change. (James C. Davies, "toward a theory of revolution." American Sociological Review, volume 27, February 1962, page 6). (Senesh—The fundamentals of the social sciences, paper delivered at the SSEC Annual Roundup, Denver, June 1989, page 1–2).

---

**Figure 9.6.** Example of a concept paper to guide differentiation for content sophistication. *Note.* From "Scarcity" (Unpublished document) by W. Stepien, 1990. Copyright 1990 by W. Stepien. Reprinted with permission.

look for deeper meaning in any subject area, including social studies. Each imperative relates to an area of fundamental knowledge or a perspective commonly used by experts as they analyze information. The imperatives are defined, along with examples, in Figure 9.8.

Another way to structure higher order thinking is through the application of Paul's (1993) model of critical thinking that includes *elements of reasoning*. Integrating elements of reasoning into lessons, students learn to seek the purpose, point of view, evidence, concepts, assumptions, inferences, implications, and questions within a body of information. A representative example uses a graphic organizer to help students visualize their thinking around several of the elements of reasoning: point of view,

| Term and Definition | Symbol |
|---|---|
| An **INSTITUTION** is an organization that is a hierarchy and has special goals. An institution can be concrete (a business) or abstract (a tradition). Regardless, it exists as a hierarchy; the top, which is the smallest point on the hierarchy, is also the most influential position. Institutions serve a purpose in society. They establish rules and govern behavior of the people inside. They outlive the individuals who create them. Marriage is an example of a tradition that is an institution. Families are institutions. Formal organizations that serve a social purpose are also institutions. Education is an institution, as is business and government. A triangle represents institutions because of its solid structure and hierarchical shape. | |
| **GROUPS** are sets of people who interact with each other and share interests, rules, expectations and/or obligations in common. They can be voluntary (a book club) or involuntary (siblings). Groups can be large (American citizens) or small (best friends). Groups can have a hierarchy but do not have to have one. Ovals work well to represent groups because they can be large or small, long if there is a hierarchy or wide if not, and they can grow to fit any number of individuals. | |
| **INDIVIDUALS** are single people. Individuals can be inside or outside of groups and inside or outside of institutions. A self-contained circle represents an individual. | |
| Many relationships exist among individuals, groups, and institutions in our world. For example, you are an INDIVIDUAL in the GROUP of students in your school. The school you attend is an INSTITUTION. Teachers are another GROUP in the same institution. Your social studies teacher is a specific individual in that group. The principal is the individual at the top of the institution. | |

**Figure 9.7.** Concrete symbols for individuals, groups, and institutions. *Note.* From *Excluded!* (p. 40), by S. Gallagher, 2012b, Unionville, NY: Royal Fireworks Press. Copyright 2012 by Royal Fireworks Press. Reprinted with permission.

207

| Icon for Content Imperative | Definition | Elementary Application | Secondary Application |
|---|---|---|---|
| **Origin** | Origin: The beginning, root, or source of something | What are the reasons we invented the job "police officer"? | Identify three factors that contributed to the Civil War, and trace the origin of each. |
| **Contribution** | Contribution: The significant part or result of something | What contributions do police make in a community? List as many as you can. | What direct and indirect contributions did the printing press make to civilization? |
| **Parallel** | Parallel: Ideas or events that are similar and can be compared to one another | Draw a parallel between a policeman and a fireman. Or a policeman and a parent/guardian. | How did Marco Polo's excursions parallel those of Lewis and Clark? |
| **Convergence** | Convergence: The coming together or meeting point of events or ideas | List some different events that combine to create a situation where you would need to call the police. | What factors converged to cause the plague epidemic of the late 1300s? |
| **Paradox** | Paradox: The contradictory elements of an event or idea | Why is it that some people do not like the police when their primary role is to help protect against lawbreakers? | How can America be home of the free and yet resist accepting different groups of immigrants? |

**Figure 9.8.** Kaplan's content imperatives. *Note.* Icons from *The Flip Book, Too* by S. N. Kaplan & B. Gould, 2005, Calabasa, CA: Educator to Educator.

assumptions, and implications. Students see that different people can have very different perspectives about a single situation, and that these varying perspectives lead to different actions. In the American history unit, *The 1920s in America: A Decade of Tensions* (College of William and Mary, 2003b), students complete a chart from the perspective of workingwomen, members of the National Women's Party, and men. The structure of the resulting assignment is presented in Figure 9.9.

Kaplan's content imperatives and Paul's elements of reasoning are generic tools that can be used across many different subject areas. It is also important to introduce students to discipline-specific ways to structure and analyze information. For instance, instead of simply studying ancient civilizations, students can learn the eight criteria that define a city and then gather information to see whether and how different ancient communities qualify as "cities." These eight criteria are presented in a sample worksheet in Figure 9.10.

Social studies are filled with many of these thinking structures that are accessible across grade levels. Primary school children could consider the functions of houses (to gather, to protect against the elements, to rest) and compare movable houses (tepees or yurts) and permanent residences (houses, apartments, or caves), or compare human houses and animal houses. Older students can be taught to "think like an anthropologist" using the criteria presented by Bruner (1965) to consider how different cultures are represented by:

- tools;
- language;
- social organization;
- childrearing; and
- the urge to explain the world through storytelling, science, art, and writing.

These thinking structures do more than provide students with a way to organize their thinking; they open the door to comparisons around the world and across the eras, providing an excellent platform for sophisticated thinking.

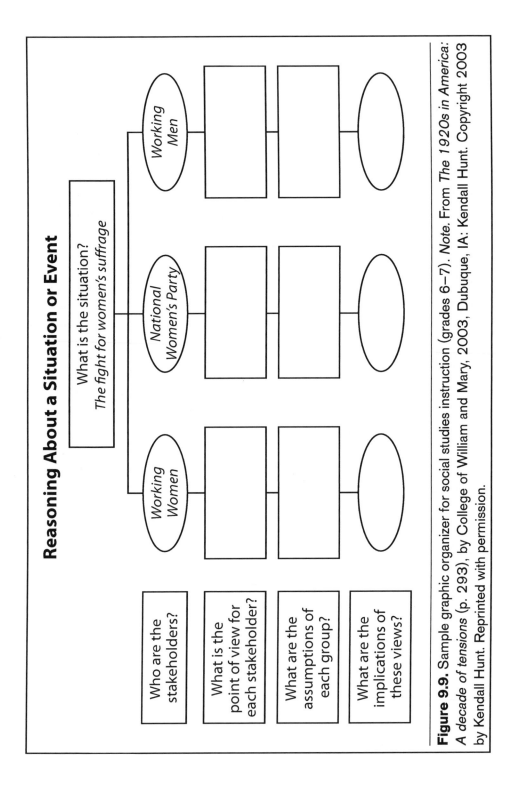

**Reasoning About a Situation or Event**

What is the situation?
*The fight for women's suffrage*

Working Women

National Women's Party

Working Men

Who are the stakeholders?

What is the point of view for each stakeholder?

What are the assumptions of each group?

What are the implications of these views?

**Figure 9.9.** Sample graphic organizer for social studies instruction (grades 6–7). *Note.* From *The 1920s in America: A decade of tensions* (p. 293), by College of William and Mary, 2003, Dubuque, IA: Kendall Hunt. Copyright 2003 by Kendall Hunt. Reprinted with permission.

| Category | Criteria | Babylon | Thebes | Alexandria | Athens | Rome |
|---|---|---|---|---|---|---|
| Population | Were there more than 5,000 people? | | | | | |
| Work | Did people have specific jobs like spear maker, apothecary, or builder? | | | | | |
| Food | Did farmers produce extra/surplus food for sale or to give as tithe to city rulers? | | | | | |
| Trade | Did people gather to trade food, cloth, spices, medicines, and other goods? | | | | | |
| Communal buildings or gathering places | Were there large community buildings such as places of worship, learning centers, and community entertainment? | | | | | |
| Writing or recorded language | Could a subgroup of people record important information? | | | | | |
| Science/ Learning | Was the place a source of new information and investigation of distance, number, time, art, history, philosophy, and/or literature? | | | | | |
| Government | Were the people, as a group, ruled in some way? Did they have common laws and rules to follow? | | | | | |

**Figure 9.10.** Eight questions to determine if a community is a city (grades 3–5). *Note. Adapted from Inquiring About Cities: Studies in Geography and Economics* by W. R. Fielder and G. Feeney, 1972, New York, NY: Holt, Rinehart and Winston.

# Authentic Social Studies Experiences

Authenticity is the modification that brings social studies to life. As already mentioned, authenticity is important for all students, but is particularly appropriate for gifted students as authentic activities often have qualities that match the open-ended, inquiring mind of the gifted learner.

A natural avenue to authentic learning experiences in social studies comes through the analysis of primary source documents. The Internet has opened the world in this respect. From the documents that formed America to political cartoons, from Supreme Court decisions to videos of influential thinkers and doers, it is increasingly easy to integrate the actual building blocks of history into classroom activities. History textbooks should take a back seat to primary documents as often as possible to help remind students that what they are studying is real.

Other authentic experiences require students to engage in social issues. For instance, instead of studying communities in the abstract, primary-aged students could be presented with the following task:

> Our school has the opportunity to improve ONE area of our school. We could:
> - Add more books and computers to the library
> - Have another school nurse
> - Add equipment to the playground
> - Add a security guard
> - Buy art for the walls
> - Add a community garden to grow vegetables and flowers
>
> We have been asked to research these and give our reasoned opinion to our principal about which would be best for our school right now.

Students research the options in groups and discuss which one is most important. The conversation would lead students into discussions of "wants" versus "needs" and how to define "important." They would also be introduced to categories of services provided by a community: education, health, communal gathering, and safety that could be transferred to the study of the larger community. Students can also be introduced to the idea that community leaders often have to make difficult decisions when allocating scare resources.

Quality experiences that emulate authentic social studies for older students sometimes come in the form of popular competitions. Chief among these are Harvard Model Congress and United Nations programs. These programs are designed to provide students with a realistic experience around the procedures of creating national or international policy. In each case, students are assigned an issue or a country to represent, which they research at their home school. Students from around the nation, and often from around the world, then convene for a "mock Congress" or "mock UN," which are staged by students at the sponsoring university, usually complete with a crisis or two. Figure 9.11 features other high-quality, authentic extra- and co-curricular experiences appropriate for gifted students in secondary school. A comprehensive list of essay contests and other opportunities for social studies honors for gifted students, including a few for elementary students, can be found at the website for the Duke University Talent Identification Program: https://eog.tip.duke.edu/home/academic_activities#Humanities.

Often authentic activities are so fun and engaging that it is easy to forget to ensure students are challenged. When working with primary resources or creating authentic activities for gifted students of any age, it is important to intentionally integrate academic rigor. Newmann and Wehlage (1993) provided helpful scales to use when rating the value of authentic activities (see Figure 9.12).

# Models That Integrate Intensity, Duration, and Authenticity

As previously mentioned, learning experiences of longer duration open the door to great intensity. The best experiences of gifted students provide the opportunity for sustained engagement with high-quality content in combination with higher order thinking and/or creative production. Often these experiences form the core of differentiated curriculum units.

It is often difficult to find high-quality curriculum resources for very young gifted children, but materials that model best practice in social

---

*Chicago Metro History Fair* (middle/high school)—http://www.chicagohistory fair.org: The Metro History Fair is an exemplary example of a community-wide, multi-district venture supporting authentic social studies research. Middle and high school students select a topic of interest, research their topic and then present their find-ings using one of a variety of possible formats. The Metro History Fair website also has a thorough repository of materials to support high-quality research, including guides on thesis development, how to develop an argument, methods of analysis, descriptions of how to analyze primary and secondary resources, and how to deliver an effective presentation. This independent umbrella organization collaborates with museums, universities, and libraries to support authentic student work. This program is easily replicable and the website includes many high-quality resources to help stu-dents engage in authentic historical research.

*National History Day* (middle/high school)—http://www.nationalhistoryday. org: National History Day is the national version of activities in Chicago Metro His-tory Day. Each year, the organization selects a theme such as "Rights and Respon-sibilities," "Turning Points," or "Conflict and Compromise." Students are encouraged to engage in an authentic project related to the theme. Student submissions are entered into regional, state, and possibly even a national competition. The National History Day website is filled with materials for students and teachers to use in creat-ing high-quality history projects.

*Harvard Model Congress* (high school)—http://harvardmodelcongress.org and *Harvard Model United Nations* (high school)—http://www.harvardmun.org: The Harvard Model Congress and Harvard Model UN started as college-level simula-tion event designed to provide undergraduate students with an authentic model of national and international governing processes. Each year, teams of students are assigned specific topics that become the focus of the weekend of collaboration and competition.

*Concord Review* (high school)—http://www.tcr.org/tcr/emerson.htm: Estab-lished in 1987, the *Concord Review* is the premiere repository of high school student writing on social studies topics. The *Concord Review* has become international in scope and readership, and has published student essays from 35 countries. Students are allowed to submit on any historical topic, allowing high school students to pur-sue their individual passions. Sample essays available online for download include "Austria-Hungary and the Compromise of 1867," "The Nazi Influence in the Formation of Apartheid in South Africa," "Francisco Franco and the Decline and Fall of Spanish Fascism," and "Writs of Assistance Trial." A submission fee supports the journal. This outlet is unique in its emphasis on having students think, write, and produce in the manner of a professional historian.

---

**Figure 9.11.** Sample authentic extra- or co-curricular activities.

---

studies investigation are available at the University Primary School (UPS) website: http://education.illinois.edu/ups. The UPS faculty have spent many years integrating gifted education practices with Reggio Emilia philosophy, resulting in several project-based curriculum units on topics including *Exploring Fire Safety, Who Measures What in Our Neighborhood,*

| Standard Category | Surface-Level Thinking | | Sophisticated Thinking |
|---|---|---|---|
| *Higher Order Thinking* | Lower Order | 1 2 3 4 5 | Higher Order |
| Depth of Knowledge | Knowledge is shallow | 1 2 3 4 5 | Knowledge is deep |
| Connected to the World | No connection | 1 2 3 4 5 | Substantially connected |
| Substantive Conversation | No substantive conversation | 1 2 3 4 5 | High-level substantive conversation |
| Social Support for Student Achievement | Negative social support | 1 2 3 4 5 | Positive social support |

**Figure 9.12.** Scales to rate the quality of authentic learning experiences.

*Exploring Communication,* and *Exploring Construction.* These units lift the ceiling on student achievement by using students' curiosity as the catalyst for learning.

The staff of the Center for Gifted Education at William & Mary spent several years developing social studies curriculum using VanTassel-Baska's Integrated Curriculum Model (VanTassel-Baska, 2003). This model combines advanced content, conceptual focus, and higher order thinking processes to create qualitatively different learning experiences for gifted students.

The primary focus of the William & Mary social studies curriculum is history, with units on topics in ancient history, European history, and American history for elementary and middle school grades. The aims of the curriculum units are to develop: (1) understanding of the concept of systems and of structure, function, and pattern as key elements; (2) understanding of the concept of cause and effect and its relationship to events and eras in history; (3) reasoning skills with application to social studies; (4) interpersonal and group process skills that are essential to 21st-century work; and (5) skills in historical analysis and primary source interpretation, encouraging students to "think like a historian." For example, in the unit *Ancient Egypt: The Gift of the Nile* (College of William and Mary, 2003a) second- and third-grade students use the concepts of *civilizations* and *systems* in the study of Ancient Egypt. Students are asked to use their imaginations and critical thinking skills to draw parallels across space and time as they compare the lives of ancient Egyptians to their own.

### Enhancing the Story of Social Studies: Problem-Based Learning

Much of social studies is a story—the story of cultural growth and dissolution, the story of invention, the story of migrating peoples, the story of strength and courage over adversity. The stories often involve complex problems and difficult decisions, including seminal decisions that changed the course of history. The study of the dilemmas and decisions that humans have encountered can bring fascination to the study of history, and naturally draw students into greater depth and complexity. It is ironic that history curriculum often focuses on a dry recounting of facts and dates, when evidence suggests that stories are more engaging and memorable (Willingham, 2004).

Problem-based learning (PBL) presents a method that integrates the benefits of storytelling with significant historical content. PBL is a model of curriculum and instruction that uses ill-structured problems as the catalyst for learning. The model is comprised of three elements: (1) initiating learning with an ill-structured problem, (2) requiring students to view the problem through the eyes of a central stakeholder, and (3) changing the teacher role to facilitator or coach. Of these, the ill-structured problem is the most important, as it creates the context for everything else that happens. Gallagher (2009a) described an ill-structured problem as (1) *authentic*—modeled on circumstances encountered in the real world; (2) *mysterious*—lacking some information needed to create a solution; (3) *flexible*—allowing many alternative paths to a solution; (4) *ambiguous*—with many possible solutions and no obvious "right" answer; and (5) *interdisciplinary*—making the integration of several dimensions of social studies relatively easy.

There is a natural synergy between the ill-structured problem and the study of history because history is a series of ill-structured problems solved by different people facing ambiguous situations. Many historical events lend themselves to presentation through an ill-structured problem, as demonstrated in the example in Figure 9.13.

Using an ill-structured problem as curriculum has a number of benefits: the structure problem places students in a story, in this case a story about child labor at the advent of the Progressive Era. The story-like quality of PBL engages students' minds and emotions by making them curious. Curiosity leads to questions and before they know it, students are telling their teacher what they need to learn about child labor, asking questions

---

**National Child Labor Commission**
**2246 Massachusetts Avenue**
**Washington, D.C. 20015**

To: Members of the National Child Labor Commission (NCLC)

From: Dr. H. Walker, Chairman

Date: October 5, 1913

Re: Welcome and information from the field

Let me be the first to thank you for agreeing to serve on this important com-mission investigating whether or how we should change the conditions of children working in U.S.

In your letter of invitation to the NCLC, I mentioned that we had already com-missioned some people to do background investigation on children's working con-ditions. Attached please find:

1.  photographs by Lewis Hine of children working in mills, and

2.  an account from John Spargo regarding children working in West Virginia mines.

Please come to our meeting prepared to give your impressions of this informa-tion. Particularly, please consider whether or not you think they provide an accurate portrayal of conditions in which children work.

Let me remind you that one of the reasons you were selected for the NCLC was your dedication to ethical decision-making. Our cause is clear—we must investigate the conditions in which children work—but we must attempt, at all times, to be fair to all parties involved. Despite the passions of those like Miss Addams, we cannot afford to ignore the needs of factory owners.

The U.S. Congress expects to hear from us within the next ten days. If changes seem to be warranted, we are to present both recommended policy and legislation. Two years after the terrible Shirtwaist incident I fear they are losing their interest.

Once again, thank you for your time and support for this cause. I look forward to working with you on this important task.

---

**Figure 9.13.** Opening scenario from a problem-based learning unit (grades 7–10). Reprinted from *All Work No Play: Child Labor in the Progressive Era* (p. 20) by S. A. Gallagher, 2013, Unionville, NY: Royal Fireworks Press.

like: Are these pictures legitimate? How many children work in conditions like this? What would happen to them if they stopped working? Moreover, because students have a problem to solve, they immediately understand the relevance of everything they are about to learn. As the story unfolds, students investigate facts about child labor and they learn about the mas-sive cultural transformation of the Industrial Revolution, the resulting confluence of a naïve immigrant labor force, new systems of mass production, unregulated economic growth, and human corruption—the growing pains associated with industrialization. As they research, the story of the ill-structured problem provides the context for remembering this complex web of content.

The story-like environment of PBL also creates a context for advanced, complex thinking. Students' research leads them into analysis of both print and visual primary resources. With quality research in hand, students think about the relationships among the individuals, groups, and institutions at play in the problem and they consider the short- and long-term consequences of different possible solutions.

# Conclusion

In this chapter, we have only dipped a toe in the vast ocean of possibility for creating content rich, substantial, challenging experiences for gifted students in social studies. Social studies is (1) inherently interdisciplinary—allowing easy connection to art, mathematics, language arts, and science; (2) represented by numerous abstract concepts already identified by the social studies professions; (3) supported by a plethora of authentic documents and experiences; and (4) easily adapted to integrate critical thinking, creativity, and ethical reasoning. The content of social studies conveys knowledge and builds identity, an ideal platform for gifted students to begin to shape a vision of their future.

# References

Bruner, J. (1965). *Man: A course of study. Occasional paper #3.* Cambridge, MA: Educational Services. Retrieved from http://eric.ed.gov/?id=ED 178390

Center for Education Policy. (2007). *Choices, changes, and challenges: Curriculum and instruction in the NCLB era.* Washington, DC: Author.

College of William and Mary. (2003a). *Ancient Egypt: The gift of the Nile.* Dubuque, IA: Kendall Hunt.

College of William and Mary. (2003b). *The 1920s in America: A decade of tensions.* Dubuque, IA: Kendall Hunt.

Fielder, W. R., & Feeney, G. (1972). *Inquiring about cities: Studies in geography and economics.* New York, NY: Holt, Rinehart and Winston.

Gallagher, J. J., & Gallagher, S. A. (1995). *Teaching the gifted child.* Boston, MA: Allyn & Bacon.

Gallagher, S. A. (2009a). Problem-based learning. In J. S. Renzulli, E. J. Gubbins, K. S. McMillen, R. D. Eckert, & C. A. Little (Eds.), *Systems and models for developing programs for the gifted and talented* (2nd ed., pp. 193–210). Waco, TX: Prufrock Press.

Gallagher, S. A. (2009b). Designed to fit: Educational implications of gifted adolescents' cognitive development. In F. Dixon (Ed.). *Programs and services for gifted secondary students* (pp. 3–20). Waco, TX: Prufrock Press.

Gallagher, S. A. (2012a). Building bridges: Using research from the Big Five, MBTI, overexcitabilites and Perry to explore personality differences of gifted youth. In C. S. Neville, M. M. Piechowski, & S. S. Tolan (Eds.), *Off the charts: Asynchrony and the gifted child* (p. 56–118). Unionville, NY: Royal Fireworks Press.

Gallagher, S. A. (2012b). *Excluded!* Unionville, NY: Royal Fireworks Press.

Gallagher, S. A. (2013). *All work, no play.* Unionville, NY: Royal Fireworks Press.

Kaplan, S. N., & Gould, B. (2005). *The flip book, too: More quick and easy methods for developing differentiated learning experiences.* Calabasas, CA: Educator to Educator.

Kirk, S. A., Gallagher, J. J., & Coleman, M. R. (2014). *Educating exceptional children* (14th ed.). Stamford, CT: Cengage Press.

Maryland Council for Social Studies. (2010, Spring). Why our students must learn social studies. *MDCSS Chronicle,* 1–4. Retrieved from http://www.gmshistory.net/MDCSS%20Spring%202010%20Newsletter.pdf

Moellering, P. (n.d.). *Layered curriculum for Separatist flight from England.* Retrieved from http://help4teachers.com/PaulSeparatistsInEngland.htm

National Council for Social Studies. (2010). *National Curriculum Standards for Social Studies.* Washington, DC: Author.

National Council for Social Studies. (n.d.). *A vision of powerful teaching and learning in the social studies: Building social understanding and civic efficacy.* Washington, DC: Author. Retrieved from http://www. socialstudies.org/positions/powerful

National Governors Association Center for Best Practices, & Council of Chief State School Officers. (2010). *Common Core State Standards for English language arts.* Washington, DC: Authors.

Newmann, F. M., & Wehlage, G. G. (1993). Five standards of authentic instruction. *Educational Leadership, 50*(7), 8–12.

Nunley, K. (2001). *Layered curriculum: The practical solution for teachers with more than one student in their classroom.* Amherst, NH: Brains. org.

Paul, R. (1993). *Critical thinking: What every person needs to survive in a rapidly changing world.* Santa Rosa, CA: Foundation for Critical Thinking.

Robinson, L. P. (2011). *Tiering to avoid tears: Developing assignments to address all learners' needs.* Retrieved from http://www.learnnc.org/lp/ editions/every-learner/6680

Stepien, W. J. (1990). *Scarcity* (Unpublished document). Illinois Mathematics and Science Academy, Aurora, IL.

Thompson, M. (2004). *Free at last.* Unionville, NY: Royal Fireworks Press.

Tomlinson, C. A. (2004). *How to differentiate instruction in mixed ability classrooms* (2nd ed.). Alexandria, VA: Association for Supervision and Curriculum Development.

VanTassel-Baska, J. (2003). Content-based curriculum for high-ability learners: An introduction. In J. VanTassel-Baska & C. A. Little (Eds.), *Content-based curriculum for high-ability learners* (pp. 1–23). Waco, TX: Prufrock Press.

Willingham, D. T. (2004, Summer). The privileged status of story. *American Educator,* 43–45, 51–53.

# The Role of Assessment in Curriculum Development

# CHAPTER 10

# Curriculum Implementation, Management, and Assessment

## Special Consideration and Best Practice

**Carolyn M. Callahan**

## Introduction

Curriculum implementation is the process of bringing to life the plans and documents that have been developed with particular learning goals in mind. Curriculum implementation and management must be viewed as a change process—that is, new curriculum requires teachers to change what and/or how they are currently teaching. Fullan's (1982, 2001) model of the change process would put curricular implementation in Phase II of the change process—the stage of first attempting to put an idea or reform into practice. Management of curriculum implementation falls into Phase III—the stage during which the curriculum becomes an ongoing part of the system or simply disappears either because a conscious decision is made that it does not work or through attrition. Although this chapter does not deal with the development and adoption of a curriculum, which Fullan considers Phase I, the activities and decisions that go on during the curriculum development phase are integrally related to the success of Phase II and Phase III. Hence, while this chapter focuses on strategies to ensure that the intended curriculum is implemented with fidelity and that the goals and objectives of the implementation are achieved, these functions are dependent on the process of curriculum development, the choice of curriculum, and/or the adaptation of the curriculum that is to be implemented.

Fullan's assertion that the implementation and management of curriculum are closely tied is reenforced in studies of curricular implementation. One of the themes that emerges in these studies is the importance of considering teacher characteristics, teacher beliefs, and level of teacher engagement in the development or selection of curriculum; this is crucial if one expects to be successful in implementing the curriculum and sustaining curricular change. Wedell (2005) concluded that any staff development or training relating to new or proposed curriculum needs to make links between the curriculum and the teachers' prior experiences and exiting beliefs.

As the particulars of planning for and implementing curriculum are considered, these factors reemerge as critical concerns.

# Curriculum Implementation

## Piloting the Curriculum

Recognizing the growing emphasis on research-based practice and the high cost of curriculum implementation (e.g., training for teachers, producing or purchasing new materials and texts, etc.), some experts recommend that curricular materials be piloted prior to full-scale implementation (UNESCO International Bureau of Education, 2009b). A pilot is considered effective in accomplishing two goals: (1) providing evidence that the curriculum will offer significant benefits and (2) offering data on whether the curriculum can be implemented successfully on a large scale in the contexts where it is to be instituted. Of particular interest in a pilot is ascertaining how different the proposed curriculum is from the curriculum currently in place, and hence, the subsequent difficulty in implementation of the new curriculum (i.e., the more removed new practice is from known curricula and instructional strategies, the more cognitive load[3] a teacher will bear in implementation, and thus, the more difficult it will be for the teacher to deliver the curriculum). Other contributions from pilot testing are greater understanding of the context and challenges that teachers may face, greater awareness of the social and/or political bases for opposition, fuller understanding of the financial implications of implementation (e.g., need for more than anticipated staff development), and signaling the unanticipated issues of conflict with other directives or expectations.

Piloting is particularly important when "others" have developed the curriculum. That is, when curriculum is given to teachers as a finished product, they may feel their role as educators has been diminished. A pilot provides the opportunity for teachers to have input into tailoring the curriculum with respect to the unique perspectives they bring to the classroom implementation phase of the process of change. This "buy in" to the process may also provide the basis for the participants to become ambassadors for change with other teachers.

### Introducing the Curriculum

Strategies for enhancing the likelihood of successful adoption and integration of new curriculum into teachers' classroom practice have been identified. Underlying the strategies to be discussed is the principle that greater effectiveness will be achieved if the focus is on building on strengths rather than emphasis on what teachers lack or need (UNESCO International Bureau of Education, 2009a).

**Beginning from an understanding of teachers' prior experiences and knowledge.** Teachers, of course, need to be formally introduced to a new curriculum. Zhao, Pugh, Sheldon, and Beyers (2002) recommended

---

3   Cognitive load, in this case, refers to the degree to which the complexity and difficulty of a learning activity is affecting the learner. Psychologists concur that people can learn most effectively if they can build on what they already know and understand and can do because the cognitive load is less.

that those responsible for introducing the curriculum and for providing training in implementation first assess teachers' previous experiences, their existing beliefs, and their current teaching practices and use that information to make connections between the new concepts, principles, and instructional practices to be introduced. If we reflect just briefly on this concept, it is akin to the preassessments we recommend to teachers for use in planning instruction for their students; really, we are advocating that we practice what we preach! In particular, being able to tie the new curriculum to existing understanding and practices—even when the new curriculum requires a considerable stretch—will provide teachers with a level of comfort that may encourage greater risk taking. Brighton, Hertberg, Moon, Tomlinson, and Callahan (2005) concluded from a 5-year study of differentiation for gifted students that success is predicated on staff development and coaching focused on ways to utilize preexisting organizational structures.

Handal and Herrington (2003) stressed the importance of taking teachers' attitudes and perceptions into account in the assessment of curriculum implementation:

> Policy makers should no longer assume that curriculum implementation is a process that translates directly into the classroom reality. Teachers are those who ultimately decide the fate of any educational enterprise. Consequently teachers' attitudes, feelings, and perceptions must be recognized well before the launching of any innovation. (p. 65)

Overlooking useful information about teachers' prior experiences and knowledge often results in one-size-fits-all professional development. Although a general presentation that introduces a new curriculum may suffice for some, it is important or recognized that some teachers will not have content background to understand the concepts and principles of the curriculum; some will not have proficiency in the use of new instructional strategies, while others may have great knowledge and others may have practiced the instructional strategies for many years. Depth of teacher content knowledge has been identified as an inhibitor to implementation of curriculum for gifted learners (Brighton et al., 2005). Therefore, appropriate staff development should go beyond an introduction to the curriculum and include scaffolding for some and advanced-level engagement for others.

Knowledge of where teachers are on a continuum of familiarity with content and instructional strategies should also influence how a new curriculum is introduced. To introduce highly unfamiliar content, totally new instructional strategies, and new classroom management expectations all at one time to teachers will likely be discouraging, and may even create a need to reject the curriculum as a means of "saving face" rather than encounter embarrassing failure.

**Beginning with understanding of teacher beliefs.** Teacher beliefs and attitudes have been confirmed as factors influencing the degree to which teachers of the gifted implement a curriculum (Azano et al., 2011; Brighton et al., 2005). In Azano and colleagues' large-scale study of curriculum implementation, teachers' perceptions of the amount of time they had to implement the curriculum and teacher expectations of students' ability to understand the content and acquire the skill of the curriculum were dominant factors influencing fidelity.

**Providing teachers with an understanding of the why behind the new curriculum.** It is not uncommon to hear teachers express the sentiment, "This too shall pass." If we cannot provide teachers with a sound rationale that is convincing to them for adopting a new curriculum, little will come of implementation. Teachers may give lip service to new ideas and practice what they are directed to teach, but when the delivery is not undergirded with a strong belief in the goals and in the proposed paths to achieving those goals, implementation is likely to fall short, and outcomes will likely be diminished. In other words, teachers need a persuasive argument and time to accept that the new curriculum will be worth the effort and investment in learning new approaches, adjusting their teaching styles, and/or learning new content or content frameworks. In an age of accountability, many teachers have been urged to adopt new curriculum because the new curriculum will improve test scores. In working with gifted students, that admonition carries little weight; teachers of gifted students regard proficient standardized test scores as something students are able to accomplish early in the school year, if not prior to the start of the school year. Hayes (2000) has documented the importance of both helping teachers understand and accept the rationale, but also the importance of bringing them to a level where they can also explain the why of the new curriculum to others.

**Effective training strategies.** Hayes (2000) also determined that implementation was more likely to occur when teachers had opportunities to experience and reflect about new ideas and activities as learners through trainer demonstrations, before being expected to teach or employ the new strategies and teach new content. Further, when teachers were provided opportunities to practice the planning and managing of new techniques and activities, honest feedback from peers and trainers *in conjunction with* the opportunity to reflect on the feedback from peers and trainers, and opportunities to suggest potential modifications based on feedback, they were more likely to implement new curriculum. Hord and Huling-Austin (1986) also found that scheduling differentiated staff-development sessions at different times was far more effective than a 3-day in-service workshop because the time between sessions allowed for assessment and responsive attention to emerging concerns and data collected during monitoring and evaluation of implementation.

However, formal training does not suffice. Hord and Huling-Austin (1986) concluded from their data that success or failure of curriculum implementation "is determined by one-to-one follow-up interactions with teachers that focus on their problems and concerns about changing their teaching practices" (p.108), and Brighton et al. (2005) concluded from a multiyear study of differentiation of curriculum that "[t]eachers in the midst of changing beliefs and practices require consistent time and honest, informed feedback about their efforts" (p. 323). Brighton et al. also noted the importance of differentiated coaching and allowing adequate time for teachers to process new ideas and practice new strategies.

# Curriculum Management

Considerations of the management of curricular implementation fall into two categories. The first is determination of the fidelity of the implementation—the degree to which teachers implement the curriculum as intended. The second is consideration of reasons why teachers may be deviating from the intended curriculum and what to do about the deviation (Orafi, 2013).

Thus, the keys to managing curriculum implementation are (1) to evaluate fidelity of implementation, (2) to understand the key factors that contribute to fidelity of implementation or deviance from expected instruction, and (3) to act to minimize inhibitors and maximize contributors to fidelity.

## Assessing Fidelity of Implementation

Eisner (2002) identified three types of curriculum. The first is the explicit or stated curriculum that includes all that is public and documented, such as specific goals and objectives, suggested activities and tasks, amount of time allocated to specific activities, procedures for evaluation, and suggested groupings. The second type of curriculum, the implicit hidden curriculum, is described by Eisner as the messages given by the way classrooms and schools are structured, including the opportunity for choice, the degree of compliance demanded, and the ways parts of the curriculum are emphasized. It can be further argued that some hidden curriculum results from the curricular modification and instructional adjustments that teachers make (or fail to make) because of unique teacher backgrounds and experiences or from accommodations made in response to the unique and diverse characteristics students bring to the classroom. For example, a teacher teaching a poetry unit may write poetry herself and bring her poetry to class to share and for analysis by her students as she encourages them to come to think of themselves as poets. Greater value is accorded to the writing of poetry when students view teachers as willing to give their time to writing poetry. As an example of adapting to student characteristics, a teacher may look for a meaningful, challenging poem not explicitly included in a poetry unit, but one that reflects and gives value to students' heritage. Conversely, a teacher who substitutes an "easier" poem out of a belief that his or her children "can't handle complex reading" may be giving a stereotypic message of lack of ability. Finally, there is the null or absent curriculum, which is comprised of those elements schools and teachers exclude from their instruction (either deliberately or unintentionally). Eisner discussed this null curriculum as value laden in terms of discipline omissions, but we may also be more specific and consider ramifications for subgroups of students. For example, teachers of the gifted may choose not to include any referents to grammar when teaching writing, even though the products of a unit may call for a level of grammar proficiency that is necessary for the level of expertise in writing that are explicit in its goals and objectives. Assessing fidelity of implementation in its most expansive interpretation is a process of determining the degree to which the explicit, hidden, and absent curriculum are present or missing from teachers' delivery of the proposed curriculum. How closely does the enacted curriculum match the written curriculum? How does the hidden or null curriculum contribute to the achievement of the goals as specified in the explicit curriculum?

The first of these questions has been the focus of efforts to assess whether or not the intended curriculum is the enacted curriculum in the classroom. However, answers to the second question will give further information on whether the intended goals and objectives of the curriculum are likely to be achieved. Initiatives that look at the first question fall in the category of assessing fidelity of implementation. The definitions of fidelity include adherence (how closely matched instruction is to the written curriculum), exposure (the completeness of delivery), quality of delivery, participant responsiveness, and program differentiation (how different the delivery is from the "old" or "standard" curriculum (Dane & Schneider, 1998). The importance of verifying curriculum fidelity in general education has been documented with increasing implementation of new curriculum paralleling increased student achievement in the general education programs (e.g., Cohen & Hill, 2002; Hord & Huling-Austin, 1986; O'Donnell, 2008; Taylor, Van Scotter, & Coulson, 2007), and the importance of fidelity in programs for the gifted was noted by Azano et al. (2011). In their study of curricular implementation, Azano et al. found that achievement test scores were higher for gifted students in classrooms with teachers who exhibited high fidelity to the curricular intervention than were the scores of students whose teachers did not exhibit close adherence to the curriculum.

There are formal models and procedures that have been developed to collect data in research projects that focus on fidelity of curriculum implementation. However, in most school-level curriculum implementation efforts, the necessary staff and intense time commitments are not available to collect this level of data. That does not diminish the importance of gathering data to determine the degree to which a curriculum is being implemented as expected. The cost of not including fidelity measures is the implementation of ineffective programs or possible rejection of effective programs (Moncher & Prinz, 1991).

One strategy that has been successful in ascertaining fidelity to curriculum for the gifted is the use of self-report logs (checklists logs with specific and detailed protocols) that accompany lessons (Foster, 2011). These protocols provide teachers with the opportunity to indicate degree of adherence to the explicit lessons, but also to indicate what they may have modified and why—thus allowing for assessment of the appropriateness of modifications.

## Understanding Why Practice Deviates From Intent or Conforms to Intent

Across disciplines, grades, and types of programs, researchers and evaluators have documented that teachers' practices often do not reflect the intended curriculum (Azano, Callahan, Missett, & Brunner, 2014; Orafi, 2013). Although classroom observation may provide a window on what is happening in the classroom, it is insufficient for understanding *why* teacher behaviors are what they are. Borg (2006) argued, "observation on its own . . . provides an inadequate basis for the study of what teachers think, know and believe. . . . [We] can draw inferences about cognition from what is observed, but verification . . . must be sought through other sources of data" (p. 247). Many sources of deviation, or even, abandonment, of new curriculum have been documented in the literature.

**Inadequate curricular exposition.** Hoover and Patton (2005) identified five essential components of effective multitiered Response to Intervention (RtI) implementation, which are generalizable to the implementation of curriculum for the gifted: clear delineation of content and skills that are research based, evidence-based interventions/instructional strategies, clearly specified instructional arrangements (e.g., various groupings, pairings, independent work), detailed classroom management procedures, and evidence of progress/outcome evaluation tied to the goals and objectives. When one or more of these factors is neglected in the curricular description, teachers are more likely to abandon the new curriculum or instructional practices and revert to the familiar. Orafi (2013) emphasized the need for clear and concrete language in the documentation provided to teachers. He is emphatic that such direction should not diminish the importance of including "conceptual and philosophical matters in curricular frameworks and related materials. It does mean, however, that the actual practices emerging from such consideration need to be outlined clearly, and with plenty of illustration" (p. 19).

**Teacher understandings of the curriculum and/or lack of skills needed to effectively deliver the curriculum.** Teacher knowledge or lack of skills as a factor in the failure to deliver curriculum as it was designed was discussed above, but must be monitored as implementation begins.

**Beliefs of teachers.** As noted above, failure to implement a curriculum is attributed to teacher knowledge or skill; however, teachers are sometimes quite capable of implementing new curriculum, but are unwilling to do so. Tomlinson (2008) identified teacher skill (discussed above) and teacher will as two inhibiting factors in the implementation of differentiated curriculum in the classroom. Teacher beliefs fall in the "will" category of inhibiting factors in implementing curriculum with fidelity; these are considered to be beliefs about student capacity, beliefs and values about what is important in a curriculum, and beliefs about their own professional capabilities (Azano et al., 2011; Brighton et al., 2005). When teachers' beliefs about their students' ability to master challenge match the challenge of gifted curriculum, the teachers are more likely to accept and attempt the lesson provided (Azano et al., 2011). Similarly, if teachers do not think their students are capable, they will likely "dumb down" the curriculum to provide students with the path of least resistance. A combination of teachers' beliefs about their students and beliefs about success and challenge interact in determining how teachers respond to curriculum. If teachers define success as not failing, then they will align their choices of curriculum to the level at which students will never fail, which often lacks the challenge necessary in a curriculum for gifted students.

Teachers' philosophies of teaching and learning also impact acceptance of and willingness to try new curriculum. For example, teachers who hold teacher-centered beliefs about teaching and learning resist using strategies that are dependent on student autonomy (Brighton et al., 2005). This is not to say that these teachers cannot learn to accept new beliefs and teaching philosophies, but they must first identify those beliefs (which often they have not articulated and recognized), and then they must be convinced of the importance, value, and effectiveness of the new philosophy (Orafi, 2013).

**Other contextual barriers to implementation.** There are other factors that may have an impact on implementation of curriculum for the gifted. One factor is the size and diversity of the classroom in which the curriculum is to be implemented and the concordance of the curriculum with those factors (Brighton et al., 2005; Wedell, 2005). For example, if a curriculum was designed as a differentiated curriculum to be used in a heterogeneous classroom, large and very diverse classrooms will present a particular challenge in management of the instruction. Teachers in pull-out classrooms in rural communities that are comprised of students of mixed grade levels will have great challenges implementing curricula designed to extend on-grade-level standards (Azano et al., 2014). Teachers of the gifted in rural classrooms also face issues of isolation (and hence, lack of perceived support) and lack of access to resources often considered readily available by curriculum developers. These teachers also attributed lack of fidelity in implementing curriculum to the challenge of teaching across many buildings and grade levels, resulting in the need to carry materials to multiple sites and having to be knowledgeable about multiple levels of curriculum; a lack of support in classroom technology; and inadequate instructional planning time because of travel among buildings or building schedules that interfered with instructional time (Azano et al., 2014). Wedell (2005) also identified incompatibility of the format of the curriculum or the requisite instructional strategies with the teaching evaluations in a school district as an impediment to fidelity of implementation.

**Limitations of supplies and resources.** Shortage of instructional materials or difficulty in accessing materials in any context will certainly limit teachers in the implementation of a curriculum (Azano et al., 2014; Brighton et al, 2005; Hord & Huling-Austin, 1986; Wedell, 2005). In examining curriculum for the gifted, one quickly is aware that the materials and resources are not those often readily available in traditional classrooms. The curricula are designed to extend learning beyond the traditional curriculum, so readings and other resources are needed. There are two potential drawbacks to curricula that do not provide the resources needed for instruction or strategies for easy access. The first is to ignore the lesson altogether because materials are not available or to alter the lesson in ways that diminish the likelihood of challenge and achievement of goals. The other is the inadequate delivery of the instruction as time is devoted to acquiring the resources rather than mastering the skills needed for curriculum fidelity. As Hord and Huling-Austin (1986) noted, when teachers are not investing time and energy in acquiring materials, they can invest that time and energy in developing the background knowledge and acquiring the skills for implementing the curriculum.

**Teacher workloads and lack of time to plan.** It is not only rural teachers of the gifted who face challenges presented by inadequate planning time. Teachers in suburban and urban districts may also face course loads that fill their day, leaving little time to plan. Brighton et al. (2005) and Wedell (2005) identified lack of planning time and consultation time as major inhibitors to curricular change and adoption. When faced with an unfamiliar curriculum and lack of time to prepare, it is easier to revert to known curriculum that has become more automatic.

# Curriculum Evaluation

The evaluation of curriculum should encompass the resources, processes, and products of evaluation.

## Resource Evaluation

Adequate and informative evaluation will provide information on whether the resources were sufficient and appropriate for development, implementation, and management of the curriculum. The curriculum development process is too seldom examined to identify whether or not those charged with the development had access to and attended to important guiding principles and information. For example:

- Were the goals and objectives of gifted services identified, and did the development team have clear and agreed upon interpretations of those goals and objectives?
- Was the development team adequately trained in developing curriculum in general and curriculum for the gifted in particular?
- Was the development team adequately trained in the model(s) of curriculum to be used in the development process?
- Did the development team have adequate time to produce high-quality curriculum?
- Did the development team have access to the resources they needed to create high-quality curriculum?

Similarly, the curriculum implementation and management functions should be evaluated in terms of adequacy of resources. Data should be collected on such questions as:

◆ Did the staff development team have adequate resources to provide the training needed?

◆ Are the curriculum materials provided to teachers in ways that are accessible and transportable?

◆ Are there adequate materials for students?

◆ Do teachers have easy access to the materials they need to teach the new curriculum (this would include both material resources and assurances that links to websites are live and appropriate)?

◆ Are coaches available to help teachers who are having difficulty with implementation?

◆ Did the curriculum developers take into consideration the contexts in which teachers must deliver the curriculum?

## Process Evaluation

A review of the factors that inhibit implementation success suggests the sort of evaluation questions that should be asked about the process of implementation:

◆ Did the staff development team preassess the teachers' knowledge, skills, beliefs, and philosophies?

◆ Did the staff development team plan the introduction to the curriculum and subsequent sessions based on preassessment information?

◆ Did the staff development team allow for practice and feedback, and was revision based on feedback?

◆ Did the introduction of the curriculum reflect strategies for accessing materials necessary for full implementation?

Questions to assess the processes of curriculum management include:

◆ Is there a clear strategy in place to monitor fidelity of implementation?

◆ Is the curriculum being implemented with fidelity? If not, why not? If yes, what factors contribute to fidelity? If needed, how can strategies used in those sites with good fidelity be replicated in those with less success in implementation with fidelity?

◆ Is there a clear strategy for increasing fidelity based on the data from monitoring fidelity?

## Product Evaluation

Evaluation of products in curriculum development and implementation is two-fold. On the one hand, the curriculum document should be carefully evaluated. Depending on the model guiding the process of curriculum development and the goals and objectives of the services being provided to the gifted, the particulars of the evaluation of the curriculum product would differ. In general, the evaluation of the curriculum documentation should include evidence that the curriculum represents high-quality curriculum for gifted learners (NAGC, 2010)[4]. Does the curriculum:

◆ provide for compacting (adapting, modifying, or replacing the core curriculum) as appropriate?

◆ reflect an articulated (comprehensive and continuous) scope and sequence of learning?

◆ align with and represent an extension of local, state, and national content standards?

◆ provide modifications for students with special needs such as twice-exceptional students, highly gifted, and English language learners?

◆ incorporate advanced, conceptually challenging, in-depth, distinctive, and complex content?

◆ include preassessments to help pace instruction based on the learning rates of students and to accelerate and compact learning as appropriate?

◆ provide for the use of information and technologies, including assistive technologies, to individualize for students, including those who are twice-exceptional?

---

4   The questions that follow are taken directly from Standard 3: Curriculum Planning and Instruction of the National Standards in Gifted and Talented Education: Pre-K to Grade 12, found at http://www.nagc.org/resources-publications/resources/national-standards-gifted-and-talented-education/pre-k-grade-12-3. The only change is to word them as evaluation questions.

- include goals and objectives in cognitive, affective, aesthetic, social, and leadership domains that are challenging and effective in achieving program goals?
- include and guide teachers in the choice of a repertoire of instructional strategies and materials that differentiate for students with gifts and talents and that respond to diversity?
- provide opportunities for students with gifts and talents to explore, develop, or research their areas of interest and/or talent?
- provide for the use of school and community resources?
- provide for the development of critical thinking, problem-solving, and inquiry strategies?
- use challenging, culturally responsive curriculum to engage all students?
- integrate career exploration experiences?
- provide for deep explorations of cultures, languages, and social issues related to diversity?

Of course, if a particular model, such as Kaplan's (2005) Depth and Complexity Model, has been used to guide curriculum development, one would create another set of unique questions revolving around the specific components of that model. The answers to the evaluation questions posed above are best looked for in expert, independent ratings of the curriculum documents. Internal or self-ratings are likely to be biased.

Finally, and perhaps most importantly, is student outcome evaluation. A well-developed curriculum will have specified goals and objectives that incorporate the principles of curriculum for the gifted articulated in the prior section of this chapter. The keys to evaluation of the outcomes are:

- Evaluate the outcomes of student learning and development: the specific goals and objectives of the curriculum. Too often the evaluation is focused only on student or parent satisfaction with services. Although this data is important, as it gives a reading of student engagement, it is insufficient without data about what students learned.
- Collect data that most directly measures the expected outcomes. Valid data will reflect the kinds and level of performance expected. If students are expected to learn accelerated content, then advanced-level content tests are the most appropriate assessment tools. If problem solving or creative product production is an out-

come, then performance or product measures should be used (see Moon, 2013, and Renzulli and Callahan, 2008).

- Be careful to use tests that have a ceiling that is high enough to measure student growth.
- Measure all outcomes (cognitive, social, emotional, psychomotor, aesthetic, etc.) of the curriculum.

# Conclusion

The curriculum implementation, management, and evaluation sections of this chapter have been written as if they were distinct processes and as if they were distinct from the curriculum development process. In reality, they are all interconnected and interdependent processes. To have an effective curriculum that achieves the desired outcomes requires that educators cycle through each of these processes and go back to the beginning to refine curriculum, adjust implementation and management strategies, and reevaluate through many cycles to maximize the effectiveness of the curriculum and to achieve optimal student learning.

# References

Azano, A. P., Callahan, C. M., Missett, T. C., & Brunner, M. (2014). Understanding the experiences of gifted education teachers and fidelity of implementation in rural schools. *Journal of Advanced Academics, 25,* 88–100.

Azano, A., Missett, T. C., Callahan, C. M., Oh, S., Brunner, M., Foster, L. H., & Moon, T. R. (2011). Exploring the relationship between fidelity of implementation and academic achievement in a third-grade curriculum: A mixed-methods study. *Journal of Advanced Academics, 22,* 693–719.

Borg, S. (2006). *Teacher cognition and language education: Research and practice.* London, England: Continuum.

Brighton, C. M., Hertberg, H. L., Moon, T. R., Tomlinson, C. A., & Callahan, C. M. (2005). *The feasibility of high-end learning in a diverse middle school* (RM05210). Storrs: University of Connecticut, The National Research Center on the Gifted and Talented.

Cohen, D. K., & Hill, H. C. (2002). *Learning policy: When state education reform works.* New Haven, CT: Yale University Press.

Dane, A. V., & Schneider, B. H. (1998). Program integrity in primary and early secondary prevention: Are implementation efforts out of control? *Clinical Psychology, 18,* 23–45. doi:10.1016/S0272-7358(97)00043-3

Eisner, E. W. (2002). *The educational imagination: On the design and evaluation of school programs* (3rd ed.). Upper Saddle River, NJ: Merrill.

Foster, L. H. (2011). *Fidelity: Snapshots of implementation of a curricular intervention* (Doctoral dissertation). Retrieved from http://search.proquest.com.proxy.its.virginia.edu/docview/908430898

Fullan, M. (1982). *The meaning of educational change.* New York, NY: Teachers College Press.

Fullan, M. (2001). *The new meaning of educational change* (3rd ed.). New York, NY: Teachers College Press.

Handal, B., & Herrington, T. (2003). Mathematics teachers' beliefs and curriculum reform. *Mathematics Education Research Journal, 15,* 59–69.

Hayes, D. (2000). Cascade training and teachers' professional development. *English Language Teaching Journal, 54,* 135–145.

Hoover, J. J., & Patton, J. R. (2005). *Curriculum adaptation for students with learning and behavior problems: Principles and practices* (3rd ed.). Austin, TX: Pro-Ed.

Hord, S. M., & Huling-Austin, L. (1986). Effective curriculum implementation: Some promising new insights. *The Elementary School Journal, 87,* 96–115.

Kaplan, S. N. (2005). Layering differential curricula for gifted and talented. In F. A. Karnes & S. M. Bean (Eds.), *Methods and materials for teaching gifted students* (2nd ed., pp. 107–132). Waco, TX: Prufrock Press.

Moncher, F., & Prinz, R. (1991). Treatment fidelity in outcome studies. *Clinical Psychology Review, 11,* 247–266. doi:10.1016/0272-7358(91)90103-2

Moon, T. R. (2013). Assessing resources, activities, and outcomes of programs for the gifted and talented. In C. M. Callahan & H. L. Hertberg-Davis (Eds.), *Fundamentals of gifted education: Considering multiple perspectives* (pp. 448–457). New York, NY: Routledge.

National Association for Gifted Children. (2010). *Pre-K–grade 12 gifted programming standards.* Washington, DC: Author. Retrieved from http://www.nagc.org/sites/default/files/standards/K-12%20programming%20standards.pdf

O'Donnell, C. L. (2008). Defining, conceptualizing, and measuring fidelity of implementation and its relationship to outcomes in K–12 curriculum intervention research. *Review of Educational Research, 78,* 33–84.

Orafi, S. M. S. (2013). Effective factors in the implementation of ELT curriculum innovations. *Scientific Research Journal, 1,* 14–21.

Renzulli, J. S., & Callahan, C. M. (2008). Product assessment. In J. L. VanTassel-Baska (Ed.), *Alternative assessment with gifted and talented students* (pp. 259–283). Waco, TX: Prufrock Press.

Taylor, J. A., Van Scotter, P., & Coulson, D. (2007). Bridging research on learning and student achievement: The role of instructional materials. *Science Educator, 16*(2), 44–50.

Tomlinson, C. A. (2008). Differentiated instruction. In J. A. Plucker & C. M. Callahan (Eds.), *Critical issues and practices in gifted education: What research says* (pp. 167–177). Waco, TX: Prufrock Press.

UNESCO International Bureau of Education. (2009a). *Module 6: Capacity building for curriculum implementation.* Retrieved from http://www.ibe.unesco.org/fileadmin/user_upload/COPs/Pages_documents/Resource_Packs/TTCD/sitemap/Module_6/Module_6.html

UNESCO International Bureau of Education. (2009b). *Module 7: Processes of curriculum implementation.* Retrieved from http://www.ibe.unesco.org/fileadmin/user_upload/COPs/Pages_documents/Resource_Packs/TTCD/sitemap/Module_7/Module_7.html

Wedell, M. (2005). Cascading training down into the classroom: The need for parallel planning. *Journal of Educational Development, 25,* 637–651.

Zhao, Y., Pugh, K., Sheldon, S., & Beyers, J. L. (2002). Conditions for classroom technology innovations. *Teachers College Record, 104,* 482–515.

# Trends and Future Directions for Curriculum for the Gifted

# CHAPTER 11

# Creativity and Curriculum for the Gifted

**Bonnie Cramond and Sarah E. Sumners**

## Introduction

The senior author of this chapter recalls:

> I stood on the tennis court frustrated. Trying to hit balls back to my former pro husband was one of the most exasperating things I had ever tried to do. He had promised me a one-hour lesson, and I was sure we must be nearing that point. I looked at my watch; 12 minutes had passed. I suddenly had an epiphany. This is how children who are not good in academics must feel in a classroom, but they have to sit there every day for hours, year after year. I was filled with empathy and regret that I had never truly understood this before. If I had to spend 6 hours a day,

Monday through Friday, playing sports and being judged
on it, I would probably drop out of school.

Why then do we concentrate almost solely on literacy and numeracy
skills in schools when we know there are so many other abilities that children have and need to develop? Whether you are a proponent of Guilford's
180 intelligences (1977), or Gardner's eight plus (1999), or even Sternberg's
three (1997), most educators and psychologists now recognize that human
abilities are multidimensional and our complex world has demands that
go far beyond competency in the three R's. Yet, teachers, increasingly bur-
dened with accountability and tasks beyond their primary job of teaching, are rightfully chagrined at the notion of adding to the curriculum.
Beleaguered educators can't be expected to be able to instruct in all areas of
human endeavor. What can be done?

One thing is to help students find their abilities and passion and connect the lessons they *must* learn to what they *want* to learn and how they
*best* learn it. It is not the job of educators to develop students into who we
want them to be, but rather to find out who they are and help them be the
best at it. This can be accomplished by tapping into students' creativity and
helping them yearn to learn and express themselves.

# Why Teach Creativity?

Educators should teach students to think creatively for the student's
personal development and for the good of society as a whole. One area that
is much debated in creativity literature is the possible link between creativity and mental illness (see for example, Silvia & Kaufman, 2010). A key reason for such diverse findings is that both constructs, creativity and mental
illness, have multidimensional meanings and levels. Accordingly, there
have been demonstrated links between high creativity in specific fields and
mental disorders, especially depression and bipolar disorder, in the individual or the family (Andreasen, 2005; Jamison, 1993). However, even the
staunchest supporters of this research do not propose that creative production *causes* mental disorders. In fact, the reverse may be true. Research from
the classic series of studies done at the Institute of Personality Assessment

and Research (MacKinnon, 1976), which compared more and less creative individuals in several fields on various psychological measures, concluded that creative individuals had higher scores on psychopathology, but they also had higher ego strength than the less creative individuals. In other words, the more creative individuals had more atypical thought patterns, but they had the ability to control and direct those thoughts for their use. More important for school applications, Cropley (1990) concluded that fostering creativity in day-to-day life most likely promotes positive mental health. There is evidence that individuals who express their creativity are both mentally and physically healthier than those who do not (Runco, 2004). Children who learn to release their emotions through creative expression can develop alternative methods to vent anger rather than fighting, to explore sorrow rather than go into depression, to conquer fears rather than cowering to them.

If educators can help children deal with their emotions through creative expression from an early age, might there be less alcohol and drug abuse, fewer suicides and homicides? The benefits of art therapy have been noted for physical and mental health (Backos et al., 2014). How much more powerful could the expressive arts be if used to prevent problems?

At the macro level, much has been written about the need for creativity and innovation in modern curriculum. From the National Advisory Committee on Creative and Cultural Education (1999) report, to the groundbreaking 2007 report from the National Center on Education and the Economy, *Tough Choices or Tough Times*, there have been arguments for changing the curriculum to one that emphasizes creativity. A major keystone of the current economy is innovation, or in psychological and educational terms, *creativity* (Council on Competitiveness, 2005; The Task Force on the Future of American Innovation, 2012). As these reports predict, the United States must change its curriculum to compete in the global economy.

Reflecting this realization, 1,500 chief executive officers from around the world responded in a survey that they regarded creativity as the most important leadership competency for success (IBM, 2010). More pertinently, the Partnership for 21st Century Skills (2008) has listed creativity, innovation, and problem solving as critical skills necessary for all students.

# Can Creativity Be Taught?

Even those who agree about the importance of creativity are often skeptical that it can be taught. However, creativity is not really taught; its development is nurtured. Creativity can be nurtured by providing psychologically safe and resourceful environments, teaching creativity techniques, providing many opportunities to use creativity in different contexts and contents, and fostering metacognition and creative dispositions.

## Environments

Although most teachers have little control over the dimensions and site of their classrooms, they do have some control over its look and a good deal over its psychological climate. Rogers (1954) may have been the first to expound upon the necessity of psychological safety for creativity to develop, but it is not hard to see that students who fear taunting or reprisals will not be likely to propose original ideas. Therefore, it is imperative that teachers create a classroom where students feel that it is safe to ask questions and develop ideas that are far from the norm. This will be discussed a little more in the section on encouraging creative dispositions.

Another component of an ideal classroom climate for creativity is one that provides the right pacing and rhythm. Such curriculum pioneers as Taba (Fraenkel, 1992) described the necessity of varying the pace and the type of activity in a lesson so that students can remain engaged. Torrance (1962) also emphasized the importance of giving students time for both stimulation and quiet reflection.

Finally, a nurturing classroom is one that has resources. Resources include material resources, people, and time. Although classrooms vary widely in the types and quantity of material resources, it is most important that students have access to the materials and know how to use them. Also, even classrooms that are not rich in material resources could be resourced with teacher time and attention, fellow students, and parent volunteers, for example. Finally, the gift of time to do creative activities, to reflect, speculate, experiment, build, imagine, and so on, is perhaps the greatest resource for the creative mind.

## Creativity Techniques

There are far too many techniques to list here; they have been described and exemplified elsewhere. However, it is probably useful to describe the main types of techniques and provide some resources. The following are not mutually exclusive categories, and they are certainly arguable, but they are used here for descriptive purposes. Most creative techniques are methods: (1) to increase ideation, such as brainstorming or analogical thinking; (2) to help one break out of the typical way of thinking, such as lateral thinking or forced relationships; (3) to make larger connections, such as mind mapping or storyboarding; (4) to consider other viewpoints and options, such as Six Thinking Hats and attribute listing; (5) to reinvigorate the mind, such as drawing, using all senses, or assumption smashing; and (6) to aid in problem solving, such as Sociodrama and Creative Problem Solving. There are many examples of these types of activities and variations within the techniques, but many of them can be found in books or online (see, for example, http://www.members.optusnet.com.au/charles57/Creative/Techniques/index.html, http://creativesomething.net/post/65040489344/the-seven-most-effective-techniques-for-creativity, and http://www.mycoted.com/Category:Creativity_Techniques).

It is not important that students know the names or "rules" of the various techniques, but rather that they know that there are a variety of techniques they can use and modify in order to choose which ones, if any, are helpful to them. This metacognitive awareness, or intentionality, of analyzing a situation and choosing a strategy to go forward is what is most important. Therefore, students might recognize that some problems are merely variations of ones they have solved successfully in other circumstances, old problems that need a new approach, or problems that are unlike any they can recall. Thus, students can learn to spend more time on analysis of the problem and being strategic and less time on trial and error. Research on expert versus novice problem solvers shows that this is the case with the experts, more time is spent on the analysis of the problem and the planning than on the actual solution (Lesgold, 1988).

## Providing Opportunities

The key to teaching creativity techniques is to educate students about when to use them as well as how. Halpern (1998) recommended that in addition to teaching students the skills of thinking, we should also teach them the metacognitive monitoring that makes them aware of the problem-solving process, the structural aspects of problems to help students recognize the types of problems that require certain strategies, and the dispositions and habits for exerting the effort to think. Halpern argued that by including these components in training, the probability of transfer of learned strategies to appropriate situations outside of the learning situation will be increased.

Although Halpern was specifically referring to critical thinking, there is no reason to think that the same would not apply to creative thinking. Students can best learn the skills and techniques of creative thinking, as well as the metacognitive monitoring and the structural aspects of different kinds of problems, by applying the techniques in different situations and with different content (Lipman, 2003). Thus, providing students with many opportunities to practice creative thinking helps them learn the techniques and when to use them.

## Fostering Creative Dispositions

Teaching students the skills and techniques to enable them to think creatively would be fruitless if students didn't choose to use them. Thus, fostering creative thinking dispositions is critical to the application and development of creative thinking beyond the classroom experience. What dispositions should be taught and how? There are various lists of thinking dispositions, or habits of mind, but The Five Creative Dispositions Model (Lucas, Claxton, & Spencer, 2013), based on a review and synthesis of the literature, was designed to be applicable in the classroom. It includes five primary dispositions with three subhabits under each one (see Figure 11.1).

This model can be used to track the 15 subhabits, or subdispositions, along three dimensions according to how the disposition is expressed by the student. These are: strength—the level of independence in expression; breadth—the ease in application in new situations; and depth—the extent and level of sophistication of application. The subhabits can also be tracked to show the extent to which students demonstrate each one, as illustrated in Figure 11.2. When students are taught to track their own dispositions, as recommended by the authors, the metacognitive aspects are addressed.

Thinking dispositions can be fostered by creating a classroom climate in which such dispositions are modeled, discussed, valued, and reinforced

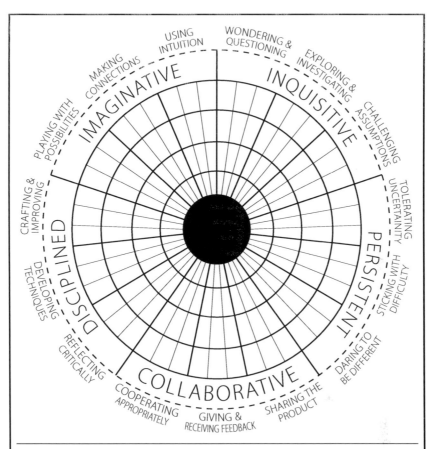

**Figure 11.1.** Part 1 of the Five Creative Dispositions Model showing the five core dispositions and three subdispositions under each. *Note.* From "Progression in Student Creativity in School: First Steps Towards New Forms of Formative Assessments" (p. 18), by B. Lucas, G. Claxton, and E. Spencer, 2013, *OECD Education Working Papers*, No. 86, OECD Publishing, Paris. Retrieved from http://dx.doi.org/10.1787/5k4dp59msdwk-en. Copyright 2013 by OECD Publishing. Reprinted with permission.

(Tishman & Andrade, 1995). This requires opportunities for students to use their creative thinking and discuss it in a class with a teacher who exhibits and values these dispositions. This also requires a psychologically safe classroom where there is zero tolerance for bullying and respect for different ways of thinking.

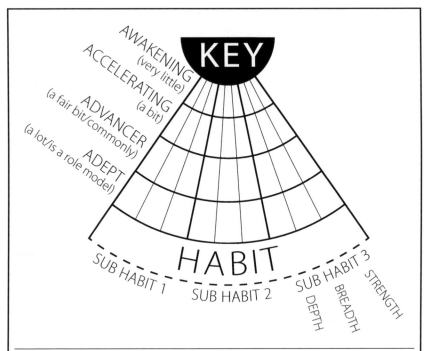

**Figure 11.2.** Part 2 of the Five Creative Dispositions Model showing how the dimensions and extent of each subdisposition can be tracked. *Note.* From "Progression in Student Creativity in School: First Steps Towards New Forms of Formative Assessments" (p. 18), by B. Lucas, G. Claxton, and E. Spencer, 2013, *OECD Education Working Papers*, No. 86, OECD Publishing, Paris. Retrieved from http://dx.doi.org/10.1787/5k4dp59msdwk-en. Copyright 2013 by OECD Publishing. Reprinted with permission.

# Creativity in the Curriculum or a Creativity Curriculum?

A central issue that plagues efforts to include creativity in the curriculum is the same one that was broadly debated during the thinking skills movement of the 1990s—to infuse or not to infuse, that is the question (see, for example, Cotton, 1991; Ennis, 1997). The argument basically boils down to infusing thinking skills into the curriculum so that it is taught in a way that is more natural and contextualized, will be more generalizable, and will not require schools to add another "subject." On the other hand, infused content and skills often become lost content and skills. When schools are not held accountable for the material, it is not taught.

Perhaps the best solution, as with most dichotomous dilemmas, lies somewhere in the middle. Or, more accurately, a solution that incorporates the best of both sides—infusing creativity into content lessons, but ensuring it is taught by specifying creative objectives along with content objectives. Schools or systems could require, as some do, that teachers include creativity objectives in their unit and lesson plans, but unless there were a systematic plan for how to do this, the result might be uneven and spotty creativity instruction. Some components would be taught over and over, and others would be ignored, thereby defeating the purpose. An alternative way to ensure the incorporation of creativity is through the use of a curriculum model that emphasizes creativity. One such model is the Incubation Model for Curriculum in which creativity is a key component of *every* unit and lesson (Cramond, 2014; Torrance, 1979; Torrance & Safter, 1990).

# The Incubation Model

In order to understand the purpose and structure of the Incubation Model (Torrance & Safter, 1990), it is important to understand the role of incubation in creative thought. Wallas (1926) and others, have described the creative problem-solving process as consisting of four steps:

1. Preparation—period during which the individual acquires the knowledge and skills necessary to solve the problem.
2. Incubation—period during which the person is not actively working on the solution of the problem.
3. Illumination—the insight as to the solution.
4. Verification—the process of determining if the solution will work and implementing it.

Although the process refers to problem solving, it can be applied to the expressive arts as well, as the inspiration and realization of a creative product can be conceptualized as a series of problems to solve. The incubation stage is one that occurs subconsciously, or as Torrance preferred to call it, a supra-rational state.

A major distinction of the Incubation Model is that it was designed to address the whole of creativity by helping students bridge the gap between the rational processes of problem solving and the subconscious or supra-rational processes activated during incubation. This is done by purposely incorporating creativity into the curriculum and engaging students' curiosity, intuition, and emotions to motivate them to keep thinking about the lessons after they leave the class. Thus, lessons prime students to use processes beyond the typical rational thinking processes and to incubate about the ideas. Although typical lessons end with some kind of closing activity, the Incubation Model lessons end with activities that are designed to keep students thinking, like a cliffhanger television show or book. The point is to open the students' minds and keep them open to learning about the topic when the formal lesson is ended (Cramond, 2014).

The model has three stages, consisting of activities at the beginning of the lesson, during the lesson, and after the lesson (see Figure 11.3). The term *lesson* is used here in a broad sense, and could refer to a unit lasting several weeks or a single activity. Although only the third stage is directly aimed at encouraging incubation, the first two stages are necessary to heighten expectation and create the knowledge base and deep involvement that lead up to incubation (Torrance, 1979). Following are the three steps of the Incubation Model and some short descriptions of instructional activities for each.

## Stage 1: Heightening Anticipation

The first stage of the model is the warm-up to the lesson. This critical step is essential to preparing students for creative thinking and is the hook that piques their interest. According to Torrance (1979), there are many ways that students may be warmed-up and intrigued at the beginning of a lesson. Any activity relevant to the lesson can be used as long as it gets the students' attention, arouses their curiosity, tickles their imagination, and gives them motivation to see connections between what they are to learn and how it may apply to their own lives. This stage is essential for priming students for the lesson to come. As such, it differs little from the activities used in many lesson plans to engage students at the beginning of a lesson.

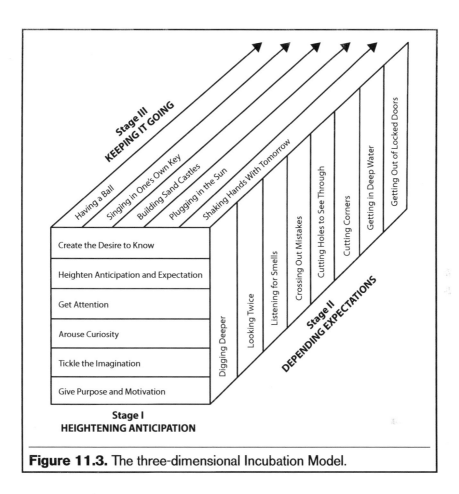

**Figure 11.3.** The three-dimensional Incubation Model.

## Stage 2: Encountering the Expected and Unexpected and Deepening Expectations

Once students are interested and motivated, it is important to keep up their energy and interest. Torrance (1979) used metaphors to explain the eight key patterns of information processing that are involved in Stage 2. The main purpose of these activities is to teach students content and deepen their interest and commitment to learning.

1. *Digging deeper* refers to making a determined effort to get beyond the surface and discover underlying information and meaning by finding problems, hypothesizing, gathering information, and thinking of divergent solutions.
2. *Looking twice* refers to staying open to multiple meanings and multiple experiences of the same information by deferring judgment.

3. *Listening for smells* employs as many of the senses as possible to experience knowing through congruence of the different sensual experiences.

4. *Listening/talking to a cat* or *crossing out mistakes* refers to the process of interacting with information on a very personal level—talking it out and reflecting on feelings about it. This includes developing hunches, and selecting and discarding proposed ideas, so mistakes will be made and should be allowed in the process to get the best result.

5. *Cutting holes to see through* involves getting to the essence of the issue and focusing on what is important.

6. *Cutting corners* requires the elimination of useless steps and information to make the "mental leaps to new insights" (Torrance, 1979, p. 30).

7. *Getting in deep water* includes thinking the unthinkable, confronting taboos, becoming overwhelmed, and becoming so absorbed as to lose track of time and awareness of self.

8. *Getting out of locked doors* involves adopting new and different solutions and really opens up the problem to a radically different solution or solutions.

## Stage 3: Going Beyond and "Keeping It Going"

This is the stage that is very different from other lessons because it is the one that really emphasizes incubation.

> to consult other people, to delve into other kinds of literature or sources of information, to get out into the community, to conduct an original experiment, to write an essay or poem, to paint an original picture, to solve a problem, or to engage in almost any kind of investigative or creative behavior. (Torrance, 1979, pp. 31–32)

There are several processes that can be employed to encourage incubation, and as with Stage 2, they are expressed as metaphors:

1. *Having a ball* emphasizes putting the fun back into education. Although this can be used at any stage, it is especially important at

this stage to encourage students to keep it going. This involves the incorporation of humor, play, fantasy, and games.

2.  *Singing in one's own key* refers to personalizing the information and helping students make connections to their own lives, current and future.

3.  *Building sand castles* employs the imagination and fantasy to create ideal solutions to problems. It frees students to imagine what would be possible if all things were possible, to break away from the present reality, and go beyond current thinking and solutions.

4.  *Plugging in the sun* involves seeking the energy needed to do the hard work that creativity requires and finding the inspiration and support to keep going. This reinvigoration can come from interaction with new people, resources, places, and ideas or through physical activities, changing the environment, forays into nature, spiritual experiences, and the like.

5.  *Shaking hands with tomorrow* involves helping students develop a future image, for themselves and for society, and empowering them to affect those futures.

The Incubation Model can be used as an organizing framework within which other creative thinking activities can be incorporated. For example, in teaching a lesson on density in a science class, the teacher heightens anticipation by showing the students a fish tank of water and two cans of soda—one diet and one regular. Ideally, the students will have an opportunity to handle the two cans and note their properties. She asks the students to speculate about whether the cans will float or sink, questioning them about why they make the predictions that they do. After the students have discussed their predictions and reasons, the teacher places the diet soda in the water, and it floats. By doing this, the teacher guides the students to encounter the expected, for those who guessed correctly, and unexpected, for those who did not, and deepens their expectations by predicting whether the regular soda can will sink or float. When the students have made their predictions, the teacher places the regular soda can into the water and it sinks. The two cans of soda could be placed on a balance to show that the regular can of soda has more mass than the diet can of soda, even though they have the same volume.

Most lessons would conclude at this point with a wrap-up and summary of why the two types of soda cans have different density. However, the idea of the Incubation Model is to keep it going, rather than wrap it up. So, before class ends, the students may be asked to think about another test they could do to discover the principle behind the difference. If students are intrigued enough, they will continue to think about the problem outside of class. Some may try to discover at home why some things float and others sink. Other students may propose another test to be conducted in class. At this point, the teacher may incorporate other creativity and problem-solving strategies by having the students brainstorm the differences in the two types of soda and create a listing of attributes to compare them. The students may also be led to think of other similar items that float (e.g., sugar-free Kool-Aid®), and some regular drinks that sink (e.g., Kool-Aid® with sugar). With guidance, and a touch of drama, the teacher should be able to lead the students to discover the principles of density. Then, the students should be able to use what they have learned to create their own drink and test whether or not it will sink or float. They can also brainstorm other examples of density outside of the science classroom, such as population density. The students have learned about the relationship that mass and volume play in determining density, but they also have learned about problem solving, hypothesizing, testing ideas, and persisting with an idea beyond the boundaries of the classroom. The lesson has resulted in a creative product that is based on sound scientific principles—a new, perhaps less sugary, drink of their own design.

# Key Components of an Incubation Lesson

The model may seem dauntingly complex, but it is really quite simple if one keeps the purpose of the model in mind—to engage students in creative thinking and keep them motivated to incubate on the learning after the lesson ends. Torrance (1979) indicated that lessons are more likely to enhance creativity and incubation when they have five key components:

1. There must be opportunities to imagine, daydream, fantasize, or the like. Such opportunities, even if they are short and intermittent, give students a chance to engage in alternative states of consciousness in addition to the rational, wakeful state of consciousness and create balance between stimulation and reflection.

2.  Students' intellect, motivation, and emotions should all be engaged. When this happens, they are more likely to continue to seek information when the class ends.

3.  Students should have realistic encounters with a problem so they can become aware, involved, absorbed, and committed to its solution.

4.  Students should be confronted with paradoxes and simultaneous antithetical concepts.

5.  At least two sensory modes should be used. Although activities involving multiple senses are common in primary grades, they tend to be abstracted as students mature, but students still need sensory stimulation to help with ideation.

The density lesson, although a simple example, has the critical components. When students are given a chance to imagine whether the cans will float or sink, they are given a brief period of reflection. When they are shown that the diet soda floats, they are either happy that their prediction was correct or confused as to why it was not. If they are given the opportunity to weigh the cans and try to float them in the fish tank, they are actively involved with the problem. The observation that the diet soda floats seems to be a paradox, especially as they can see that the two cans are the same and feel that they weigh fairly the same when they pick them up. Finally, they use this information to create a new drink flavor of their own.

More complex and longer lessons can include the components in more depth and variety. The key is to emphasize creative thinking and alternate opportunities for rational and supra-rational states.

# Conclusion

The nurturing and maximization of creative potentials can easily be taught if the right variables exist in the school and the classroom. By providing psychologically safe and resourceful environments through celebrating and appreciating creative efforts, educators can teach children the tolerance needed for creativity to bloom. Teaching creative tactics and techniques that incorporate both the affective and cognitive aspects of the creative process are also essential to the creative process, as is providing many opportunities for students to practice creativity in different contexts and contents. Lastly, fostering metacognitve and creative dispositions through modeling creative behaviors in the classroom is essential to developing creative production in the future.

Addressing the question of infusing creativity into the current curriculum versus designing a stand-alone creativity curriculum, this chapter offers a holistic approach of a curriculum model that emphasizes creativity. Several publications have shown the effectiveness of models and strategies to enhance creative potential such as Torrance's (1979) Incubation Model of Teaching that focuses on collaborative learning in a three-stage process designed to foster creativity within each step.

Whether infusing creativity into lessons or adopting a curriculum in which creativity is a key component, it is the responsibility of educators to foster students' creativity. By doing so, we nurture the expression that may provide a framework for lifelong physical and mental health and help students imagine their future and that of their society. As Torrance (1979) said, "the images of the future held by today's young people will determine what the future will be like" (p. 11).

# References

Andreasen, N. C. (2005). *The creating brain: The neuroscience of creativity.* New York, NY: Dana Press.

Backos, A., Betts, D., Bermudez-Rodriguez, S., Collie, K., Deaver, S., Gerber, N., . . . van der Vennett, R. (2014). *Art therapy outcome bibliography.* American Art Therapy Association Research Committee. Retrieved from http://www.arttherapy.org/upload/outcomebiblio graphyresearchcmte.pdf

Cotton, K. (1991, November). Teaching thinking skills. Close-Up #11. *School Improvement Research Series (SIRS).* NW Archives, Regional Educational Laboratory. Retrieved from http://hppa.spps.org/up loads/teaching_thinking_skills.pdf

Council on Competitiveness. (2005). *Innovate America: National innovation initiative summit and report.* Washington, DC: Author.

Cramond, B. (2014). Torrance's Incubation Model. In F. Morais, S. Wechsler, & L. Miranda (Eds.), *Criatividade: Aplicacoes practicas em contextos internacionais*. Brasilia, Brazil: Editora Vetor.

Cropley, A. (1990). Creativity and mental health in everyday life. *Creativity Research Journal, 3,* 167–178.

Ennis, R. H. (1997). Incorporating critical thinking in the curriculum: An introduction to some basic issues. *Inquiry: Critical Thinking Across the Disciplines, XVI*(3), 1–9. Retrieved from http://faculty.education.illinois.edu/rhennis/documents/IncorpY400dpiBWNoDropPp1-9PrintD.pdf

Fraenkel, J. R. (1992). Hilda Taba's contributions to social studies education. *Social Education, 56,* 172–178.

Gardner, H. (1999). *Intelligence reframed: Multiple intelligences for the 21st century.* New York, NY: Basic Books.

Guilford, J. P. (1977). *Way beyond the I.Q.* Buffalo, NY: Creative Education Foundation.

Halpern, D. F. (1998). Teaching critical thinking for transfer across domains: Dispositions, skills, structure training, and metacognitive monitoring. *American Psychologist, 53,* 449–455.

IBM. (2010). *Capitalizing on complexity: Insights from the global chief executive officer study.* Somers, NY: IBM Global Business Services. Retrieved from http://www.ibm.com/common/ssi/cgi-bin/ssialias?infotype=PM&subtype=XB&htmlfid=6BE03297USEN

Jamison, K. R. (1993). *Touched with fire: Manic-depressive illness and the artistic temperament.* New York, NY: The Free Press.

Lesgold, A. M. (1988). Problem solving. In R. J. Sternberg & E. E. Smith (Eds.), *The psychology of human thought* (pp. 188–213). New York, NY: Cambridge University Press.

Lipman, M. (2003). *Thinking in education.* New York, NY: Cambridge University Press.

Lucas, B., Claxton, G., & Spencer, E. (2013). Progression in student creativity in school: First steps towards new forms of formative assessments. *OECD Education Working Papers, 86,* OECD Publishing. doi:10.1787/5k4dp59msdwk-en

MacKinnon, D. W. (1976). Architects, personality types, and creativity. In A. Rothenberg & C. R. Hausman (Eds.), *The creativity question* (pp. 175–189). Durham, NC: Duke University Press.

National Advisory Committee on Creative and Cultural Education. (1999). *All our futures: Creativity, culture & education.* Suffolk, England:

Department for Education and Employment. (ERIC Document Reproduction Service No. ED440037)

National Center on Education and the Economy. (2007). *Tough choices or tough times: The report of the New Commission on the Skills of the American Workforce.* San Francisco, CA: John Wiley & Sons.

Partnership for 21st Century Skills. (2008). *21st century skills, education, and competitiveness: A resource and policy guide.* Tucson, AZ: Author. Retrieved from http://www.p21.org/storage/documents/21st_century _skills_education_and_competitiveness_guide.pdf

Rogers, C. R. (1954). Toward a theory of creativity. *ETC: A Review of General Semantics, 11,* 249–260.

Runco, M. A. (2004). Creativity. *Annual Review of Psychology, 55,* 657–687. doi:10.1146/annurev.psych.55.090902.141502

Silvia, P. J., & Kaufman, J. C. (2010). Creativity and mental illness. In J. C. Kaufman & R. J. Sternberg (Eds.), *The Cambridge handbook of creativity* (pp. 381–394). New York, NY: Cambridge University Press.

Sternberg, R. J. (1997). A triarchic view of giftedness: Theory and practice. In N. Colangelo & G. A. Davis (Eds.), *Handbook of gifted education* (pp. 43–53). Boston, MA: Allyn and Bacon.

The Task Force on the Future of American Innovation. (2012, December). *American exceptionalism, American decline: Research, the knowledge economy, and the 21st century challenge.* Washington, DC: Author. Retrieved from http://www.innovationtaskforce.org/docs/ Benchmarks%20-%202012.pdf

Tishman, S., & Andrade, A. (1995). *Thinking dispositions: A review of current theories, practices, and issues.* ACCTION report #1. Washington, DC: ACCTION. Retrieved from http://learnweb.harvard.edu/alps/ thinking/docs/Dispositions.htm

Torrance, E. P. (1962). *Guiding creative talent.* Englewood Cliffs, NJ: Prentice-Hall.

Torrance, E. P. (1979). An instructional model for enhancing incubation. *The Journal of Creative Behavior, 13,* 23–35. doi:10.1002/j.2162-6057.1979. tb00186.x

Torrance, E. P., & Safter, H. T. (1990). *The incubation model of teaching: Getting beyond the aha!* New York, NY: Bearly, Ltd.

Wallas, G. (1926). *The art of thought.* New York, NY: Harcourt Brace.

# CHAPTER 12

# The Role of Technology in Curriculum for the Gifted

## *From Little Acorns Grow Mighty Oaks*

**Brian C. Housand**

Since the dawn of time, humans have created technologies to allow them to do more, be more, and learn more. Technology has allowed us to travel at a faster rate; to record thoughts, ideas, dreams; and to capture moments in time and preserve them for future generations. Technology allows us to communicate with others across great distances, and to bring the world not only into our homes, but into the palms of our hands. Today's digital devices are only the latest developments in a long evolutionary history that is constantly changing and ever growing. What exists only in our imagination today may very likely be part of reality tomorrow.

Although we may feel that today we are altering our world at an unprecedented rate, this perhaps has always been the case. In 1970, Alvin Toffler described the condition of "too much change in too short of a time" as "future shock." If one examines life and the technological changes in

1970 in terms of our current time, 1970 seems simple. We must also consider that future generations will look back at our present time and feel very much the same. For further illustration of this point, one could use Amazon to stream the BBC television series *Downton Abbey* to a digital device, which is something that has only recently become possible. As you are viewing across the series, pay close attention to how technology begins to enter this English country estate and be amused at how the safety of electricity and the need for a telephone are discussed among the Downton staff. That being said, each generation is met with new innovations and technologies that have the potential to either complicate or simplify our lives. Our generation is no different.

In 1915, John Dewey and Evelyn Dewey published a book entitled *Schools of To-Morrow* which criticized the schools of the early 20th century and declared that education should reorganize curriculum standards and employ new instructional approaches that emphasized individuality and freedom in learning along with emphasizing the needs of the society and the changing requirements for future employment. A century later, the call by the Common Core State Standards Initiative for College and Career Readiness sounds remarkably similar. Indeed, we are still coming to terms with Dewey's idea that, "If we teach today's students as we taught yesterday's, we rob them of tomorrow." (Dewey, 1944, p. 167)

The purpose of the chapter is to examine the role of technology in curriculum for the gifted. This is no small task, as one of the great challenges of writing about technology is that it seemingly changes every day. There is the real danger that what is written today may seem obsolete or trite and antiquated by the time of publication. Even as this is being written or read, the latest release of an operating system, iPhone, or tablet device may be only weeks away. Rather than viewing technology as a collection of apps or Internet resources or simply focusing on technology for the sake of technology, teachers should direct their attention toward the possible learning outcomes that are more readily achieved because technology is utilized as the tool it was designed to be.

Technology is an all-encompassing term that could refer to any number things, including computer software, mobile applications, Internet resources, and social media. The ever-growing number of devices available, including cameras, cell phones, mobile devices, GPS, robotics, 3D printers, and circuit board computers, further complicates attempting to define technology. To try to address all of technology would extend well beyond the scope of a single chapter or even a single book. Instead, this chapter will focus on the role that technology can meaningfully play in curriculum for gifted students.

# Technology and Gifted Learners

In 2012, Periathiruvadi and Rinn conducted an in-depth review of the literature related to the use of technology in gifted education and found that vast majority of publications focused on the use of technology by gifted students and their teachers. However, a paucity of empirical research studies had been published on the topic. Periathiruvadi and Rinn categorized 23 publications into the following categories: technology for learning and development, technology for assessment, curriculum and instruction planning with technology, programming with technology tools, technology in varied learning environments, and professional development using technology. The key findings from this review indicate that gifted students reported positive perceptions about using technology for their learning.

However, Housand and Housand (2012) asserted that it is not the technology itself that enhances motivation in gifted students. Instead, it is the opportunities that are afforded by technology that provide motivation particularly when aligned with authentic experiences.

## Technology Integration

The role of technology in curriculum for the gifted is further complicated by the fact that policies related to gifted education not only vary state by state, but also within states and districts and even from school to school. Furthermore, there is often little agreement regarding what type of curriculum is best for gifted students. A multitude of systems and models for gifted education exist with varying levels of implementation. VanTassel-Baska (2003) reflected on the theory, research, and practice in gifted education and synthesized five tenets that provide a set of exceptions for meeting the needs of gifted learners.

♦ All learners should be provided curriculum opportunities that allow them to attain optimum levels of learning.

♦ Gifted learners have different learning needs compared with typical learners. Therefore, curriculum must be adapted or designed to accommodate these needs.

♦ The needs of gifted learners cut across cognitive, affective, social, and aesthetic areas of curriculum experiences.

♦ Gifted learners are best served by a confluent approach that allows for both accelerated and enriched learning.

♦ Curriculum experiences for gifted learners need to be carefully planned, written down, implemented, and evaluated in order to maximize potential effect.

With this as the lens of quality curriculum for the gifted, the quality of integration of technology into the learning environment will be examined. In 2007, the International Society for Technology in Education (ISTE) released the National Educational Technology Standards for Students (NETS-S) for the purpose of leveraging the use of technology in K–12 education to enable students to learn effectively and live productively in an increasingly digital society. The NETS-S contains a set of six standards:

1. **Creativity and Innovation.** Students demonstrate creative thinking, construct knowledge, and develop innovative products and processes using technology.

2. **Communication and Collaboration.** Students use digital media and environments to communicate and work collaboratively, including at a distance, to support individual learning and contribute to the learning of others.

3. **Research and Information Fluency.** Students apply digital tools to gather, evaluate, and use information.

4. **Critical Thinking, Problem Solving, and Decision Making.** Students use critical thinking skills to plan and conduct research, manage projects, solve problems, and make informed decisions using appropriate digital tools and resources.

5. **Digital Citizenship.** Students understand human, cultural, and societal issues related to technology and practice legal and ethical behavior.

6. **Technology Operations and Concepts.** Students demonstrate a sound understanding of technology concepts, systems, and operations. (ISTE, 2007)

Note that only the last standard deals exclusively with technology. Instead, ISTE chose to create standards that highlight the possibility of what students are capable of doing with technology. Created in the age of No Child Left Behind when there was an overwhelming emphasis on all students meeting a set of minimum standards, ISTE composed a set of standards that employ many of the aspects that have traditionally been the domain of gifted education programs including creativity, critical thinking, and problem solving. The major differences between curriculum for the gifted and that proposed by the NETS-S is that ISTE suggests that "all" students be expected to achieve these goals by meaningfully using technology with purpose.

## TPACK Framework

Developments in technology are not only changing society but also redefining the role of the teacher. According to the 2014 Horizon Report for Schools from the New Media Consortium,

> Teachers are increasingly expected to be adept at a variety of technology-based and other approaches for content delivery, learner support, and assessment; to collaborate with other teachers both inside and outside their schools; to routinely use digital strategies in their work with students; to act as guides and mentors to promote student-centered learning; and to organize their own work and comply with administrative documentation and reporting requirements. (Johnson, Adams Becker, Estrada, & Freeman, 2014, p. 6)

This is further convoluted by the expectations of students and even families to have teachers use technology to instruct, organize, and communicate on a daily basis.

In simpler times, teachers were only required to have knowledge of the content they taught and knowledge of how to teach it. Now, teachers must also possess a working knowledge of technology. However, none of these three components exist in isolation of themselves. Instead, they are three interacting factors all situated within a variety of ever changing contexts for learning. This interaction is illustrated in Figure 12.1: Technological

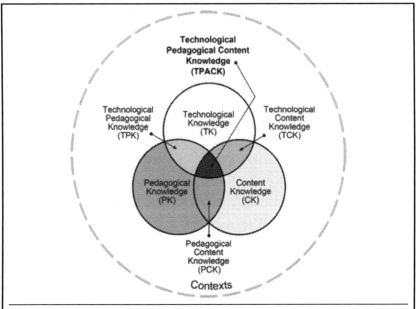

**Figure 12.1.** TPACK. *Note.* Reproduced by permission of the publisher, © 2012 by tpack.org

Pedagogical Content Knowledge Framework (TPACK; Mishra & Koehler, 2006).

Koehler and Mishra (2009) readily admitted, "Teaching with technology is a difficult thing to do well" (p. 67), as the TPACK framework emphasizes that content, pedagogy, technology, and teaching have roles to play both individually and collectively. Expert teachers recognize the unique combination of each of these factors and realize that there is not a single technological solution that will work for every teacher in every situation. Instead, Koehler and Mishra felt that solutions rest in the ability of a teacher to be cognitively flexible and adapt to the ever-changing interaction of the TPACK model. To be truly effective in our use of technology, we must realize that none of these factors can be viewed in isolation, but instead they serve to form a symbiotic relationship in which the whole is greater than the sum of its parts.

The developers of the TPACK framework believe that effective technology integration requires that teachers be sensitive to the dynamic and transactional relationship of each of the components of the model. Mishra and Koehler (2006) also contended that every situation is unique and distinct from every other. With this in mind, we must be cautious in oversimplifying or attempting to generalize, as what will work for one teacher may not work for another. The addition of gifted learners as a variable only serves to further complicate the situation.

With all of that being said, we are truly living in a remarkable time with access to unprecedented amounts of information thanks to the Internet and digital information devices. However, if we are not careful, we run the real risk of becoming victims of our own technology and blinded by all of the possibility without fully realizing the real potential of available technologies. The power of technology to motivate does not rest in the devices themselves, but in what we are able to do with the devices (Housand & Housand, 2012). When considering the role of technology in gifted education, the focus should be not on what teachers are doing with technology, but on what students can "DO" with technology. Put another way, rather than running the risk of leaving gifted students to their own "devices" and assuming they will utilize technology to its and their fullest potential, teachers can serve as the bridge in connecting technology to meaningful learning experiences for students.

## SAMR Model

To stratify the levels of complexity of how technology is integrated in a learning environment, Puentedura (2009) devised the SAMR Model to focus on the varying levels of student engagement with technology and to help teachers seek out ways to better infuse technology into teaching and learning. The model is composed of a continuum of four levels of technology integration ranging from uses that merely enhance the lesson to those that transform the learning experience.

**Substitution.** Puentedura (2009) defined substitution as the lowest level in which computer technology is used to perform the same task as it was done before the use of computers. This level is characterized by technology acting as a direct tool substitute with no functional change. Substitution tends to be focused on the teacher rather than the student. For example, students might use a word processor to compose an essay rather than using pencil and paper.

**Augmentation.** Augmentation is the point at which technology acts as a direct tool substitution with functional improvement. Like the level of substitution, Puentedura sees augmentation as an enhancement to the learning activity rather than a transformation of the task. For example, a teacher might use Google Forms and Flubaroo to create a self-grading quiz rather than administering a paper quiz. At this level, the use of technology tends to remain teacher focused.

**Modification.** Modification is the use of technology for significant redesign of the task. Unlike the previous two levels, which only allow for enhancement, the third and fourth levels provide for transformation of the learning task. There also tends to be a transition from teacher use to student use in the higher levels of the model. For example, rather than writing an essay, students are asked to create an audio recording complete with a musical soundtrack that will be posted on the class website for a wider and more authentic audience.

**Redefinition.** Finally, technology is capable of allowing for the creation of new tasks previously inconceivable or for redefining the way we think and behave. For example, students might be asked to use digital tools to collaborate and create a documentary answering an essential question related to important concepts. By utilizing tools for collaboration, teams of students would take on different subtopics and collaborate to create one final product. Teams are expected to contact outside experts for information.


## From ACORNs to Mighty Oaks

To illustrate the potential and promise of technology in the role of curriculum for the gifted, consider the acronym and metaphor of A.C.O.R.N. Teachers of the gifted should work to plant the seeds of possibilities for the use of technology for purpose and meaning. Regardless of how gifted or talented they are, students may not be able to determine the best means for utilizing the technology they possess. Instead, it is up to teachers to help cultivate students' effective and meaningful use of technology. Teachers of the gifted can more effectively integrate technology into their curriculum by:

- providing gifted students with greater *access* to Internet resources,
- promoting the use of technology for *creativity*,
- supplying *opportunities* for the development of interests,
- emphasizing the importance of *responsibility* when using technology, and
- viewing technology as a *necessity* rather something superfluous.

# Technology Access

We are currently in the midst of a rapid expansion in our level of access to the Internet and the skyrocketing of Internet connection speeds. With every passing year, the availability of access to the Internet is significantly increasing. In early 2015, the Federal Communications Commission changed the definition of broadband Internet by raising the minimum download speed from 4Mbps to 25Mbps. Meanwhile, ConnectED, an educational initiative launched by the White House in June 2013, set out to deliver Internet speeds of at least 100Mbps to 99% of all schools in the United States within 5 years (The White House, n.d.). Although these increases in speed are significant increases over the days of DSL and dial-up connections, they still pale in comparison to the fiber networks being built by Google and other Internet Service Providers that deliver speeds of 1000Mbps. Although the Internet used to trickle into our homes via the equivalent of a garden hose, within the next few years our homes and schools will see access to the Internet at speeds akin to the flow of Niagara Falls.

Thanks to the availability of the Internet, today's gifted students have unprecedented access to information and online resources. We are living in a time where no one has to wonder about the answer to common questions as long as there is a device connected to the Internet within reach. Gone are the days of having to travel to a library to access reference materials. According to a Pew Internet Research report, with all of this access, students have been conditioned to expect to be able to find information quickly and easily (Purcell et al., 2012). However, the amount of information available online is overwhelming to most students, and even though the world is available at their fingertips, today's digital technologies may actually be discouraging students from using a wide range of sources when conducting research. Asking students to conduct "Internet research" without equipping them with the necessary skills and strategies is equivalent to dropping students off at the Library of Congress and asking them to retrieve a book.

Instead of assuming that students know how to effectively access information on the Internet, teachers must teach students how to do so by developing a set of "New Literacies" (Coiro, Knobel, Lankshear, & Leu, 2008). The New Literacies framework is based around five practices: (1)

identify important questions, (2) locate information, (3) evaluate information critically, (4) synthesize information, and (5) communicate information. For students to be effective and efficient in using the Internet, they must develop the ability to successfully employ these five practices when reading online in addition to the required skills for offline reading comprehension. By providing students with training and opportunities to practice searching for answers to questions, we are able to better equip them to utilize the access they possess to the Internet.

Aside from Internet access, we must also consider gifted students' access to devices. However, this is something that is often well beyond the control of a gifted teacher. Ideally, students would be at least one-to-one with an Internet connected device. Although many schools have invested in this endeavor and others have embraced a bring your own device solution, it is up to teachers to lead the way in helping gifted students effectively utilize their devices to access information and content based on their interests and passions. However, beyond merely accessing information, we should strive to help gifted students do something.

# Creativity

Although today's digital youth may have been conditioned to expect Google or their smartphone to answer almost any question that they have, Gardner and Davis (2013) contended that this "app mentality" has created two technological mindsets. The first group is "app-dependent" and utilizes available technology for information purposes, texting, and casual game play. The second group is "app-enabled" and utilizes technology to pursue new possibilities and to creatively express themselves.

In curriculum for the gifted, technology can play the role of bolstering our students' creativity. Gifted education has strong roots in the inclusion of creativity in its curriculum and programs, but somewhere in the age of accountability, gifted education seemingly forgot about this important branch of study. Meanwhile, other fields such as educational technology and the 21st century skills framework (Partnership for 21st Century Skills, n.d.) picked up the gauntlet and heralded the importance of creativity for all students. Although many may worry that technology is making our students less creative, Resnick, Bruckman, and Martin (1996) advised us to consider computers to be more like pianos and less like stereos. Today's technology not only allows us to play the music that others have created as a stereo does, but more importantly, we are able to utilize technology as an instrument to create and compose our own music. This is not only limited to music but to all forms of art.

Gardner and Davis (2013) examined digital media's effect on students' creativity in the area of fiction writing and visual art. In a comparative analysis of middle school and high school fiction writing from the early 1990s to writing samples from the 2010s, today's students produced more traditional stories with less fantasy elements that tended to feature a protagonist of a student and set in a school. By comparison, the early works feature far more fantasy elements. The authors concluded that time spent on students mastering the five paragraph essay has perhaps discouraged students from being creative in an effort to do what is safe.

However, when it came to visual arts, Gardner and Davis (2013) found exactly the opposite. The percentage of "conservative" pieces declined from 33% in the early 1990s to 19% in the more recent works. In addition, the percentage of "unconventional" pieces increased from 19% to 28%. Gardner and Davis concluded that digital media has played an important role in increasing students' creativity specifically in the visual arts. Today gifted students have access to powerful tools for creative and personal expression.

Gifted education has long been concerned with the issue of transitioning students from being merely consumers of information to producers of new knowledge (Renzulli, 1978). Teachers of the gifted should provide opportunities for students to use technology to create rather than simply consume information. To accomplish this, teachers must be willing to step aside from the role of "sage on the stage" to help facilitate learning more as "the guide on the side." For many, the idea of asking students to create using technology is one that solicits a fair amount of anxiety for teachers because of all the unknowns. Teachers should become comfortable with the ambiguity that is often present in these situations and position themselves to learn alongside students. Rather than directing instruction toward a known product or outcome, teachers should provide opportunities for gifted students to utilize technology to create and produce products and solutions that are beyond preconceived possibilities or expected outcomes.

One way to focus on using technology for creativity is to introduce students to coding or computer programming. As long as computers have been in schools, this is an idea that has been present. With the first Apple

II computers, students were introduced to the programming language LOGO, and in the 1980s, there was a rush to have students learn to program using BASIC. Beginning in 2013, Code.org created a vast number of free resources to introduce computer science to a wide array of students. The resources at Code.org provide an easy entry point into the world of coding and can serve as a springboard into a much more advanced pursuit of computer programming. The Hour of Code (http://code.org/learn) teaches some basic concepts of computer science using a drag and drop programing tool called Blockly. While working through the game-like tutorial, students learn from actual computer programmers like Bill Gates and Mark Zuckerberg. The resources provided by Code.org can serve as a perfect Type I experience (Renzulli, 1978) to introduce gifted students to the world of computer science. Even if only a few students decide to pursue a career in computer programming, all students have been taught a basic understanding of programming concepts that employ problem solving, critical thinking, and creativity.

Technology is currently fueling the creative fire of the do-it-yourself culture in the form of the Maker Movement. What started as *Make* magazine in 2005 spawned the first Maker Faire in 2006 as a gathering of individuals' and small groups' engineering projects focused on the creative and innovative use of electronics, robotics, and other technologies such as 3D printing. By 2012, the Maker Faire attracted more than 120,000 people to the festival, and since that time, hundreds of local Maker Faires have been established in cities around the world. As an extension of this idea, many schools and libraries have begun creating Makerspaces designed to "represent the democratization of design, engineering, fabrication and education" (http://spaces.makerspace.com). These spaces represent an idealized environment for providing the opportunities, resources, and encouragement based on students' interests, which is a central component of the Schoolwide Enrichment Model (Renzulli & Reis, 2014). Gifted education is uniquely poised to be a leader within this burgeoning technology revolution, as the pedagogy on which this movement is built is precisely the type of learning that our field has been promoting for decades. For more information, see The Makerspace Playbook (http://spaces.makerspace.com), a free PDF that provides advice and instructions for building a Makerspace in your school.

# Interest-Based Opportunities

The role of technology in the curriculum for the gifted is to provide opportunities for students to more deeply explore their own interests. In 1988, science fiction author and futurist, Isaac Asimov, was interviewed by Bill Moyers for the PBS show *World of Ideas*, Asimov shared his ideas regarding the role that technology would play in education in the future. He spoke of a time in the not too distant future when every home would have a computer connected to an information network that would allow anyone to access information from libraries and research centers. One has to keep in mind that the time was 1988, and that computers were still very large machines that were primarily sold by RadioShack. This was also a time when cell phones were like bricks, no one had an e-mail address, and virtually no one had either heard of or had access to the Internet. Asimov envisioned that computers would revolutionize learning because we would be free to direct our own learning at our own pace and in our own time. Asimov said:

> Today, what people call learning is forced on you. Everyone is forced to learn the same thing on the same day at the same speed in class. But everyone is different. For some, class goes too fast, for some too slow, for some in the wrong direction. But give everyone a chance, in addition to school, to follow up their own bent from the start, to find out about whatever they're interested in by looking it up in their own homes, at their own speed, in their own time, and everyone will enjoy learning.

This approach to interest-based learning is one that is a hallmark of gifted education programs such as the Schoolwide Enrichment Model (Renzulli & Reis, 2014). Today we are living in precisely the age that Asimov described, and yet one has to wonder if everyone is truly enjoying learning as he had hoped. Teachers of the gifted can help foster a love for learning and develop the talents of students by connecting them to opportunities that will allow them to deeply investigate their own interests.

Today we have the opportunity to learn how to do almost anything because of the Internet—regardless of what we might be interested in—and this goes far beyond the traditional text formats that Asimov had envisioned in 1988. In a 2015 Google consumer survey of 385 millennials aged 18–34, 67% of them agreed that they can find a YouTube video on anything they want to learn more about (Mogensen, 2015). In a separate study, Google reported that 91% of individuals turn to their smartphone while doing a task (Mogensen, 2015). With access to this type of information and resources, gifted education should be focused on providing opportunities for students to connect with high-level resources to meet their academic and intellectual needs.

Although hundreds of millions of hours of videos are watched on YouTube every day (Mogensen, 2015), the vast majority of those hours would probably not qualify as quality content. However, YouTube can play an important role in curriculum for the gifted by providing opportunities to learn about a wide range of interest-based content and resources. For example, using technology, teachers can bring expert speakers into the classroom (i.e., TedTalks) where gifted students can hear compelling presentations from some of the greatest minds of our time. It is suggested that teachers seek out or have their students seek out quality content on YouTube based on interests and topics being studied. To supplement instruction or for independent investigations, the following online video resources are recommended:

- *TED: Ideas Worth Spreading*—http://www.ted.com
- *TED Ed: Lessons Worth Sharing*—http://ed.ted.com
- *Crash Course*—https://www.youtube.com/user/crashcourse
- *Crash Course Kids*—https://www.youtube.com/user/crashcourse kids

Finally, gifted educators are highly encouraged to explore the opportunities presented by iTunes U. This ever-growing collection of educational content, from institutions around the world, contains 800,000 resources on almost every topic imaginable. What started as a collection of recordings of lectures from actual courses taught at some of the most prestigious universities, has expanded to include a wealth of digital resources from organizations like the Library of Congress, Metropolitan Museum of Art, NASA, and National Geographic. iTunes U also contains an outstanding collection of primary source materials that can bring new life to almost any history lesson (http://bit.ly/itunesu-primarysource).

Thanks to interest-based Internet resources such as these, there exists boundless opportunities for gifted students to deeply explore powerful and timely content.

# Responsibility

Since the very first appearance of Spider-Man in 1962, creators Stan Lee and Jack Kirby have cautioned us that "with great power there must also come—great responsibility." This is especially true when it comes to the great power of the Internet and social media that has the ability to not only mirror but to magnify all that is both wonderful and horrible in life. We must be cautious in assuming that simply because today's youth were born in a digital world, that they fully understand or are capable of using technology to its fullest capacity in a responsible and meaningful manner.

Schools have traditionally helped to instruct students on the merits of good citizenship and community involvement. Children have been taught not to take candy from strangers and to be kind to others. Teachers must also help students develop similar behaviors in digital environments. According to the ISTE (2007) NETS-S, as good digital citizens all students should "understand human, cultural, and societal issues related to technology and practice legal and ethical behavior" (p. 2). In addition, all students should

a.  advocate and practice safe, legal, and responsible use of information and technology;
b.  exhibit a positive attitude toward using technology that supports collaboration, learning, and productivity;
c.  demonstrate personal responsibility for lifelong learning, and;
d.  exhibit leadership for digital citizenship.

Although the daily news is routinely filled with stories of cyberbullying, educators should be cautious in the temptation to demonize the technology, but instead, work to create a positive school climate that meaningfully integrates opportunities for students to develop as digital citizens. To combat cyberbullying, educators should take a proactive approach to developing a positive school climate. A multitude of resources are available from organizations such as the Cyberbullying Research Center (http://cyberbullying.us) or from the U.S. Department of Health and Human Services (http://www.stopbullying.gov/cyberbullying).

Perhaps the most meaningful way to develop good digital citizens is to provide students with the opportunity to practice the desired behaviors using social media for educational purposes. Edmodo (https://www.edmodo.com) provides a free and private community built for educators to use with their students. With a look and feel similar to Facebook, Edmodo is a powerful course management tool that can be used to facilitate class discussions and collaboration both in and outside of the classroom. Likewise, Shelfari (http://www.shelfari.com) is a social media site devoted to a community of book lovers. A teacher might have his or her students utilize this site not only to engage in book discussions, but also to build students' digital citizenship skills.

In a generation that is often criticized as being self-absorbed and addicted to posting selfies, why not encourage students to utilize social media for good? The use of hashtags on social media sites such as Twitter has created a growing awareness of a number of campaigns and causes that may have gone unnoticed. #ArabSpring brought attention to protests and civil unrest in countries throughout the Middle East. Meanwhile, the #IceBucketChallenge of 2014 raised record-breaking amounts of donations for the ALS Association. Educational consultant Kevin Honeycutt (see http://kevinhoneycutt.org) suggests using students' fondness for selfies to create and post 30-second videos using #soulselfie to promote those causes they care about and begin constructing their own legacy. It is precisely these types of altruistic activities that can be an important building block toward what Renzulli (2002) referred to as the co-cognitive traits of giftedness that promote social capital.

# Conclusion

The role that technology plays in curriculum for the gifted is that of necessity. In *The Road Ahead*, Bill Gates wrote, "We don't have the option of turning away from the future. No one gets to vote on whether technology is going to change our lives" (Gates & Myhrvold, 1995, p. 74). Indeed, if we consider how far our relationship with technology has come since the year 1995, I am not sure that even Bill Gates could have imagined the world in which we are currently living. Technology is an integral part of every aspect of our daily lives. Try to imagine even a single thing that in some way or another technology does not impact. Looking toward the future, there most likely will not be a single job that will not involve technology in some way. Schools are currently preparing students for future jobs that have yet to be invented.

To prepare students for their future roles, it is necessary to provide them with ample opportunities to develop the ability to adapt in the ever-changing landscape of technology. If students are to develop their talents, it is necessary that technology is kept in their hands along with a curriculum that engages them in meaningful activities that encourage thinking, feeling, and acting like a practicing professional, while also utilizing the technological tools of the discipline.

In designing curriculum for the gifted, teachers should continually seek ways to best integrate technology by planting this "acorn" for future success. By providing gifted students with opportunities, resources, and encouragement for firsthand investigative or creative endeavors (Renzulli, 2002), we are sowing the seeds for a new generation of mighty oaks.

# References

Coiro, J., Knobel, M., Lankshear, C., & Leu, D. J. (Eds). (2008). *Handbook of research on new literacies.* Mahwah, NJ: Lawrence Erlbaum.

Dewey, J. (1944). *Democracy and education.* New York, NY: Macmillan Company.

Dewey, J., & Dewey E. (1915). *Schools of to-morrow.* New York, NY: E. P. Dutton & Company.

Federal Communications Commission. (2015). *2015 broadband progress report and notice of inquiry on immediate action to accelerate deployment* (FCC Publication No. FCC 15-10). Washington, DC: Author.

Gardner, H., & Davis, K. (2013). *The app generation: How today's youth navigate identity, intimacy, and imagination in a digital world.* New Haven, CT: Yale University Press.

Gates, B., & Myhrvold, N. (1995). *The road ahead.* New York, NY: Viking Press.

Housand, B. C., & Housand, A. M. (2012). The role of technology in gifted students' motivation. *Psychology in the Schools, 49,* 706–715.

International Society for Technology in Education. (2007). *National Educational Technology Standards for Students.* Arlington, VA: Author. Retrieved from http://www.iste.org/standards/iste-standards/standards-for-students

Johnson, L., Adams Becker, S., Estrada, V., & Freeman, A. (2014). *NMC Horizon Report: 2014 K–12 Edition.* Austin, TX: The New Media Consortium.

Koehler, M. J., & Mishra, P. (2009). What is technological pedagogical content knowledge? *Contemporary Issues in Technology and Teacher Education, 9*(1), 60–70.

Mishra, P., & Koehler, M. J. (2006). Technological pedagogical content knowledge: A framework for teacher knowledge. *Teachers College Record, 108,* 1017–1054.

Mogensen, D. (2015, March). I want-to-do moments: From home to beauty. *Think With Google.* Retrieved from https://www.thinkwithgoogle.com/features/i-want-to-do-micro-moments.html#utm_source=Twitter&utm_medium=social&utm_campaign=Think

Moyers, B. (1988). *An interview with Isaac Asimov.* Retrieved from http://www.pbs.org/moyers/journal/blog/2008/03/bill_moyers_rewind_isaac_asimo_1.html

Partnership for 21st Century Skills. (n.d.). *Framework for 21st century learning.* Retrieved from http://www.p21.org/our-work/p21-framework

Periathiruvadi, S., & Rinn, A. N. (2012). Technology in gifted education: A review of best practices and empirical research. *Journal of Research on Technology in Education, 45,* 153–169.

Puentedura, R. R. (2009). *As we may teach: Educational technology, from theory into practice.* Retrieved from http://tinyurl.com/aswemayteach

Purcell, K., Rainie, L., Heaps, A., Buchanan, J., Friedrich, L., Jacklin, A., . . . Zickuhr, K. (2012). *How teens do research in the digital world.* Washington, DC: Pew Research Center. Retrieved from http://www.pewinternet.org/files/old-media/Files/Reports/2012/PIP_TeacherSurveyReportWithMethodology110112.pdf

Renzulli, J. S. (1978). What makes giftedness? Reexamining a definition. *Phi Delta Kappan, 60,* 180–184, 261.

Renzulli, J. S. (2002). Expanding the conception of giftedness to include co-cognitive traits and to promote social capital. *Phi Delta Kappan, 84,* 33–58.

Renzulli, J. S., & Reis, S. M. (2014). *The Schoolwide Enrichment Model: A how-to guide for talent development* (3rd ed.). Waco, TX: Prufrock Press.

Resnick, M., Bruckman, A., & Martin, F. (1996). Pianos not stereos: Creating computational construction kits. *Interactions, 3*(6), 40–50.

Toffler, A. (1970). *Future shock.* New York, NY: Random House.

VanTassel-Baska, J. (2003). What matters in curriculum for gifted learners: Reflection on theory, research, and practice. In N. Colangelo & G. A. Davis (Eds.), *Handbook of gifted education* (3rd ed., pp. 174–183). Boston, MA: Allyn & Bacon.

The White House. (n.d.). *ConnectED Initiative.* Retrieved from https://www.whitehouse.gov/issues/education/k-12/connected

# CHAPTER 13

# Service-Learning in Gifted Education

## Addressing Cognitive and Affective Domains

**Kristen R. Stephens, David Malone,
and Alissa P. Griffith**

## Introduction

> Educating the mind without educating the heart is no
> education at all.         —Aristotle

Many curriculum and instructional models seek to address the cognitive needs of gifted students; however, few also attend to their psychosocial needs. The beauty of service-learning, both as a pedagogy and a framework for designing curriculum, is that it addresses the whole student—the academic, intellectual, social, and emotional self. Service-learning also targets those characteristics of gifted students that are often overlooked in academic settings such as compassion, sense of social justice, and altruism.

This chapter introduces the reader to service-learning, summarizes the research supporting service-learning experiences for students, highlights the role service-learning plays in curriculum development for gifted learners, and shares teachers' experiences with implementing service-learning in schools and classrooms. Although a growing body of research exists on the benefits of service-learning for students, a paucity of studies have addressed the impact of service-learning on gifted students. Because the components of service-learning are strongly tied to many of the best practices articulated within the gifted education literature, service-learning has great potential to inform curriculum development and modification for the gifted and requires further consideration.

# What Is Service-Learning?

Educator Robert Sigmon is credited with coining the term *service-learning* in 1967. The use of service-learning in schools has grown significantly over the past two decades. The passage of the National Community Service Act of 1990 under President Bush and the National and Community Service Trust Act of 1993 under President Clinton provided support for the development of educational programs that utilized service-learning. The National Youth Leadership Council, founded in 1983, also promotes service-learning in schools and hosts an annual National Service-Learning Conference.

Simply put, service-learning can be defined as an approach to teaching and learning that integrates classroom instruction and curriculum with meaningful community service for the purpose of enhancing student learning while addressing a community need. Yet, as Clayton, Bringle, and Hatcher (2013) rightly indicated, "there are many definitions of service-learning and each may emphasize a slightly different orientation to, or aspect of, the pedagogy" (p. 5). These different ways of thinking about service-learning grow out of the varying purposes for which teachers use service-learning. One teacher may choose to emphasize the service aspect of service-learning, another teacher might focus on the learning aspect of service-learning, and a third teacher might strive to find a more equal balance between service and learning. For each of these three teachers, service-learning represents something different. The fact that the term service-learning has been used to describe such a wide variety of activities that link community service and learning may represent one reason why some teachers seem unconvinced about the efficacy and usefulness of service-learning as a high impact instructional strategy and curricular approach. Defining this term more precisely may be the first step in convincing teachers that service-learning is a powerful transformative pedagogy.

When used in a school setting, for example, the term service-learning has become a label for describing many different kinds of community-oriented activities, including volunteering, community service, civic engagement, community needs assessment, and all types of community-based approaches to teaching and experiential learning. For example, in one middle school, service-learning refers to the activities students are required to complete and count toward a required number of "service-learning hours." A list of volunteer placements is posted and students sign up to do certain activities on particular days and times. One student signs up to shelve books in the school library and another helps clean tables in the cafeteria. A third student volunteers a few hours each week reading to elderly residents at a nearby retirement home. Students must log their hours, obtain verification, and write a brief paragraph describing their "service-learning" and what they learned.

In one elementary school, the term service-learning is used to describe class-based activities that address community needs—teachers organize a Thanksgiving food drive and sponsor a competition among students to see which grade level can collect the most canned foods. The children are told by their teachers that there are families in the community that need food; children are reminded that as members of the community they have a civic responsibility to help others. At the end of the food drive, the entire school meets in the auditorium and each class shares what has been collected; the school principal then speaks briefly about citizenship and civic duty.

In another elementary school, service-learning is the term used by teachers who want to connect classroom instruction directly with the local community. For example, several fifth-grade teachers collaborate to plan a unit focused on levels of government (municipal, state, federal); they invite police officers, firefighters, and other local government employees to visit the school and to work with the children on identifying issues facing the community. These teachers then plan a field-trip to city hall where they observe a city council meeting. The students visit a local community-health center where they learn about healthcare challenges facing the community. At the end of the unit, the fifth graders work in teams and create research-based presentations in which they identify a community need and offer strategies to ameloriate the selected community problem.

Each of these examples involves school-based activities that combine learning, community engagement, and, to some degree, service. In each case, teachers in the school use the term service-learning to describe the activities—yet, in terms of best practice, none of the examples above represents well-designed, effectively implemented, high-quality service-learning.

With these ideas in mind, it is useful for teachers who plan to integrate service-learning into the curriculum to be able to clearly distinguish among community service, community-based learning, and service-learning. *Community service* includes activities that are primarily service-oriented such as volunteering to assist others and collecting money or goods for charitable causes. *Community-based learning* involves efforts to connect the classroom to the local community through activities such as field trips, fieldwork, guest speakers, and immersive experiences such as internships. Both community service and community-based learning often involve service and learning, but there is no intentional effort on the part of the teacher to integrate, in sustained and meaningful ways, academic content and related service. In *service-learning*, on the other hand, the teacher involves the students from the beginning in giving voice to the connections between the academic learning and service to the community. Service-learning then can be seen as a project-based experiential approach to teaching (Stanton, Giles, & Cruz, 1999) and curriculum development, which always includes intentionality, integration, and structured critical reflection. The purpose of service-learning is to address community needs while concurrently fostering student development in multiple areas (academic, civic, ethical, motivational, personal-social).

# Theoretical Underpinnings of Service-Learning

Although the term service-learning has not been widely used until relatively recently, the integration of active real-world experience and academic learning is one of the pillars of the educational philosophy of John Dewey (1938). As a proponent of progressive education, Dewey understood the value of designing learning environments that placed children in situations in which they actively construct knowledge and develop skills as opposed to being passive recipients of information. David Kolb and Ron Fry (1975), drawing on the work of Dewey and Jean Piaget (1970), developed the Experiential Learning Model, which outlines four elements (concrete experience, reflection on that experience, formation of abstract concepts, testing new ideas through experimentation). For Dewey and Kolb, critical reflection on experience is an essential ingredient of meaningful learning. The ideas of Dewey, Piaget, Kolb, and others provide the theoretical underpinnings for service-learning, which can be seen as a subset of the educational approaches of experiential learning and constructivism. In this regard, service-learning is closely connected to other high impact innovative instructional strategies and curricular approaches such as active learning, problem-based learning, project-based learning, and place-based learning. What distinguishes service-learning from these other approaches is its balanced emphasis on learning and service. In service-learning, students and teachers make a commitment to addressing social justice issues and contributing to the public good while also attending to academic learning goals.

## Service-Learning Frameworks

Scholars (Furco, 1996; Sigmon, 1994; Terry & Bohnenberger, 2003) have developed frameworks for analyzing community-based approaches to teaching. Such analytical frameworks can be helpful to teachers who wish to embed high-quality service-learning activities within the curriculum.

### Degree of Service—Degree of Learning

Service-learning pioneer Robert Sigmon (1994) promoted high-quality service-learning by utilizing four service-learning typologies (service-LEARNING, SERVICE-learning, service-learning, and SERVICE-LEARNING). In designing service-learning instructional activities, teachers can use these typologies to determine the degree to which activities involve little service but significant learning (service-LEARNING), significant service and little learning (SERVICE-learning), little service and little learning (service-learning), and (optimally) significant service and significant learning (SERVICE-LEARNING).

### Beneficiary—Focus

Similarly, Furco (1996) has developed a framework that asks teachers to reflect on who is the primary beneficiary of the service: The provider of the service or the recipient? Is the activity designed to benefit the student or the receiver of the service? Furco also asked what is the chief focus or purpose of the activity: To provide service or to enhance learning? In volunteerism and community service, the beneficiary tends to be the recipient of the service—and the focus is on providing service. In field-based, community-oriented education, the beneficiary is typically the student and the focus is on learning. Only in a true, well-designed service-learning experience is there balance and reciprocity between student learning and community service.

### Degree of Involvement

Terry and Bohnenberger (2003) classified service-learning into three typologies or classifications based on the degree of student involvement and service to the community. The initial level, *Community Service,* is characterized by a high degree of community involvement with a lesser degree of learning (similar to Sigmon's SERVICE-learning typology described previously). At this level, students may volunteer at an organization or work as a tutor. The interaction between the school and the community goes one way—from school to community. The next level, *Community Exploration,* involves further engagement with the community where students go out into the community or community members come into the classroom to share information, thus a two-way relationship between the school and community exists. Learning receives more emphasis at this level as students explore and engage with real-world issues. Many experiential learning activities like internships would be classified at this level. At the highest level, *Community Action*, students not only become engaged with the community, but they also start making a positive difference in the community. The student gains valuable learning experiences whereas the community is enhanced through the efforts of the student—both the student and the community benefit from the experience (reciprocity). A high degree of both learning and service occur at this level (similar to Sigmon's SERVICE-LEARNING typology).

## Service-Learning Standards

The National Youth Leadership Council (NYLC; 2008) has identified a set of K–12 Service-Learning Standards for Quality Practice, which can also serve as a valuable tool for designing effective service-learning experiences. The standards include eight critical elements:

1. **Meaningful Service**—experience is personally relevant to students;
2. **Link to Curriculum**—meets learning goals and content standards;
3. **Reflection**—is ongoing and prompts analysis of oneself and one's relationship to society;
4. **Diversity**—promotes understanding and mutual respect of others;
5. **Youth Voice**—students plan, implement and evaluate the experience;
6. **Partnerships**—are collaborative and mutually beneficial to students and community;
7. **Progress Monitoring**—ongoing assessment of progress; uses results for improvement and sustainability; and
8. **Duration and Intensity**—sufficient to meet community needs and reach intended outcomes.

Each of the above elements includes a set of indicators to ensure service-learning experiences are implemented with fidelity. The standards and indicators are "clear, measurable, and actionable" (NYLC, 2008, p. 9) and should be considered to ensure the larger goals of service-learning are met.

Teachers seeking to learn more about high quality service-learning can utilize the following resources housed on the National Youth Leadership Council's website (https://nylc.org): Generator School Network (https://gsn.nylc.org) and the National Service-Learning Clearinghouse (https://gsn.nylc.org/clearinghouse). Other useful resources include:

◆ *The Corporation for National and Community Service*—http://www.nationalservice.gov
◆ *Kids Consortium*—http://www.kidsconsortium.org
◆ *The International Association for Research on Service-Learning and Community Engagement*—http://www.researchslce.org
◆ *The International Center for Service-Learning in Teacher Education*—http://educationprogram.duke.edu/icslte

# Benefits of Service Learning

A number of research studies have reported the benefits of service-learning for students (Andersen, 1998; Billig, 2000; Conrad & Hedin, 1991; Eyler & Giles, 1999; Furco, 1994; Kahne & Sporte, 2008; Shumer, 2005). As Furco and Root (2010) indicated: "Indeed, reviews of K–12 service-learning research include close to 70 studies, most of which have found positive impacts on participating students' academic, civic, personal, social, ethical, and vocational development." In a *Phi Delta Kappan* article entitled "Research on K–12 School-Based Service-Learning: The Evidence Builds," Billig (2000) outlined the many positive ways service-learning can impact students and communities. Billig concluded that service-learning:

◆ has a positive effect on the personal development of students;
◆ decreases "risk" behaviors in students;
◆ has a positive effect on students' interpersonal development and the ability to relate to culturally diverse groups;
◆ helps develop students' sense of civic and social responsibility and their citizenship skills;
◆ provides an avenue for students to become active, positive contributors to society;
◆ assists students in acquiring academic skills and knowledge;

- helps students to become more knowledgeable and realistic about careers;
- results in greater mutual respect between teachers and students;
- improves the overall school climate;
- leads to discussions of teaching and learning and of the best ways for students to learn; and;
- promotes positive perceptions among community members of schools and youths.

Billig and other researchers have emphasized that these types of impacts are only likely to occur when service-learning adheres to high-quality standards such as those outlined by National Youth Leadership Council (2008).

A paucity of research exists on the impact of service-learning specifically on gifted students; however, favorable effects have been reported across existing studies. Terry (2000) found that following a service-learning experience, gifted students reported increased self-confidence and perseverance, an appreciation of new perspectives, and improved teamwork and cooperation skills. Lee, Olszewski-Kubilius, Donahue, and Weimholt (2007) found that students participating in a service-learning program had a higher sense of civic responsibility and personal connection to the community than their peers who did not participate in the program. Gifted students participating in service-learning also reported learning the value of group cooperation and the collaborative learning process (Trebilcox, 1997; Willard, 1984). It should be noted that much of the research pertaining to gifted students and service-learning is anecdotal. Empirical evidence on the effects of service-learning on gifted students is needed.

# Why Is Service-Learning a "Good Fit" for Gifted Learners?

When aligning the goals of service-learning with the characteristics of gifted learners, a "hand-in-glove" relationship emerges. Table 13.1 depicts how the primary features of service-learning help address some of the learning characteristics often exhibited by gifted students. For example,

**Table 13.1**

*Alignment of Service-Learning to the Characteristics of Gifted Learners*

| Service-Learning Components | How Does Service-Learning Meet the Needs of Gifted Students? |
| --- | --- |
| | **Characteristics of Gifted Students** |
| Authentic experience | Demonstrate leadership; exhibit a wide range of interests; venturesome; entrepreneurial and resourceful; able to extend learning to other areas; interest in fairness and justice; seek and value assistance from experts |
| Problem-based learning | Solve problems in unique ways; inquisitive about the world; enjoy exploration; ask many questions; generate multiple solutions; fluid in elaborating ideas; sense when problems exist; employ higher level thinking skills |
| Investigates from a variety of perspectives | Understand how people feel and groups function; interest in cause/effect relationship; perceptually open to the environment; exhibit a broad perspective; embrace being different or expressing unique ideas |
| Fosters teamwork and collaboration | Stimulate others' interests; organize others; recognize and articulate group goals; adopt nonleadership roles in a group; support others in a group when recognized; coordinate the work of others |
| Links to curriculum and standards | Explore areas of interest; voluntarily spend time beyond ordinary assignments; flexible thinking patterns; extend learning from key areas to other areas; pursue innovation; demonstrate superior judgment in evaluating; learn rapidly, efficiently, and easily |
| Encourages and models citizenship | Possess a keen sense of judgment; ask questions of a provocative nature; globally aware; understand how groups function; listen to others empathetically; strive to adapt and improve conditions; curious about the world |

the problem-based nature of service-learning appeals to gifted students' natural inquisitiveness and need for opportunities to think at high levels. Furthermore, gifted students' keen sense of justice is addressed through not only the authenticity of the service learning experience, but also through the opportunity to model effective citizenship.

Dabrowski's theory of emotional development (positive disintegration) addresses the intersection of the cognitive and emotional domains. Scholars in gifted education have embraced Dabrowski's theory as a means for examining the relationship between personality traits and high ability (see Hébert, 2011). According to Dabrowski's theory, gifted individuals exhibit higher levels of empathy, sensitivity, moral responsibility, and self-reflection (Nelson, 1989). Service-learning can be a productive and meaningful way to channel these characteristics, as it directly responds to students' personalities, interests, and their desire to make the world a better place.

Renzulli (2002) has referred to some personality traits as co-cognitive factors. Co-cognitive factors "interact with and enhance the cognitive traits that we ordinarily associate with success in school and with the overall development of human abilities" (Renzulli, Koehler, & Fogarty, 2006, p. 18). Terry, Bohnenberger, Renzulli, Cramond, and Sisk (2008) argued that co-cognitive traits should receive just as much attention as cognitive characteristics in school. Operation Houndstooth—a theory proposing that the interaction between personality traits and the environment influence the development of abilities, creativity, and task commitment (Renzulli et al., 2006)—identifies the following co-cognitive traits as important for academic achievement: optimism, courage, romance with a topic, sensitivity to human concerns, physical/mental energy, and vision/sense of destiny. Unlike many traditional pedagogies and curricular practices, service-learning can help foster the development of these co-cognitive factors. For example, students' altruism and their sensitivity to human concerns might be addressed through a service-learning project addressing community and/or global humanitarian issues. Tackling issues pertaining to education, the environment, health, and poverty can affirm that a student's efforts can produce positive change while also supporting his or her sense of hope about the future.

Many recognized traits of good citizenship can be nurtured through service-learning experiences. For example, the International Baccalaureate program (IB; 2013) identified 10 attributes that are believed to help individuals become responsible members of their community. The IB program aims to help learners strive to be:

- Inquirers
- Knowledgeable
- Thinkers
- Communicators
- Principled
- Open-Minded
- Caring
- Risk-Takers
- Balanced
- Reflective

Service-learning has great promise for developing these aspirational qualities in students. For example, reflection is a key component of most service-learning models and consideration of diverse perspectives around community issues serves to foster open-mindedness among students.

Service-learning taps into those co-cognitive traits, personality characteristics, and/or psychosocial qualities often associated with gifted students. In fact, service-learning may be the only means for really targeting and nurturing these domains within an academic context.

# Curricular Considerations

Service-learning gives the curriculum relevance. Students are better able to see connections across content areas, are exposed to real problems in their original context, and acquire real-world skills as they engage in community-related issues. Service-learning also provides a useful framework for interdisciplinary problem solving and authentic engagement. Passow (1989) emphasized that the affective domain must be considered along with the cognitive when planning learning experiences so that students are sensitized to the problems that exist in our world. In addition, such problems do not exist in a vacuum (one content area)—they permeate across many fields and domains. Service-learning allows for meaningful interdisciplinary study and supports both cognitive and affective development in students.

## Existing Curricula Frameworks That Align With Service-Learning

There are several national frameworks that consist of elements that can be successfully addressed through service-learning experiences. Although many are within the context of social studies (i.e., citizenship), other content areas are not precluded from the benefit of service-learning. For example, environmental stewardship can address learning goals in science; projects can incorporate language arts through interviewing, writing, reading, and speaking; and math learning is enhanced through service-learning projects that employ survey and statistical analysis, modeling, cost-benefit analysis, and fundraising.

**C3 Framework.** The National Council for the Social Studies (NCSS; 2013) has developed the C3 Framework as a guide for states to enhance the rigor of their K–12 civics, economics, geography, and history curricula. The nature of inquiry is central to the framework, which consists of four dimensions:

1. Developing questions and planning inquiries,
2. Applying disciplinary concepts and tools,
3. Evaluating sources and using evidence, and
4. Communicating conclusions and taking informed actions.

These dimensions seem to encompass both the service (Dimension 4) and the learning (Dimensions 1–3) that comprise a high-quality service-learning experience. According to the C3 Framework, "Active and responsible citizens identify and analyze public problems; deliberate with other people about how to define and address issues; take constructive, collaborative action; reflect on their actions; create and sustain groups; and influence institutions both large and small" (NCSS, 2013, p. 19). The emphasis on collaboration and reflection is critical, as both are essential to sustaining a strong connection between the *service* and the *learning* components of service-learning.

**P21 Framework for 21st Century Learning.** The P21 Framework (Partnership for 21st Century Skills, 2015) was developed to identify the knowledge and skills needed by students to succeed in work, life, and citizenship. There are several skills acknowledged in the framework that can be cultivated through engagement in service-learning. Some of these include: working collaboratively with others, understanding the obligations of citizenship and the implications of civic decisions, taking individual and collective action toward addressing environmental challenges, creating new and worthwhile ideas, being open and responsive to new and diverse perspectives, reflecting critically on learning experiences, communicating effectively in diverse environments, working effectively and respectively with a diverse team, and managing goals and time.

Teachers are encouraged to review their state curriculum documents across content areas to determine additional points of alignment between student learning outcomes and service-learning. Generally, numerous content and skill goals can be addressed through a single service-learning experience, making service-learning an efficient means for achieving curricular goals.

## Service-Learning Models

In planning service-learning experiences, there are several service-learning models to consider. These models help teachers best determine how to initiate service-learning experiences in the classroom.

Kolb and Fry's (1974) experiential learning cycle has served as a foundation for many subsequent service-learning models. Kolb and Fry's cycle is represented by four stages:

1. Concrete Experience (engaging in an experience—*Feeling*),
2. Reflective Observation (reflecting on the experience—*Watching*),
3. Abstract Conceptualization (learning from the experience—*Thinking*), and
4. Active Experimentation (trying out what was learned—*Doing*).

Kolb (1976) viewed each stage of the cycle as feeding into the next, and one can enter the cycle at any one of the four stages, continuing in sequence. All four stages must be completed for effective learning to occur.

The NYLC (2009) service-learning cycle provides another useful format to consider. The cycle consists of three stages: pre-service, service, and post-service. During the pre-service stage, the teacher identifies academic goals, establishes evidence of learning, and plans and prepares necessary resources. It is also important that students identify community needs and set goals during the pre-service stage. The service stage of the cycle constitutes the execution of the meaningful service experience. During the final stage, post-service, participants evaluate the effects of the experience and whether academic and service goals were achieved. Outcomes of the service-learning experience are also shared with the others and consideration is given to next steps to sustain efforts.

Kaye (2010) identified five stages of service-learning:

1. *Investigation*—gathering information about student interest and collecting relevant data around the issue to be addressed;
2. *Preparation*—organizing a plan and clarifying roles and responsibilities;
3. *Action*—implementing the plan, engaging in direct or indirect service;
4. *Reflection*—reflecting on thoughts and feelings regarding the total experience (Note: Reflection occurs between all stages of the model as well as summatively); and
5. *Demonstration*—telling the story of what took place, capturing the totality of the experience, and sharing what has been learned and accomplished.

Even though each of the stages is presented separately, they are each connected and may actually be experienced simultaneously.

## Points of Entry

In addition to examining the different cycles and models for service-learning, several implementation approaches also warrant consideration. Kaye (2010) identified these as "points of entry" into a service-learning experience. Teachers might:

1. Transform an existing program into a service-learning experience.
2. Find an extension into service from the content and/or skills that need to be taught.
3. Identify a connection to service from a general theme or unit of study.
4. Connect a student-identified community need with a service-learning experience.
5. Take a community-identified need and design a service-learning experience.

Teachers are encouraged to use the "point of entry" that makes sense for their respective situation. A good place for teachers just beginning service-learning to start may be to transform an existing program into a more authentic service-learning experience, while the more seasoned professional may begin by seeking ways to connect student interests, passions, and concerns with a community need.

## Additional Considerations

Due to the time required in both designing and implementing a service-learning project, it is recommended that service-learning be fully integrated into the curriculum rather than just perceived as an "add-on" project within a curriculum. Best practices are well-represented in the theoretical underpinnings of service-learning, thus service-learning should be viewed as a critical and viable means to achieve student learning goals. It must also be acknowledged that content can still be "covered" through a service-learning experience. In fact, because service-learning places content into a meaningful and relevant context, it can be argued that students will engage with the content on a much higher level and with greater intensity, thus ensuring the rigor appropriate to gifted learners and increasing the likelihood that students will retain the newly acquired knowledge, skills, and understandings.

It is recommended that teams of teachers work and plan service-learning experiences for students together. In the elementary school, this could be teachers working together to connect grade-level content with a service-learning experience that serves to deepen student understanding around the content, helps students practice targeted skills, and provides opportunities for students to engage in service to their community while they learn. At the middle and high school level, grade-level teams across content areas can work together to design interdisciplinary service-learning experiences. For example, a service-learning project pertaining to poverty/homelessness might include topics and activities associated with English language arts (i.e., journaling, letter writing, interviewing), social studies (i.e., geography, public policy, history), mathematics (i.e., economics, budgeting), science (i.e., health-related issues, brain development), and art (i.e., photography). In these examples, the service-learning experience is at the core of the curriculum with each teacher linking his or her subject area back to the experience while also highlighting connections between and across disciplines.

# Stories From the Field: Teachers' Experiences With Service Learning

Teachers often want to know "stories from the field"; in other words, they are interested in ideas for service-learning experiences, successful ways of integrating service-learning into the curriculum, as well as possible pitfalls that may occur in a service-learning experience. Teachers want to know what works and what does not work in classrooms and how to share the benefit of service-learning with parents, colleagues, and administrators. The most authentic source for this information is through teachers who have actually implemented successful service-learning experiences with their students. The following are real examples of service-learning experiences that have been planned and implemented in schools and classrooms.

## Reduce, Reuse, Recycle

Fourth and fifth graders identified a problem at their school—the cafeteria was generating too much trash! Students decided to research possible methods of trash disposal to help reduce the amount of trash produced in the cafeteria. This investigation led them to discover the value of reduce, reuse, and recycle. First, they watched students dispose of trash during lunch and collected data about the types of trash being discarded. After analyzing their data, students decided they needed to educate others in the school about more effective ways of disposing of their garbage as a means of helping the school community. They produced posters to hang in the cafeteria as a reminder of how to reduce, reuse, and recycle trash. Students met with school administrators and custodians to talk about the disposal of trash and provide possible solutions to the trash problem at their school. As a result of the students' data analysis, additional trashcans were purchased and labeled for different kinds of trash to be reused, reduced, or recycled. Once again, students collected data following the installation of the new trash bins. The result: The school eliminated the need for two of the huge dumpsters outside. This freed more room for students' outside activities and exemplified the fact that student voice has power! Students celebrated their success by announcing their result to the superintendent and board of education of the school system.

This project incorporated goals and objectives in mathematics, science, and English language arts, while building self-confidence and providing a sense of greater good in students. Students learned to critically reflect after each stage of their project to determine what worked well and what didn't. They learned about their own community and how to problem solve to benefit their community.

How impactful was the experience for students? Students who were in the fourth grade insisted on recreating the project the following year as a way to reeducate peers who forgot the importance of reduce, reuse, and recycle and to provide training for the kindergarteners new to the school. Students who were in the fifth grade during the initial project reported their experience to their sixth-grade teachers, suggesting they implement service-learning into their sixth-grade year as well. Below are some statements from the teacher who spearheaded this service-learning project.

**The result.** "My students were totally engaged. Their behavior improved because they were so invested in their project. We were able to cover many skills required in our curriculum in an economical manner. By integrating content, students were able to work on several skills at once while seeing their application in the real world. Students were able to make connections and feel a part of 'change' for the greater good."

**The challenges.** "It can be 'messy.' Things may not always go as planned because the students are driving the show while the teacher becomes the facilitator. . . . You do not always know what is around the corner."

**The advice.** "Just do it. The economy of time and the benefit for students makes it worthwhile."

## The Essence of a Person

While one teacher was resolving a trash problem, another was working with writing, descriptive writing to be exact, with his students. The teacher shared obituaries of 9/11 victims appearing in *The New York Times* with his class as examples of descriptive writing. These obituaries not only contained demographic information about these men and women, but also included personal touches—descriptions that captured the "essence" of the person, as a way of paying tribute to life and legacy. Students decided they, too, wanted to capture the "essence" of a person to demonstrate their ability to write descriptively. They brainstormed to identify a population with whom this might be appropriate. Whose story needed to be shared? They researched local agencies and residents. Then, they found it! Within walking distance of the school was an assisted living facility. Its residents were elderly residents who had contributed as active citizens to the community during their lives. Students began sharing stories about their own grandparents, elderly neighbors, and senior citizens they observed in their community. Students recognized these individuals had history and memories to share, perfect subjects for capturing the "essence" of a person. They explored children's literature in order to better understand the culture of the elderly. Stories such as *Song and Dance Man* by Karen Ackerman and *Wilfred Gordon McDonald Partridge* by Mem Fox inspired the students' journey into understanding the need for celebrating this often neglected group. Students began preparing interview questions and researching best practices for interviewing. Students researched geriatric characteristics of individuals in order to prepare for their interviews, to know how to speak with these residents, and to know what to expect from them. When students had their prepared questions finalized and research completed, they made their first visit to the assisted living environment. Small groups of students interviewed selected residents. Students took pictures of each resident they interviewed. Students returned to school with interview notes, memories, and photographs. They crafted, edited, and revised biographical sketches of the residents they interviewed. The goal: Descriptive writing that would capture the "essence" of the individual. With the help of one student's parent, a graphic artist, a poster was designed and printed for each interviewee boasting the picture of the resident and the final copy of his or her story—the "essence" of the individual. Students returned to the assisted living facility to present the story posters to the residents. The seniors were elated to receive such thoughtful gifts from the students. Rather than being presented with sketches of their lives, residents received carefully articulated moments of their lives that captured who they were. Some resulting story titles included *The Library Lady*, *Marble Man*, *Hometown Girl*, and *Enthusiastic Scholar*, to name a few.

The project incorporated goals and objectives from several areas of the language arts curriculum. Students researched and honed the skills of an interviewer and worked with mood and theme as they crafted their descriptive biographical sketches. Social studies was incorporated as students learned about their community and the firsthand accounts of the historical events experienced by their interviewee. Following are some excerpts from the reflections of the teacher and students.

**The Result.** "This service-learning experience answered the question for my students and me, 'What was a service we could render that would somehow be lasting and meaningful, that would go beyond the superficial here today, gone tomorrow care baskets of soap, oranges, and lavender potpourri?' It fit nicely into the school's new writing initiative. Students learned that feeling you get about yourself and others when you give. Students learned to reflect on their experiences and their practices." . . . "Though I have been a witness to and experienced the remarkable rewards of service-learning for all concerned, there is, I admit it, an inkling of dread as we are now in the middle of navigating all the messy logistics of pulling off another service learning project this spring. I am dreading it and I will *love* it!"

**Student comments.** "It taught us the generosity of giving and the great feelings you get from giving." . . . "It taught us about another generation of people." . . . "It taught us about the difference between a long biography and a short biography that tries to capture the essence of a person." . . . "We learned a lot about writing and interviewing."

## Change Over Time

A first-grade class of gifted students participating in a pull-out enrichment program brainstormed ways of representing change over time. They targeted their school community or neighborhood as a place that had indeed changed over time. What were the results of change over time? How had change over time impacted their school/neighborhood community? In order to answer these questions, students began researching their school community. They invited a local historian into their classroom to talk about the history of the community. Students walked several blocks into the nearby business area, which was part of the original community. Students interviewed some of the small business owners who knew the history of the buildings in which their shops were operating. They learned about the buildings and visited the former pharmacy-turned-gift shop to view relics from the original store. Students interviewed members of the community who attended their school 40 years earlier. They also interviewed firefighters from the fire station next to the school, researched the streets within the community and how they got their names, and located old pictures of the community spanning a 40-year period. Students then created a PowerPoint and picture book using their research findings—including photographs, data and facts about the community, and the results of their interviews. They presented their research at the local history center.

The project included goals and objectives related to English language arts and social studies required in first-grade curriculum. Students addressed the use of technology through their research and in the creation of their final products, learned about the impact of change over time, as well as cause-effect relationships. Writing, interviewing, and presenting were skills embedded in this service-learning project. Student experiences were authentic as they interviewed people and visited actual places within their community. The following is a reflection about the project by the teacher.

**The result.** "Through our service-learning experience, lessons were learned which were valuable to academics (reading, writing, math, science, and social studies), but also in life skills such as problem solving, interviewing skills, working with a group, caring for the environment, community, and others. K–12 standards are concept-based which lends itself to a wide variety of service-learning experiences. Students learn to see the value of teaching and learning from others. Students become active participants in learning, not just receivers of facts."

## Pediatric Cancer and Its Impact on Society

A middle school teacher recognized the need for providing enrichment for a group of gifted seventh graders. Students identified their interest in the problem of pediatric cancer. The seventh graders researched the different types of pediatric cancer and made presentations and public service announcements within their school community. Feeling the mission was not complete, students continued their research and deepened their study by analyzing statistics about the disease in relation to such factors as gender, ethnicity, age, geography, and impact on society. A field trip for students to the pediatric cancer unit at the local medical research center was arranged. Through this experience, students not only learned more about the different forms of pediatric cancer, but they also increased their awareness about medical research, facilities for medical research, and the professionals who work in the field of medical research. Students created pamphlets about pediatric cancer, held an awareness day about the impact of cancer on society, and collected money for the local Ronald McDonald House—an organization that supports the families of pediatric cancer patients.

This project addressed science, math, social studies, and language arts goals and objectives as outlined in the state's curriculum. Students used technology during their research and when reporting and displaying their findings. They learned about their local community and had the opportunity to further engage with the topic through a meaningful field experience. The social-emotional needs of these seventh graders were fostered as they recognized and discussed ethical considerations faced by medical professionals and compassion and empathy were addressed as students learned firsthand about the experience of living with pediatric cancers.

# Conclusion

Service-learning experiences provide meaningful, unique learning challenges and environments for gifted learners that can be authentically integrated into the curriculum. Such integration facilitates economy of time, a commodity that teachers rarely have enough of. Through service-learning, students are encouraged to make connections between academic goals and objectives (curriculum and content) and real-world application (authentic experience) and come to realize their "voice" is a powerful tool in positively impacting the world. For all students, this instructional strategy is appropriate, but for gifted learners, it is a "hand-in-glove" fit due to their heightened sense of justice and fairness and emotional intensity, sensitivity, and passion.

# References

Andersen, S. M. (1998). *Service learning: A national strategy for youth development.* A position paper issued by the Task Force on Education Policy. Washington, DC: Institute for Communitarian Policy Studies, George Washington University.

Billig, S. H. (2000, May). Research on K–12 school-based service learning: The evidence builds. *Phi Delta Kappan, 81,* 658–664.

Clayton, P. H., Bringle, R. G., & Hatcher, J. A. (Eds.). (2013). *Research on service learning: Conceptual frameworks and assessment* (Vols. 2A & 2B). Arlington, VA: Stylus.

Conrad, D., & Hedin, D. (1991, June). School-based community service: What we know from research and theory. *Phi Delta Kappan, 72,* 743–749.

Dewey, J. (1938). *Experience and education.* New York, NY: Macmillan.

Eyler, J., & Giles, D. E. (1999). *Where's the learning in service-learning?* San Francisco, CA: Jossey-Bass.

Furco, A. (1994, August). A conceptual framework for the institutionalization of youth service programs in primary and secondary education. *Journal of Adolescence, 17,* 395–409.

Furco, A. (1996). Service-learning: A balanced approach to experiential education. In *Expanding boundaries: Service and learning* (pp. 2–6). Washington, DC: Corporation for National and Community Service.

Furco, A., & Root, S. (2010). Research demonstrates the value of service learning. *Phi Delta Kappan, 91*(5), 16–20.

Hébert, T. P. (2011). *Understanding the social and emotional lives of gifted students.* Waco, TX: Prufrock Press.

International Baccalaureate Organization. (2013). *IB learner profile.* Retrieved from http://www.ibo.org/contentassets/fd82f70643ef4086b7d3f292cc214962/learner-profile-en.pdf

Kahne, J., & Sporte, S. (2008). Developing citizens: The impact of civic learning opportunities on students' commitment to civic participation. *American Educational Research Journal, 45,* 738–766.

Kaye, C. B. (2010). *The complete guide to service learning* (2nd ed.). Minneapolis, MN: Free Spirit Publishing.

Kolb, D. A. (1976). *The learning style inventory: Technical manual.* Boston, MA: McBer & Co.

Kolb, D. A., & Fry, R. E. (1974). *Toward an applied theory of experiential learning*. Boston, MA: MIT Alfred P. Sloan School of Management.

Kolb. D. A., & Fry, R. (1975). Toward an applied theory of experiential learning. In C. Cooper (Ed.), *Theories of group process*. London, England: John Wiley.

Lee, S.-Y., Olszewski-Kubilius, P., Donahue, R., & Weimholt, K. (2007). The effects of a service learning program on the development of civic attitudes and behaviors among academically talented adolescents. *Journal for the Education of the Gifted, 31,* 165–197. doi:10.4219/ jeg-2007-674

*National and Community Service Trust Act of 1993*, Pub. L. 103-82, 107 Stat. 785.

*National Community Service Act of 1990,* Pub. L. 101–610, 104 Stat. 3127, codified as amended at 42 U.S.C. 12501 et seq.

National Council for Social Studies. (2013). *The college, career, and civic life (C3) framework for social studies state standards: Guidance for enhancing the rigor of K–12 civics, economics, geography, and history.* Silver Spring, MD: Author. Retrieved from http://www.socialstudies.org/ system/files/c3/C3-Framework-for-Social-Studies.pdf

National Youth Leadership Council. (2008). *K–12 service-learning standards for quality practice.* Retrieved from https://nylcweb.files.word press.com/2014/08/standards_oct2009-web.pdf

National Youth Leadership Council. (2009). *The service-learning cycle.* Retrieved from https://www.ceesa.org/phocadownload/servicelearn ing/part_3_organizations_resources/7_NationalYouthLeadership Council/6_nylc_gsn_handout-whatissl.pdf

Nelson, K. C. (1989). Dabrowski's theory of positive disintegration. *Advanced Development, 1,* 1–14.

Partnership for 21st Century Skills. (2015). *P12 framework definitions.* Retrieved from http://www.p21.org/storage/documents/docs/P21_ Framework_Definitions_New_Logo_2015.pdf

Passow, A. H. (1989). Educating gifted persons who are caring and concerned. *Gifted Education International, 6,* 5–7.

Piaget, J. (1970). *Science of education and the psychology of the child.* New York, NY: Orion Press.

Renzulli, J. S. (2002). Expanding the conception of giftedness to include co-cognitive traits and to promote social capital. *Phi Delta Kappan, 84*(1), 33–58.

Renzulli, J., Koehler, J., & Fogarty, E. (2006). Operation Houndstooth intervention theory: Social capital in today's schools. *Gifted Child Today, 29*(1), 15–24.

Shumer, R. (2005). Service learning research: What have we learned from the past. In *Growing to greatness: The state of service learning report* (pp. 48–53). St. Paul, MN: National Youth Leadership Council.

Sigmon, R. (1994). *Serving to learn, learning to serve. Linking service with learning.* Washington, DC: Council for Independent Colleges.

Stanton, T., Giles, D., & Cruz, N. (1999). *Service learning: A movement's pioneers reflect on its origins, practice, and future.* San Francisco, CA: Jossey-Bass.

Terry, A. W. (2000). An early glimpse: Service learning from an adolescent perspective. *The Journal of Secondary Gifted Education, 11*, 115–134.

Terry, A. W., & Bohnenberger, J. E. (2003). Service-learning: Fostering a cycle of caring in our gifted youth. *The Journal of Secondary Gifted Education, 15*(1), 23–32.

Terry, A. W., Bohnenberger, J. E., Renzulli, J. S., Cramond, B., & Sisk, D. (2008). Vision with action: Developing sensitivity to societal concerns in gifted youth. *Roeper Review, 30*, 61–67. doi:10.1080/02783190701836478

Trebilcox, P. S. (1997). S.O.S.: A gifted class responds. *Gifted Child Today, 20*(5), 42–45.

Willard, D. E. (1984). A "social" social studies model for gifted students. *Teaching Exceptional Children, 17*, 18–22.

# CHAPTER 14

# Affective Curriculum
## Proactively Addressing the Challenges of Growing Up

### Jean Sunde Peterson

## Introduction

Attention to the social and emotional development of gifted children and adolescents in the gifted-education literature is not new. Strang, in 1951, referred to the "mental hygiene" of this population in an edited book, and later noted the emotional conflict related to the intensity of their interaction with the environment. However, it was not until a few decades later that the idea of formally addressing affective concerns gained traction.

The positive conclusions from the Terman (1925) longitudinal study of an intellectually exceptional population likely contributed to the unfortunate myth that gifted individuals need less assistance than others for social and emotional development (Blackburn & Erickson, 1986). Perhaps as a result, attention to well-being within gifted education curriculum was tardy. Both Silverman's *Counseling the Gifted and Talented* (1993) and Hébert's (2011) *Understanding the Social and Emotional Lives of Gifted Students* many years later were exceptions to the lack of consideration of the social and emotional development of gifted students. However, *affective curriculum* has become a familiar phrase. VanTassel-Baska, Cross, and Olenchak's (2009) edited volume is focused on affective curriculum. Cross and Cross's (2012) edited handbook on development, relationships, school issues, and counseling interventions serves to inform that curriculum.

Among pioneers in devising strategies for nurturing social and emotional development were Treffinger, Borgers, Render, and Hoffman (1976), who used the phrase *affective development* in their compendium of techniques and resources. In the 1980s, Webb, Meckstroth, and Tolan's (1982) classic *Guiding the Gifted Child* became an enduring resource. Betts (1986) cited pertinent counseling literature when promoting affective education for gifted youth. However, few models have emerged beyond the Autonomous Learner Model (ALM; Betts & Kercher, 1999) and Peterson's (2008) small-group curriculum. Mendaglio and Peterson's (2007) edited *Models of Counseling Gifted Children, Adolescents, and Young Adults* is geared mostly to mental health counseling and clinical and counseling psychology, not school counseling, although basic tenets apply in schools. Peterson and Lorimer's (2011, 2012) studies are rare in examining students' and teachers' receptivity to the implementation of affective curriculum.

The neglect of affective curriculum may be due to constraints inherent in education for gifted students. Inclusion and emphasis on test-oriented instruction (cf. Adams, 2009; Scot, Callahan, & Urquhart, 2009) can limit time and inclination to address affective (or other) needs of gifted students. Teacher training may not focus sufficiently on these needs either. Gifted students may not be perceived as even having a social-emotional self. Educators may believe that high ability can be applied adequately to meet personal challenges (Broughton, 2006).

# What Is Affective Curriculum?

Affective curriculum is proactive, prevention-oriented, and developmental (VanTassel-Baska, 2009). Regardless of format and target population, it is intended to help children and teens self-reflect, reflect about others, develop positive school relationships, learn expressive language, explore careers, self-regulate, make decisions, and progress with developmental tasks.

## In the Classroom

Affective curriculum for gifted students can be embedded into core academic classroom curriculum, focused on personal response to literature, political leaders' value-laden responses to historical events, moral dilemmas, or feelings related to intense learning, for instance. It can be integrated into cluster-grouping, self-contained classrooms for gifted students, or small pull-out groups. VanTassel-Baska (2009) encouraged self-assessment of beliefs and values, affective insight through books, and writing about emotions. Hébert and Hammond (2006) recommended using film to generate discussion of social and emotional development and concerns. Themes in embedded components might be sustained across grade levels. However, if such curriculum occurs only in advanced classes, some gifted students will not have access to it, as discussed here later.

Truncated examples of how social and emotional development can be embedded into existing curriculum follow. The first five were created by preservice and veteran teachers enrolled in a university course focused on the social and emotional development of gifted students. Some components from Peterson's (2008) affective curriculum for adolescents were adapted for young age levels for some of the plans.

**Grade 1, language arts: When "bad" happens.** Materials were a book, *A Chair for My Mother* (Williams, 1982), a paper "mood meter" to color, and a "My Story" activity adapted from Peterson (2008, p. 77). Engagement involved discussion about "hard times" in the book, how class members "made it through" stressful times, feelings during the shared stories, and "what to remember when something bad happens."

**Grades 1–3, language arts: Anger.** Materials were *The Day Leo Said I HATE YOU!* (Harris, 2008) and a worksheet. Engagement involved discussion of the main book character's feelings of anger and hurtful behaviors, as well as the worksheet (i.e., situations provoking anger and responses); discussion groups with 3–4 children each; whole-class discussion of coping, self-calming, "stuffing" anger; and creating a poem, song, skit, comic strip, or poster about anger.

**Grade 4, language arts: Relationships.** Material was the film *Wide Awake* (Konrad, Woods, & Shyamalan, 1998). The rationale referred to loss, forgiveness, and friendship. Objectives were related to self-understanding, strong feelings, and identifying the main character's feelings. Engagement involved journaling (not shared) about a favorite family member and discussion about "influencers," asking for help, and adults who help.

**Grade 7, health/language arts: Stress (two classes, two teachers collaborating).** Materials were a book about stress, *Don't Sweat the Small Stuff for Teens: Simple Ways to Keep Your Cool in Stressful Times* (Carlson, 2000) and a worksheet about sensitivity (Peterson, 2008, p. 98). Engagement involved discussing how stress affects performance, mood, and attitudes; how sensitivity (associated with giftedness) can increase stress level; and coping with feeling overwhelmed. Students listed personal stressors, identified the top three, and wrote a paragraph about coping.

**Grades 11–12, writing: Disordered eating.** Materials were online resources, a persuasive essay organizer, and citation format. Engagement involved researching, whole-group discussion using Peterson's (2008) suggestions for questioning, using the organizer to formulate arguments, and writing a letter to self or someone else (read aloud to a small group in class).

**Grade 8, gifted classroom: Identity development/Perspective taking.** Materials included a career assessment; information about college majors; two field trips (one to a nearby eldercare facility to listen and learn from the residents, adjusting language and pace accordingly, and the other to an advanced auto-mechanics class at a nearby school to observe sophisticated digitical automotive tehnology, in order to promote respect for undervalued intelligences); a speaker about the mental health of adolescents; "career panels" (e.g., adults who had changed careers, women and men in gender-untypical careers, adults in unfamiliar science careers); official materials for Future Problem Solving (FPS) competitions; and moral-dilemma scenarios. Engagement was in the form of either FPS participation or filmmaking (student choice), policy debates, and activities related to moral dilemmas, learning styles, writing and research, and weekly small-group discussion.

**Grade 10, language arts: Novel.** Materials in this course for above-average (including gifted) students were four required and three self-selected novels, a vocabulary program based on the required novels, and documentary films and community speakers to give context to the novels. Engagement involved choice of one of four options for an analytical paper at the end of each unit, with latitude for breadth and depth within length limits. In addition, two weekly journal pages (not intended to be personal narratives) responding to readings were not evaluated, but instead allowed written dialogue between students and teacher. Students could, for example, react to a character's choices and change, offer an insight, or comment about their own emotional responses. The films, speakers, journals, and study of vocabulary essentially replaced teacher presentations and oral discussion. Students felt heard, and their discussion of their own and characters' social and emotional development was open-ended. Pertinent here, gifted students were free to immerse themselves in literature at their preferred pace, pursue other works by an author on their own, and gain skills in self-reflection and writing with no "ceiling" (see Peterson, 1981, for a more thorough description of this approach).

## Outside of the Usual Curriculum

Stand-alone affective curriculum can help a pull-out program embrace the whole child and increase participation of gifted students uncomfortable with advanced classes at a particular developmental stage. Some may begin to feel connected to intellectual peers—and to school.

Actually, a broad range of highly capable students can be involved, including stellar leaders in talent areas and academics. Arranging to borrow 10 minutes from the preceding or next class might make a homeroom or lunch period long enough for substantive, semistructured discussion about development, perhaps initially cofacilitated by a school counselor and a gifted education teacher. Because counselor preparation typically gives scant, if any, attention to gifted youth as a special population (Peterson & Wachter, 2010), the teacher might share information about giftedness. The counselor might share resource catalogs and model basic listening skills.

It is usually appropriate to inform parents when affective curriculum will be implemented, regardless of format, with topics listed and purpose clearly articulated. Reference to the connection between positive relationships in school and academic success might be part of the rationale. Parents' distrust or uneasiness might be assuaged by this kind of information.

**Discussion groups.** Small groups might be formed for topic-focused discussion and activities with prevention in mind (i.e., not organized as an intervention for a problem shared by all members). A quiet, comfortable, private, uninterrupted space is best, with developmentally appropriate meeting length. Group size should be conducive to building trust, giving each member opportunity to speak, and generating social information. Ideal size is 3–4 for primary-level groups, 4–5 for intermediate level, 6–7 for middle school, and no more than 8 for high school. When larger group size is unavoidable, discussions are likely to resemble the whole-classroom guidance lessons that elementary-level counselors often conduct, valuable in a different way. Regardless, organizing a series of weekly meetings for one or more groups (e.g., for 6–12 weeks), and then organizing new groups for a new series, can ultimately give many students a rare small-group experience. However, context often determines how long groups continue.

For several years, the Purdue Gifted Education Resource Institute (GERI) summer commuter and residential programs have included an affective curriculum in the form of small-group discussion. Young adults, after a few hours of training and with debriefings then interspersed, facilitate the discussions. The rationale for this curriculum refers to developing expressive language, affirming personal strengths, nurturing identity development, normalizing feelings and developmental challenges, and making social connections. Suggested topics for the discussions, by grade level, follow here.

***Kindergarten through grade 4.*** Differentiated across this age range, a "rhythm game," in which clapping and remembering one's own and another's "label" (aligned with the topic of the day, such as worries, strengths, coping strategies) requires concentration. Other topics and activities include 13 intelligences, personality "parts," changes, a future self-portrait, stress, relaxation, self-talk, tossing a paper airplane with worries written on it, a My Story adaptation (see Peterson, 2008, p. 77), perfectionism, and assessing moods and mood range with an "emotional thermometer."

***Grades 5–6.*** Sample topic titles are Best Advice, Influencers, Uniquenesses and Similarities, Personal Strengths and Limitations, Change, Bullying, Intelligence, Needs, Resumé, Finding Satisfaction, and Having Fun. See *The Essential Guide to Talking With Gifted Teens* (Peterson, 2008) for additional topic details.

***Grades 7–8.*** The 13 intelligences, mood range, and stress topics are revisited. Added are Fear, Worry, Anger, Encouragers and Discouragers, Maturity, Values, Change and Loss, Family Roles, College, Future Lifestyle, and Gender Expectations.

***High school.*** Some earlier topics are revisited in new formats. Sample topics are Do the Stereotypes Fit, What Defines Us, Sensitivity, Perfectionism, Permission, Rating My Self-Esteem, Influencers, Competition, Compliments, My Story, College, Choosing a Career, Moods, Small Talk, Needs, Satisfaction, and Leaving Home.

*Other topics.* In small-group work, the content comes from group members, facilitated by the adult leader, who avoids a didactic posture. However, gifted youth may welcome information that helps them make sense of themselves. Therefore, after members explore a topic such as those above, they might welcome psychoeducational information, with discussion—about intelligence, the concept of "flow" (Csikszentmihalyi, 1996), resilience (Higgins, 1994), perfectionism (Greenspon, 2000), Dabrowski's theory of positive disintegration (see Mendaglio, 2008), learning styles (Samardzija & Peterson, 2015), depression (Jackson & Peterson, 2003), and the impact of negative (Peterson, Duncan, & Canady, 2009) and positive (Peterson, Canady, & Duncan, 2012) life events, for example. VanTassel-Baska (2009) advocated for information about, and exploration of, emotional intelligence.

# For Whom Is Affective Curriculum Appropriate?

Affective curriculum is appropriate for a broad range of gifted students across cultural groups, socioeconomic strata, talent domains, personality types, school social groups, and motivation levels. Actually, self-reflection related to development can be a social leveler; because it is unlikely that anyone excels in this realm in a competitive, hierarchic sense. High achievers, underachievers, superstars, risk-takers, risk-avoiders, bullies, trauma survivors, and students who are shy, twice-exceptional, or socially, economically, or culturally marginalized usually find common ground—including that giftedness is paradoxically both an asset and burden (Peterson, 2012). High achievers might be amazed and humbled by underachievers' insights and skills with expressive language, realizing that they themselves need practice. Affective curriculum can help to increase respect for otherwise unacknowledged gifted peers.

Supported by scholarships, young gifted children from low-income families were approximately 18% of the total population in the GERI commuter program at one point. Learning and social experiences were similar, regardless of economic status (Miller & Gentry, 2010). School counselors who were hired to lead the affective curriculum and assist in the classrooms made similar observations (Peterson, 2013).

# What Affective Curriculum Is Not

Affective curriculum is likely to be "therapeutic" (i.e., contributing to well-being), but is not intended to be "therapy." Yet it is appropriate for students with significant problems, because, like anyone else, they are developing. Distress may, in fact, be ameliorated by noncompetitive, non-evaluative interaction with peers and a caring, trustworthy adult. *All* students have concerns that might be diminished through listening, talking, feedback, and connection. However, not all problems are obvious. This curriculum offers a place to reflect, even silently, on concerns.

School personnel who are not trained counselors or psychologists can deliver affective curriculum. In fact, the Peterson (2008) group curriculum was created for either counselors or teachers. However, teachers should not present themselves as counselors, because then they have commensurate liability. It is also inappropriate for them to engage in cause-effect speculation about behavior, "diagnosing," or approaches for which they are not trained.

# Self-Aware Teachers

School personnel who are involved in affective curriculum, including those whose classes students leave to participate in it, should self-reflect and self-monitor. They may have complex biases about high achievers or underachievers, based on their own school experiences. Adults who facilitate discussions may suddenly feel intimidated, envious, or competitive with one or more students. To be in awe of gifted students is also not beneficial. When teachers, counselors, and parents are highly impressed, a student may not feel permission to show limitations, needs, concerns, or distress—potentially life threatening in a crisis. Ideally, invested adults recognize that even the most capable students have doubts, fears, uneasiness, and sadness.

# Assumptions

When planning to implement affective curriculum in some format, the following assumptions offer guidance. They argue for, and can inform, affective curriculum.

## Gifted Students Are Socially and Emotionally Complex

High expectations (Greenspon, 2000) and protection of public image (Peterson et al., 2009; Peterson & Rischar, 2000) may contribute to stress. Bullying (Peterson & Ray, 2006a), anxiety about sexual orientation (Peterson & Rischar, 2000), or unsettling existential questions (Webb et al., 1982) may add layers of concern. Peterson (2000) found social challenges and leaving home to be major concerns for gifted graduates. In the Mendaglio and Peterson (2007) book, clinical professionals reported a wide range of presenting issues, most of them pertinent to the school years: underachievement, depression, adjustment to life events, perfectionism, social difficulties, learning disabilities, isolation, substance abuse, sexual-orientation and sexual-identity issues, relationship difficulties, thought disorders, and oppositional defiance. Hébert (2001), studying bright, underachieving urban male students, learned about problems at home, negative peer pressure, poor organization, unsuitable and ineffective coping, procrastination, and mismatched learning and teaching styles. In the study of life events and stress (Peterson et al., 2009), the most passionate comments were about social challenges. However, the greatest stressors were related to academics, activities, and college decisions. Regular (perhaps weekly) discussion in a small group fairly homogeneous in ability can affirm and normalize this complexity, generate genuine connections with peers, and be a safe and noncompetitive place to talk about challenges related to growing up.

## Gifted Youth May Be at Risk for Poor Personal and Educational Outcomes

Most highly able students are likely do well personally and academically during the school years and beyond. However, future performance and well-being for both high achievers and underachievers are difficult to predict (Peterson, 2000, 2001a, 2001b, 2002). Some mental health concerns may not be apparent until young adulthood. Depression may be a challenge during the school years, but be hidden by skilled self-presentation (Jackson & Peterson, 2003; Peterson & Ray, 2006a; Peterson & Rischar, 2000). When a school shooter is identified as highly intelligent, or suicide by a gifted student shocks a community, or a promising graduate performs poorly in college, or a gifted young adult is exposed as a dangerous political radical, educators and parents may be reminded that no societal strata are immune. These are extreme outcomes. A "poor outcome," in the view of some, might instead be simply disappointing invested adults. Regardless, a substantive affective curriculum can at least be a venue for self-reflection during the formative school years. Small-group discussion, here, too, can help gifted kids develop expressive language, receive personal feedback, anticipate change, learn about individual strengths, and be appreciated as unique. Such an experience might help them be resilient when facing setbacks and disappointment.

## Gifted Students May Have Difficult Life Circumstances

Any health concern, accident, tragedy, death or other loss, and family dysfunction are possible for gifted kids, even in seemingly ideal circumstances. In the study of life events (Peterson et al., 2009), parents of 91 students who generally fit common positive stereotypes related to giftedness (e.g., high achievement, middle-to-upper-class socioeconomic status, dominant culture) reported the following on an annual checklist: death (94) or serious illness (77) in the extended family, new or chronic serious illness in the family (13) or a major health change in the student (7), a major family-structure change (13), a "scary" accident (10), death of a friend (6), parental incarceration (5), fault in a car accident (4), mental illness in self (2), and family financial reversal (2), for example. A national study of bullying of and by eighth graders identified as gifted (Peterson & Ray, 2006b) revealed that 67% had been bullied in at least one of 13 listed ways between kindergarten and grade 8, with the percentage steadily increasing. In a study of 30 successful adults who had been underachievers during adolescence, motivation to achieve was often delayed until late college or beyond, coinciding with developmental task accomplishments.

A longitudinal study of a gifted student leader who survived multiple traumas (Peterson, 2012) revealed that characteristics associated with giftedness both helped and hindered as she struggled with identity, direction, peer relationships, autonomy, domestic violence, sexual abuse, ostracism, harassment, and an abusive boyfriend. In studies of six gifted females in high-stress circumstances (Peterson, 1998), 11 bright middle school students at high risk for poor outcomes (Peterson, 1997), and 14 at-risk gifted young adults postgraduation (Peterson, 2002), some were high achievers, seeming to pour energy into achievement to maintain control of one aspect of an otherwise chaotic life. One of the six females was class valedictorian, but was the caregiver of siblings in a complicated home affected by substance abuse.

Affective curriculum, especially in the form of small groups, can help students like these, and their more advantaged peers as well, connect positively with each other about nonacademic, nonextracurricular life, regardless of whether they reveal their personal circumstances. For some, simply having a positive, noncompetitive social outlet in school may balance high-stress situations elsewhere. Affective components in the regular classroom can also acknowledge social and emotional aspects of learning, emotional complexities in biographies, and psychology reflected in fiction, for instance, all of which might help to normalize developmental struggles and offer hope in difficult circumstances.

## Gifted Students May Not Seek Help, Even When in Distress

Wood (2010) noted that little is known about whether and how much school counselors work with gifted students. Because some may believe that the counselors are for *other* kids (Peterson, 1990), gifted adolescents may approach them only for recommendation letters or scheduling. They may also believe they should be able to solve their own problems. In addition, they may have valid concerns that no one can understand them (Yermish, 2010). When teachers embrace affective curriculum, students may view them as concerned and compassionate—and trustworthy. Then distressed students may feel comfortable approaching them for help.

## Gifted Youth Face Common Developmental Tasks, But Experience Them Differently

Gifted youth face the same general developmental tasks as anyone else their age. However, heightened sensitivity to environmental stimuli (Mendaglio, 1995), intensity (Daniels & Piechowski, 2009), asynchronous development (Alsop, 2003), stress from expectations (Peterson et al., 2009), overexcitabilities (Piechowski, 1999), perfectionistic tendencies (Neumeister & Finch, 2006), and interpersonal challenges because of extreme ability levels (Gross, 2004) differentially affect how gifted youth *experience* development (Peterson, 2009b). That reality can be discussed in an affective curriculum: providing important psychoeducational information *about* development to help gifted kids make sense of themselves.

When gifted youth are preoccupied with the future, affective curriculum can help them focus on thoughts and feelings in the present (Peterson, 2009a). Learning how to verbalize feelings "in the now," including intense emotions, may enhance current and future relationships. The curriculum can also help to reduce anxiety about the future. In a classroom or a small group, discussion about college and career development can focus on self-assessment instead of on career decision-making, as identity is central to career development (Hébert & Kelly, 2006).

## Gifted Youth May Struggle With Developmental Tasks

Developmental tasks are related to identity, direction, relationships, autonomy, and competence, among several challenges (cf. Erikson, 1968; Marcia, 1993; Vondracek, Lerner, & Schulenberg, 1986). Both high achievers and underachievers may struggle with these. High achievers may foreclose prematurely on a career because of family pressure (Hébert & Kelly, 2006) or because of low tolerance of ambiguity, without considering the fit of the career with personality, interests, needs, and values. These achievers may also not have much sense of self beyond academic performance, and extended education might delay autonomy. Underachievers may explore identity more actively, focusing intensely on peer relationships. A low sense of competence and direction (Peterson, 2001b, 2002) and lack of goals may interfere with motivation to achieve academically, although it should not be assumed that underachievers have a poor academic self-concept (McCoach & Siegle, 2003).

Considering development might help invested adults meet underachievers "where they are" (Peterson, 2009a), embrace their complexity, and not be preoccupied with fixing them. Formal and informal conversations about development, per se, can be rare for gifted children and teens otherwise.

Gifted youth will not always be as they are during the school years. Researchers have shown that underachievers can change (Emerick, 1992; Peterson, 2000, 2001a, 2001b; Peterson & Colangelo, 1996), perhaps as circumstances change or developmental tasks are accomplished. High achievers may also change (Grobman, 2006; Peterson, 2000). Without affective curriculum, neither may have opportunities for dialogue about development.

## Gifted Students May Not Be Referred Because They Do Not Demonstrate "Gifted Behaviors"

In a study of the oral referral language of dominant-culture middle-school teachers as they nominated students for a hypothetical program for gifted youth (Peterson & Margolin, 1997), verbal strengths, organization skills, knowledge, production, eagerness to learn, academic achievement, competitiveness, perfection, winning, and domain-specific strengths were valued and needed to be demonstrated. Behavior, verbal ability and verbal assertiveness, family status, work ethic, and social skills were actually their main themes, with implications for children who do not fit common stereotypes of giftedness.

In a follow-up study (Peterson, 1999), when adults in five U.S. minority cultures (African American, Latino, Southeast Asian, American Indian, low-income White) were asked to nominate "the most gifted" individuals they had known, none of the behaviors the dominant-culture teachers valued were mentioned. In fact, humility was highly valued by Latino interviewees, and "not standing out" was a value of American Indians. Helping others, artistic expression, and wisdom (in contrast to knowledge) were other themes that differed from those of the teachers.

Not being referred and selected for a program has social and emotional implications for students with high ability. If they are denied access to program elements or if their quietness in the classroom is viewed as lack of ability, for example, they may miss information important to their sense of self as well as opportunities to develop interests and skills through interaction with intellectual peers. An affective curriculum, with discussion about the universals of human development in large or small groups, can break down barriers among cultures and social and economic groups, help students be known beyond performance or nonperformance, help them demonstrate strengths more comfortably than when showing knowledge overtly and competitively, and provide opportunities to learn *from* each other.

# Listening and Responding Skills

Basic listening and responding skills are important in both whole-classroom and small-group affective curriculum—and not just because teachers are expected to facilitate discussion. If educators show interest in the internal world of gifted youth, they may be viewed as safe to confide in, individually, outside of the class or group, when life circumstances feel dire. At such times, when the adult is in a position of power, the focus should be on the speaker(s), not on the listener. It is helpful to have some guidelines for how to be, what to say, and what to do. Some gifted education teachers arrange initially to facilitate small-group discussion collaboratively with a school counselor in order to observe how the latter responds, asks questions, and behaves in a nondidactic manner. However, some rudimentary skills and general guidelines can support any adult in a nonpeer position with youth, gifted or not gifted. When appropriate, teachers in the classroom can use these admonitions to move nimbly out of an informing posture ("one-up") and into a "teach-me" mode ("one-down"), during which students inform each other *and* the adult about how they are experiencing a particular stage of development. The same guidelines apply particularly during small-group discussion. Regardless of context, the students benefit. Some guidelines are summarized next.

In general, effective listeners convey that they are attentive, focused on the speaker, not distracted, and not self-absorbed. The following are several ways to show attention and hearing.

1. **Nonverbals.** The listener communicates with face and body (e.g., leaning forward slightly; facing the speaker, with arms unfolded; using eyes, eyebrows, frowning, mouth position, facial expressions), trusting that these can be eloquent in themselves. Monosyllabic "encouragers" (e.g., "mmm," "wow," "um-hum") fit into this category.

2. **Reflecting feelings.** The listener makes statements that capture one or more feelings being conveyed by the speaker, including naming the feeling (e.g., "That sounds frustrating/sad/unsettling/disappointing/hurtful"; "It makes sense that you felt hurt").

3. **Checking for accuracy.** In addition to nonverbals and reflection of feelings, the listener might hold up a hand, with palm facing outward, and say, "I want to make sure I'm getting this. You went . . . and then you . . . ? Is that correct?"

4. **Paraphrasing and/or asking for more.** In addition to the above, the listener might show understanding by summarizing what the speaker has said (e.g., "So what I'm understanding is that you . . . " [one or two short sentences only] and, if appropriate, "I'd like to hear more about that").

5. **Open-ended questions.** Closed questions, beginning with "small words" (e.g., *Do/Did/Does; Has/Have/Had; Is/Are/Was/Were*), often lead to just *yes* or *no* responses. In contrast, questions or statements beginning with *When, Who, How, How much, What, Tell me more about,* or *Help me understand* are more optimal. Actually, statements are often more effective than questions for generating discussion. Questions reflect the listener's agenda, not the speaker's. The goal is to *facilitate* conversation, not control it.

The following are some general imperatives for listeners:

◆ Focus on listening. When uncertain, focus more intently on listening and maybe just nod.

◆ Don't assume you know what you need to know. Give away some power. It's OK to "be clueless," a nonexpert.

◆ Respond with statements. ("That sounds hard." "That makes sense." "I'm so sorry to hear that." "Many kids your age don't have a career in mind." "You've had a rough week.")

◆ Accept, calmly and with poise, what is said—no matter what it is. Your poise tells them it *is* OK to speak about it. Your seeming uncomfortable may confirm that it is *not* OK.

◆ Don't be afraid of their feelings. Don't be upset by tears. Just give them a tissue.

◆ Don't be afraid of pauses. Silence may help them organize thoughts or stay calm.

◆ Be nonjudgmental. Let them talk. Accept what they say as important from their perspective. If they are talking nonstop, and if time is a concern, apply #2, #3, and #4 above in order to stop the narrative and nudge the conversation in a different direction.

◆ Don't be preoccupied with accomplishing something specific—a "product."

◆ Don't talk about yourself, even if you once had a similar experience. It's often difficult to move the focus back to them if you do. The interaction is about them, not you.

◆ Don't criticize, preach, judge, shame, blame, give advice, or bombard.

◆ Avoid *should* and *shouldn't* and *why* and *yes, but*.

◆ Don't invalidate their feelings with "That's nothing to be upset about."

◆ Don't say, "I know exactly what you mean," because you don't.

◆ Don't say, "Don't you think it would be better if . . ." Advice can be disempowering.

◆ Don't rescue them. Struggle is not "bad." Focus on validating their unique experience.

◆ Focus on strengths—credibly. ("You're a good problem solver." "You're observant." "You know what's important." "You've got the ability to bounce back." "You were smart enough to talk with someone.") Base your comments on what you have observed in them.

◆ Thank them for talking with you.

◆ Be alert to depression, suicidal ideation ("Should I worry about you—that you'll hurt yourself?"), cutting or other self-harm, and thoughts of violence.

It is important that group facilitators *self*-monitor for tendencies such as voyeuristically needing group members to share private information and asking questions accordingly. Students are usually discreet. However, if someone shares information that raises concerns, the facilitator can meet privately with the student afterward. A school counselor may need to be consulted—ideally, with the student present.

If a semi-structured curriculum is carefully prepared, and if these guidelines are followed, gifted children and teens are likely to be safe. In a group, a semi-structured curriculum has parameters and provides an excuse to return to a topic if someone is straying or dominating. However, because group dynamics and shared information cannot be controlled, at the first small-group meeting leaders should say something like this:

> Because we're going to be talking about growing up, we might hear serious personal comments now and then. It's important to respect privacy. That means we don't talk to anyone outside of the group about what someone says here. We need to trust each other, and we need to be trustworthy ourselves. Following this rule can help make your group special. I, too, will not talk with anyone else about what is said, but, if I sense, or if you say, that you are a danger to yourself or to someone else, or if you have experienced abuse or neglect, I must, by law, report that to someone who can help you or someone else be safe. I would talk with you first.

If a group member says something like "I'm going to tell you something I've never told anyone," an alert leader might say to the group (with hand forward, palm out), "Hang on a minute. Remember what we said at our first meeting about trust and privacy? It sounds as if _____ has something serious to say. Are you trustworthy? OK. Do you still want to share this information?" This pause protects the speaker in several ways and slows down and formalizes the moment.

---

## When Affective Curriculum Is Central

In a multifaceted program for gifted adolescents in an urban high school, affective elements were central. In addition to advanced academic classes were approximately 20 other options, with the goal of broadening perspectives. During one of two lunch hours (each including a half-hour study hall), 85% of students involved in the program met weekly in small, stable-membership, age-homogeneous groups to discuss a development-oriented topic. A school counselor and gifted education teacher cofacilitated these for one semester, after 30 students responded to an invitation "for high-ability kids like you to talk about stress from high expectations." Numbers increased to 60, then 90, and then well past 100 by year 4. By the fifth year, 30% of involved students were gifted underachievers, usually found by perusing school files. Most had been identified earlier, but not involved.

Several program components were *indirectly* affective because of purposeful social interaction: Future Problem Solving (FPS) teams; noon-hour philosophy and classical music appreciation classes; afterschool mime and dance groups; poetry writing and sharing before school; collaboration with the art teacher on school and community exhibitions; weekly afterschool lectures by community volunteers (open to any student); one-time, full-day career-shadowing; field trips to interact with engineers; foreign-language and sign-language teaching at elementary schools; and afterschool Chinese and Russian language classes. Underachievers were engaged in all of these.

These options, none requiring class absence, were led by either teachers or unpaid community volunteers. The social benefits were obvious. Activities illuminated career options not previously considered. Career shadowing sometimes led to summer apprenticeships. These gifted adolescents welcomed opportunities to connect with peers about social and emotional development. Teachers commented that the lectures enhanced respect for intellect and learning. Some gave extra credit and attended themselves. Teachers also credited the discussion groups with decreasing arrogance and reminding them that gifted students were not just performers.

# Conclusion

If a program for gifted students is understaffed and underfunded, and only one dimension is possible, an affective curriculum is a worthy option—regardless of grade level. It can address an important common denominator: social, emotional, and career development. Because gifted kids are idiosyncratic in learning preferences, interests, strengths and limitations, personality, life experiences, family situations, stressors, and mental and physical health, no one academic curriculum or approach is likely to be satisfactory or effective with all who have high capability.

Appropriate academic programming is certainly important and should be part of any plan. However, incorporating affective dimensions into classrooms, clusters, nonclass periods, activities before and after school, or pull-out programming is likely to address critical needs of *all* students who are identified as gifted. All are growing up. Interaction for many may otherwise be focused mostly on performance or nonperformance, with neither adults nor age peers embracing the complex whole child. With current and future well-being in mind, affective curriculum needs to respond to that complexity—with open-ended exploration of self, others, and developmental tasks. A good affective curriculum may even help gifted kids be more competent and effective as parents, spouses/partners, leaders, employers, employees, and friends in the future.

# References

Adams, C. M. (2009). Waiting for Santa Claus. *Gifted Child Quarterly, 53,* 272–273.

Alsop, G. (2003). Asynchrony: Intuitively valid and theoretically reliable. *Roeper Review, 25,* 118–127.

Betts, G. T. (1986). Development of the emotional and social needs of gifted individuals. *Journal of Counseling & Development, 64,* 587–589.

Betts, G. T., & Kercher, J. K. (1999). *Autonomous learner model: Optimizing ability.* Greely, CO: ALPS Publishing.

Blackburn, A. C., & Erickson, D. B. (1986). Predictable crises of the gifted student. *Journal of Counseling & Development, 64,* 552–555.

Broughton, L. S. (2006). Training elements of elementary teachers in social and emotional development of gifted students. *Dissertation Abstracts International, 66(9A),* 3207.

Carlson, R. (2000). *Don't sweat the small stuff for teens: Simple ways to keep your cool in stressful times.* New York, NY: Hatchette Books.

Cross, T. L., & Cross, J. R. (2012). *Handbook for counselors serving students with gifts and talents.* Waco, TX: Prufrock Press.

Csikszentmihalyi, M. (1996). *Creativity: Flow and the psychology of discovery and invention.* New York, NY: Harper Perennial.

Daniels, S., & Piechowski, M. M. (2009). *Living with intensity: Understanding the sensitivity, excitability and emotional development of gifted children, adolescents and adults.* Scottsdale, AZ: Great Potential Press.

Emerick, L. J. (1992). Academic underachievement among the gifted: Students' perceptions of factors that reverse the pattern. *Gifted Child Quarterly, 36,* 140–146.

Erikson, E. H. (1968). *Youth and crisis.* New York, NY: Norton.

Greenspon, T. S. (2000). Healthy perfectionism is an oxymoron! Reflections on the psychology of perfectionism and the sociology of science. *Journal of Secondary Gifted Education, 11,* 197–208.

Grobman, J. (2006). Underachievement in exceptionally gifted adolescents and young adults: A psychiatrist's view. *Journal of Secondary Gifted Education, 17,* 199–210.

Gross, M. U. M. (2004). *Exceptionally gifted children* (2nd ed.). London, England: Routledge Falmer.

Harris, R. (2008). *The day Leo said I hate you.* New York, NY: Little Brown & Company.

Hébert, T. P. (2001). "If I had a new notebook, I know things would change": Bright underachieving young men in urban classrooms. *Gifted Child Quarterly, 45,* 174–194.

Hébert, T. P. (2011). *Understanding the social and emotional lives of gifted students.* Waco, TX: Prufrock Press.

Hébert, T. P., & Hammond, D. R. (2006). Guided viewing of film with gifted students: Resources for educators and counselors. *Gifted Child Today, 29*(3), 14–27.

Hébert, T. P., & Kelly, K. R. (2006). Identity and career development in gifted students. In F. A. Dixon & S. M. Moon (Eds.), *The handbook of secondary gifted education* (pp. 35–64). Waco, TX: Prufrock Press.

Higgins, G. O. C. (1994). *Resilient adults: Overcoming a cruel past.* San Francisco, CA: Jossey-Bass.

Jackson, P. S., & Peterson, J. S. (2003). Depressive disorder in highly gifted adolescents. *Journal for Secondary Gifted Education, 14,* 175–186.

Konrad, C. & Woods, C. (Producers) & Shyamalan, M. N. (Director). (1989). *Wide awake* [Motion picture]. USA: Woods Entertainment.

Marcia, J. E. (1993). The ego identity status approach to ego identity. In J. E. Marcia, A. S. Waterman, D. R. Matteson, S. L. Archer, & J. L. Orlofsky

(Eds.), *Ego identity: A handbook for psychological research* (pp. 3–21). New York, NY: Springer-Verlag.

McCoach, D. B., & Siegle, D. (2003). Factors that differentiate underachieving gifted students from high-achieving gifted students. *Gifted Child Quarterly, 47,* 144–154.

Mendaglio, S. (1995). Sensitivity among gifted persons: A multi-faceted perspective. *Roeper Review, 17,* 169–172.

Mendaglio, S. (2008). Dabrowski's theory of positive disintegration: A personality theory for the 21st century. In S. Mendaglio (Ed.), *Dabrowski's theory of positive disintegration* (pp. 13–40). Scottsdale, AZ: Great Potential Press.

Mendaglio, S., & Peterson, J. S. (2007). *Models of counseling gifted children, adolescents, and young adults.* Waco, TX: Prufrock Press.

Miller, R., & Gentry, M. (2010). Developing talents among high-potential students from low-income families in an out-of-school enrichment program. *Journal of Advanced Academics, 21,* 594–627.

Neumeister, K. L. S., & Finch, H. (2006). Perfectionism in high-ability students: Relational precursors and influences on achievement motivation. *Gifted Child Quarterly, 50,* 238–250. Retrieved from http://dx.doi.org/10.1177/001698620605000304

Peterson, J. S. (1981). *Teaching the novel: Mainstreaming the gifted and jet-streaming the average.* (ERIC Document Reproduction Service No. ED199764)

Peterson, J. S. (1990). Noon-hour discussion groups: Dealing with the burdens of capability. *Gifted Child Today, 13*(4), 17–22.

Peterson, J. S. (1997). Bright, troubled, and resilient, and not in a gifted program. *Journal of Secondary Gifted Education, 8,* 121–136.

Peterson, J. S. (1998). Six exceptional young women at risk. *Reclaiming Children and Youth, 6,* 233–238.

Peterson, J. S. (1999). Gifted—through whose cultural lens? An application of the postpositivistic mode of inquiry. *Journal for the Education of the Gifted, 22,* 354–383.

Peterson, J. S. (2000). A follow-up study of one group of achievers and underachievers four years after high school graduation. *Roeper Review, 22,* 217–224.

Peterson, J. S. (2001a). Gifted and at risk: Four longitudinal case studies. *Roeper Review, 24,* 31–39.

Peterson, J. S. (2001b). Successful adults who were once adolescent underachievers. *Gifted Child Quarterly, 45,* 236–249.

Peterson, J. S. (2002). A longitudinal study of post-high-school development in gifted individuals at risk for poor educational outcomes. *Journal for Secondary Gifted Education, 14,* 6–18.

Peterson, J. S. (2008). *The essential guide for talking with gifted teens.* Minneapolis, MN: Free Spirit.

Peterson, J. S. (2009a). Focusing on where they are: A clinical perspective. In J. VanTassel-Baska, T. R. Cross, & R. Olenchak (Eds.) *Social-emotional curriculum with gifted and talented students* (pp. 193–226). Waco, TX: Prufrock Press.

Peterson, J. S. (2009b). Myth 17: Gifted and talented individuals do not have unique social and emotional needs. *Gifted Child Quarterly, 53,* 280–282.

Peterson, J. S. (2012). The asset-burden paradox of giftedness: A 15-year phenomenological, longitudinal case study. *Roeper Review, 34,* 1–17.

Peterson, J. S. (2013). School counselors' experiences with children from low-income families and other gifted children in a summer program. *Professional School Counseling, 16,* 194–204.

Peterson, J. S., & Colangelo, N. (1996). Gifted achievers and underachievers: A comparison of patterns found in school files. *Journal of Counseling and Development, 74,* 399–407.

Peterson, J. S., Canady, K., & Duncan, N. (2012). Positive life experiences: A qualitative, cross-sectional, longitudinal study of gifted graduates. *Journal for the Education of the Gifted, 35,* 81–89.

Peterson, J. S., Duncan, N., & Canady, K. (2009). A longitudinal study of negative life events, stress, and school experiences of gifted youth. *Gifted Child Quarterly, 53,* 34–49.

Peterson, J. S., & Lorimer, M. R. (2011). Student response to a small-group affective curriculum in a school for gifted children. *Gifted Child Quarterly, 55,* 167–180.

Peterson, J. S., & Lorimer, M. R. (2012). Small-group affective curriculum for gifted students: A Longitudinal Study of teacher-facilitators. *Roeper Review, 34,* 158–169.

Peterson, J. S., & Margolin, L. (1997). Naming gifted children: An example of unintended "reproduction." *Journal for the Education of the Gifted, 21,* 82–100.

Peterson, J. S., & Ray, K. E. (2006a). Bullying among the gifted: The subjective experience. *Gifted Child Quarterly, 50,* 252–269.

Peterson, J. S., & Ray, K. E. (2006b). Bullying and the gifted: Victims, perpetrators, prevalence, and effects. *Gifted Child Quarterly, 50,* 148–168.

Peterson, J. S., & Rischar, H. (2000). Gifted and gay: A study of the adolescent experience. *Gifted Child Quarterly, 44,* 149–164.

Peterson, J. S., & Wachter, C. A. (2010). Understanding and responding to concerns related to giftedness: A study of CACREP-accredited programs. *Journal for Education of the Gifted, 33,* 311–336.

Piechowski, M. M. (1999). Overexcitabilities. In M. A. Runco & S. R. Pfirtzker (Eds.), *Encyclopedia of creativity* (Vol. 2, pp. 325–334). San Diego, CA: Academic Press.

Samardzija, N., & Peterson, J. S. (2015). Learning styles and classroom preferences of gifted eighth graders: A qualitative study. *Journal for the Education of the Gifted, 38,* 233–256.

Scot, T. P., Callahan, C. M., & Urquhart, J. (2009). Paint-by-number teachers and cookie-cutter students: The unintended effects of high-stakes testing on the education of gifted students. *Roeper Review, 31,* 40–52.

Silverman, L. K. (Ed.). (1993). *Counseling the gifted and talented.* Denver, CO: Love Publishing.

Strang, R. (1951). Mental hygiene of gifted children. In P. Witty (Ed.), *The gifted child* (pp. 131–162). Boston, MA: Heath.

Terman, L. M. (1925). *Genetic studies of genius, Vol. 1: Mental and physical traits of a thousand gifted children.* Stanford, CA: Stanford University Press.

Treffinger, D. J., Borgers, S. B., Render, G. F., & Hoffman, R. M. (1976). Encouraging affective development: A compendium of techniques and resources. *Gifted Child Quarterly, 20,* 47–65.

VanTassel-Baska, J. (2009). Affective curriculum and instruction for gifted learners. In J. L. VanTassel-Baska, T. L. Cross, & F. R. Olenchak (Eds.). *Social-emotional curriculum with gifted and talented students* (pp. 113–132). Waco, TX: Prufrock Press.

VanTassel-Baska, J. L., Cross, T. L., & Olenchak, F. R. (2009). *Social-emotional curriculum with gifted and talented students.* Waco, TX: Prufrock Press.

Vondracek, F. W., Lerner, R. M., & Schulenberg, J. E. (1986). *Career development: A life-span developmental approach.* Hillsdale, NJ: Lawrence Erlbaum Associates.

Webb, J. T., Meckstroth, E. A., & Tolan, S. S. (1982). *Guiding the gifted child: A practical source for parents and teachers.* Dayton, OH: Ohio Psychology Press.

Williams, V. B. (1982). *A chair for my mother.* New York, NY: Greenwillow Books.

Wood, S. M. (2010). Nurturing a garden: A qualitative investigation into school counselors' experiences with gifted students. *Journal for the Education of the Gifted, 34,* 261–302.

Yermish, A. (2010). *Cheetahs on the couch: Issues affecting the therapeutic working alliance with clients who are cognitively gifted.* ProQuest Dissertations and Theses Database (UMI NO. 3415722)

# CHAPTER 15

# Culturally Responsive and Relevant Curriculum

## *The Revised Bloom-Banks Matrix*

**Donna Y. Ford and Michelle Frazier Trotman Scott**

## Introduction

African American and Hispanic students are underrepresented in gifted education. And in general, many are underachieving in schools partly due to a lack of interest personally and culturally in the content and topics being taught. This chapter briefly discusses the underrepresentation of African American and Hispanic students in gifted programs, and then hones in on curricula and program challenges, issues, and needs using Bloom's taxonomy and Banks' multicultural curriculum model. The chapter merges these two models and provides a discussion of the revised Ford-Harris Matrix (Ford, 2011) also known as the revised Bloom-Banks Matrix, and describes a color-coded layout of the matrix modified by

Trotman Scott (2014a, 2014b) accompanied by pros and cons of certain components of the matrix.

Michael (a pseudonym) is a fifth-grade African American student at Johnson Elementary School in Georgia. He lives with his mother and interacts frequently with his father who lives in Texas. Michael is a young fifth grader who turned 10 in October. Michael enrolled in kindergarten when he was 4 years old because he attended a private school and faired well in school, earning A's and B's in most of his academic classes.

According to his mother, Shannon, Michael does not exhibit age-appropriate behaviors. As a matter of fact, Michael receives low scores in behavior conduct from his teachers—all of whom are White. Although his work is satisfactory, it tends to be sloppy and at times is not turned in. Shannon has observed his interactions with peers and describes his behavior as selfish or self-centered. She attributes this behavior to him being a "spoiled only child." However, his mother does not consider Michael's behavior disrespectful, disobedient, or defiant.

Shannon was pleased with her son's scholastic progress until he entered third grade; at that time, he was placed with a White female teacher entering her first year in the profession. The novice teacher lacked classroom management skills and, according to Michael's mother, the teacher called or e-mailed her at least two times per week with negative reports ranging from Michael not turning in homework to him talking in class and being "overly active." Shannon was upset about this, but her anger turned to indignation and frustration upon learning that several parents of African American students enrolled in this class had received the same types of communication. Nonetheless, she disciplined Michael accordingly (e.g., loss of television, gaming system, and/or music privileges) in her desire to support teachers and improve her son's academic experiences.

Michael is also very athletic and excels in multiple sports. He enjoys interacting with teammates and traveling to related games and activities. Shannon used sports as leverage and has threatened to impose a suspension from extracurricular activities if he did not show more effort and improved behavior (according to his teacher) in class. Yet, Michael's lack of motivation persists. Michael thrives when working on assignments that focus on topics of interest to him. This young student eventually confessed to his mother that he hates school. He does not see himself (a Black male) in the books, stories, and lesson plans in most cases and bemoans that Black History Month and focusing on dead Black heroes are not enough and trouble him. He questions why President Obama is not talked about in his classes and wonders why teachers seem to be uncomfortable talking about Black people and contemporary issues.

There are many students of color like Michael in our classrooms. They show up to school with a canvas ready to be painted with the colors of knowledge, heritage, and power. However, when the paint of knowledge mainly or only consists of one hue, it becomes uninteresting, and for many, the paint is deemed useless or colorless. However, if teachers are equipped with *and use* different colors to show students how to make new colors and/or use different mediums, students like Michael will be eager to learn and engage.

Throughout the nation, African American students are underrepresented in gifted education by almost 50% and Hispanic students by some 40% (Ford, 2010, 2011, 2013). When combined, more than 500,000 Black and Hispanic students are being denied gifted education classes and services. These national statistics are troubling and prevalent in most states and districts.

Teachers must differentiate instruction to meet the needs of gifted students, and differentiation must include consideration of culture. However, it is highly likely that most differentiated content has a monocultural focus, and thus may not peak the interest of those students whose culture is not reflected in the curriculum. The academic performance of gifted students would likely increase if culture was prioritized when differentiating instruction and developing curriculum.

Differentiation is discussed extensively in gifted education, which is a recognition that instruction that may be effective with one student or group of students may also be ineffective or not work as well with another student or group of students. Ineffective instruction leads to poor performance and academic outcomes. Ineffective instruction includes instruction that is not responsive to students' culture and racial identity (Ford, 2011). As such, differentiation via multicultural education holds potential for increasing rigor and relevance for all students, but in particular for gifted Black and Hispanic students, many of whom complain about being disinterested in school and not seeing themselves positively reflected in the literature, materials, and lesson plans (see Ford, 2011; Grantham, Trotman Scott, & Harmon, 2013). Differentiated multicultural education, using the work of Ford who created the original and updated Bloom-Banks Matrix (Ford, 2011; Ford & Harris, 1999), is one means of addressing the needs of all gifted students. With students of color in mind, especially Black and

Hispanic students, the matrix can be used to differentiate instruction to include rigor (Bloom, 1956) *and* relevance (Banks, 2009).

# Differentiation: Rigor and Relevance

All instructional procedures—materials, lectures, daily assignments, summative and formative assessments—should be culturally fair and responsive. Teachers must ensure that assignments and materials accurately, equally, and equitably represent the experiences, realities, and views of culturally different students, and that they do not contain biased, discriminatory, or offensive language, materials, and examples. Only then are we on the essential journey to making sure that instruction is culturally responsive and to increasing the likelihood that gifted students of color, like Michael, are engaged and motivated by what is being taught.

To add relevance and rigor to assignments, multiple levels of outcome criteria must be planned. Gifted students should be provided with critical thinking and problem-solving opportunities that embrace the characteristics of culturally different students, meet their needs, and include culturally responsive practices, theories, and research.

Students become more interested and want to be engaged when the curricula is rigorous and relevant. Disengaged students may begin to underachieve and/or disrupt the class. In some districts, if students underachieve, they may be dismissed from the gifted program; this practice is objectionable because the students are still gifted even if their performance is low. High performance is not the hallmark of being gifted (Ford, 2010). Students, including those who are gifted, underachieve for a host of reasons (e.g., peer pressures, self-efficacy, special education need such as a learning disability, lack of challenge, personal and family transitions, health, and more; Siegle, 2012; Siegle & McCoach, 2005; Whitmore, 1980). Given that they have been identified as gifted but are underperforming, educational professionals must invest in them—not give up on them. If not, the waste of gifts and talents takes its toll on students and society at large (Grantham et al., 2013). A multicultural gifted approach developed by Ford (2011) and Ford and Harris (1999) can be used to increase the interest, engagement, and achievement of gifted students who are disconnected from what they are learning and experiencing in schools.

Much of the curriculum used in typical classrooms fails to represent the population served by teachers. That is, too few schools have adopted multicultural curricula. Moreover, few teacher preparation programs have trained teacher candidates with the necessary skills to create lesson plans that are culturally responsive. The same holds true for professional development opportunities offered to teachers (Ford, 2011).

Selected resources and materials must be carefully examined to ensure that specific cultural groups are not negatively represented, stereotyped, and/or completely omitted from the proposed curriculum (Ford, 2011; Gay, 2010; Ladson-Billings, 2009). The authenticity and integrity of the curriculum content and materials must also be evident to make sure that the roles reflected within the curricula do not promote superiority, inferiority, and/or minimize and trivialize a specific racial and cultural group.

In the following section, Ford's revised Bloom-Banks Matrix is described. To begin with, an overview of the revised Bloom's taxonomy (Krathwohl, 2002) will be addressed followed by Banks' (2009) model of how to infuse rigorous multicultural content into the curriculum for all students.

## Bloom-Banks Matrix: An Overview

When teachers differentiate, the content, process, product, and learning environment are considered in meaningful ways. To successfully or effectively differentiate, teachers must modify the curriculum, instruction, and outcomes to meet the needs of individual and groups of students (Adams & Pierce, 2010; Tomlinson, 2001, 2009); when implemented using a cultural lens, this allows students to master academic content while also addressing their diverse academic, cultural, and learning needs. Cultural diversity or differences are important and must be addressed in a culturally responsive manner. In other words, colorblindness is ineffective for students and fails to promote educational experiences that are rigorous and relevant.

**Rigor and Bloom's taxonomy.** Bloom's taxonomy (original: Bloom, 1956; revised: Krathwohl, 2002) is often used to ensure rigor, meaning, critical thinking, and problem solving are addressed in the curriculum. When teachers use either version of Bloom's taxonomy to differentiate, they adapt activities related to the same academic content based on students' abilities, skills, and readiness to engage in certain cognitive tasks.

Utilizing the cognitive domains of the revised Bloom's taxonomy (Krathwohl, 2002; see Figure 15.1), teachers can: (1) determine if students are able to recall information presented in the curriculum (knowing); (2) assess if students understand the concepts of the curriculum as evidenced by their ability to explain what they learned (understanding); (3) evaluate the students' ability to demonstrate what they learned (applying); (4) gauge students' ability to understand what was learned by being able to form views, make predictions, and compare-contrast information (analyzing); (5) decide if students are able to study, judge, critique, and support what was taught and learned (evaluating); and (6) consider students' ability and skills to use information to develop new, original, and/or improved approaches (creating). Clearly, the first three levels lack rigor (i.e., knowing, understanding, and applying) as opposed to the latter three levels (i.e., analyzing, evaluating, and creating).

In many instances, teachers must rely on the formal curriculum provided by their district. Although Bloom's taxonomy (Bloom, 1956; Krathwohl, 2002) provides teachers with a means to develop differentiated lessons and activities, it does not provide them with the tools needed to infuse multiculturalism at all or in a meaningful way. When teachers differentiate curriculum, they must always infuse multicultural or culturally responsive content. Rigorous content alone is not sufficient. All content must be reflective of the world in which we live and respond to the lives and needs of our students. Banks' (2009) approach to integrating multicultural content into the curriculum allows this to happen, by giving teachers a framework to infuse high-quality diversity content into daily lesson plans, activities, and readings.

**Banks' Multicultural Curriculum Model.** Banks' (2009) multicultural curriculum model addresses four levels (also called approaches) of integration to help Michael and all students increase their level of awareness, enthusiasm, knowledge, and understanding about cultural and racial diversity, as well as attain a sense of social justice (Gay, 2010). This model is useful to teachers and curriculum specialists as they develop a framework for high-quality (rigorous) multicultural lessons. It offers different levels/approaches of integration, ranging from the very simplistic and pervasive contributions approach, an approach in which teachers are not required to change the curriculum and can create and/or reinforce stereotypes and misperceptions about people of color, to the more complex and often

| Level | Meaning and Goal | Sample Action Verbs | Sample Products |
|---|---|---|---|
| Remembering | To remember/recall | List, recall, identify, label, repeat, match, name, outline, select, tell | Exams/tests, reports of facts |
| Understanding | To understand/ comprehend | Describe, recognize, explain, extend, generalize, identify examples, restate, paraphrase, summarize | Diagrams, drawings, outlines |
| Applying | To apply/use | Change, demonstrate, illustrate, interpret operate, predict, prepare, relate, sketch, solve | Demonstrations, models, reports, recipes |
| Analyzing | To analyze/compare | Break down, compare and contrast, categorize, debate, experiment, differentiate, distinguish, examine, illustrate | Venn diagrams, plans or prospectuses, questionnaires, reviews |
| Evaluating | To evaluate/study/ critique | Appraise, conclude, criticize, defend, describe, discriminate, explain, justify, interpret, relate, summarize, support, value | Critiques, decision making, debates, editorials, study |
| Creating | To create/solve problems | Arrange, assemble, collect, combine, compile, compose, create, design, develop, devise, plan, produce, propose | Creations, inventions, poems, songs, stories |

**Figure 15.1.** Revised Bloom's taxonomy: An overview.

neglected social action approach, where teachers empower all students to identify and solve problems through a social justice/equitable lens.

The first and basic level of Banks' (2009) Multicultural Curriculum Model is the Contributions Approach. This approach integrates cultural content into the curriculum and is most commonly used within classrooms because it requires minimal planning to implement. The contributions level focuses on heroes, holidays, food, fashion, and other discrete elements within a culture, making this level of integration the least authentic regarding the quality of multicultural engagement, rigor, and substance. At this low-level approach, students are unable to expand their knowledge base regarding culturally different groups because the delivered information is often superficial, stereotypical, and insufficient to help students gain an accurate and detailed understanding of others. The result can be new or reinforced stereotypes promoted among students by the lessons, activities, materials, and resources.

The Additive Approach is the second level on Banks' continuum; it is slightly better than the Contributions Approach. Here, multiculturalism is implemented using the existing curriculum without changing its basic or fundamental structure. The Additive Approach does not conceptualize the content, concepts, themes, and perspectives of the culturally different students, people, and events. The opposite occurs—teachers add safe and noncontroversial cultural content to the curriculum, making the background knowledge needed to understand the content minimal and devoid of depth and substance. Although the information presented at this level is more substantive than that of the Contributions Approach, teachers typically add an assignment to the existing curriculum that requires students to engage in and obtain minimal knowledge of non-White groups and of themselves, meaning lack of self-reflection. Therefore, students will not be challenged or required to understand the significance of the culturally different individuals and groups in the larger scheme of things.

The third level of multicultural integration, the Transformation Approach, represents high-quality content per Bloom's taxonomy. Yet, unlike the previous two levels, Transformation presents the significance of events, issues, problems, and themes using substantive multicultural content and material. This level or approach changes the basic goals, structure, and nature of the curricula used in the classroom, and allows students to obtain a deeper knowledge base—one that promotes multiple views, opposing views, empathy, and deep or critical understanding of people, issues, and events. When multiculturalism is infused at this level, students are able to and empowered to view and critique content from the perspectives of groups that differ from their own and examine what they are learning from more than one viewpoint. This is, of course, critical thinking; it is also empathy and compassion for oppressed individuals and groups. In other words, the Transformation Approach addresses—in deep and authentic ways—events, facts, and characteristics that enable *all* students to become more aware of and gain meaningful knowledge and resources about different cultural groups, especially those who are marginalized.

The fourth and highest level of Banks' approach to multicultural integration is Social Action. At this level, students are able to identify, analyze, and clarify important social problems and issues, make decisions, and take action to help resolve the issues or problems. When taught at this level, students are able to develop and improve their problem-solving skills, as well as skills in working with and supporting culturally different groups. At this approach, students are provided with essential information and resources needed to take actions that enhance the lives of others.

To reiterate, curriculum is incomplete and not culturally responsive if students are not provided with opportunities to think critically *and* act equitably in culturally responsive ways. Curriculum must provide students with the skills and abilities to think and learn beyond themselves and to see the world from the viewpoints of others (i.e., empathy). The revised Bloom-Banks Matrix (Ford-Harris Matrix) marries the components of the revised Bloom's taxonomy and Banks' Multicultural Curriculum Model to provide teachers with a framework that allows them to create curricula that provide a multitude of critical thinking levels while integrating multicultural content; this provides all students with a culturally responsive and rigorous education.

Ford (2011) defined a culturally responsive education as one that: (a) has an educational philosophy among educators that is not colorblind, (b) appreciates and values the cultural differences of students, (c) utilizes a curriculum that is multicultural and addresses culturally different ways of learning and understanding, and (d) assesses students using testing/evaluation that is culturally and linguistically relevant. Gifted students must be able to access a flexibly paced and advanced curricula that provides depth and breadth in their area(s) of strength, as well as curriculum and instruction that is of interest and relevance to their lives (i.e., culturally responsive education). Following these protocols will help eliminate ineffective and culturally assaultive curriculum and instruction.

# Merging Bloom and Banks for Rigor and Relevance: Ford-Harris Matrix

To reiterate, the original Bloom-Banks Matrix, developed by Ford and Harris (1999) and updated by Ford (2011), combines Bloom's taxonomy (Bloom, 1956) and Banks' Multicultural Curriculum Model (2009) to provide educators with a multicultural gifted education model that reflects the goals, objectives, and perspectives of differentiated, gifted, and multicultural education. The result is 24 cells or 4 quadrants based on the six levels of Bloom by the four levels of Banks (see Figures 15.2 and 15.3). Trotman-Scott (2014a, 2014b) also color-coded the four quadrants of the matrix.

The lowest cell is knowledge-contributions (part of Quadrant 1). The highest and most substantive cell is transformation-social action; this is the cell (part of Quadrant 4) that all students and teachers are urged to reach, especially because instruction on this level enables students to engage in the highest level of critical thinking *and* multiculturalism.

The Bloom-Banks Matrix, a 4 x 6 matrix, has been color-coded for conceptual reasons as follows:

◆ **Red/Stop = Quadrant 1:** Low on both Bloom's taxonomy and Banks' multicultural level. When low on Bloom's taxonomy (understanding, remembering, and applying) and low on Banks' multicultural levels (contributions and additives), students will know, understand, and apply information about cultural elements, groups, and concepts but in a superficial way. Gifted students may not be challenged in either way. Moreover, the content provided within the red section (Quadrant 1), rarely provides students with multicultural growth and substance. Instruction on the red level is very common and many students may have been exposed to similar information in previous settings.

◆ **Yellow/Caution = Quadrant 2:** High on Bloom's taxonomy and low on Banks' multicultural levels. Students taught in this quadrant are able to compare and contrast, create, and critique information about cultural groups, concepts, and themes. This level requires that students use higher level critical thinking (analyzing, evaluating, and creating) skills. Although instruction is at a high

|  | Remembering | Understanding | Applying | Analyzing | Evaluating | Creating |
|---|---|---|---|---|---|---|
| Contributions | Students are taught and are able to remember about cultural artifacts, events, groups, and other cultural elements. | Students are taught and show evidence of understanding information about cultural artifacts, groups, etc. | Students are asked to and can apply information learned on cultural artifacts, events, etc. | Students are taught to and can analyze (e.g., compare and contrast) information about cultural artifacts, groups, etc. | Students are taught to and can evaluate facts and information based on cultural artifacts, groups, etc. | Students are required to and can create a new product from the information on cultural artifacts, groups, etc. |
| Additive | Students are taught and are able to remember concepts and themes about cultural groups. | Students are taught and show evidence of understanding cultural concepts and themes. | Students are required to and can apply information learned about cultural concepts and themes. | Students are taught to and can analyze important cultural concepts and themes. | Students are taught to and can critique cultural concepts and themes. | Students are asked to and can create important information on cultural concepts and themes. |
| Transformation | Students are able to remember information on important cultural elements, groups, and so forth, and can understand this information from different perspectives. | Students are taught to understand and can demonstrate an understanding of important cultural concepts and themes from different perspectives. | Students are asked to and can apply their understanding of important concepts and themes from different perspectives. | Students are taught to and can analyze important cultural concepts and themes from more than one perspective. | Students are taught to and can evaluate or judge important cultural concepts and themes from different viewpoints (e.g., racially and culturally different groups). | Students are required to and can create a product based on their new perspective or the perspective of another group. |
| Social Action | Based on their ability to remember information about cultural artifacts, students make recommendations for social action. | Based on their understanding of important concepts and themes, students make recommendations for social action. | Students are asked to and can apply their understanding of important social and cultural issues; they make recommendations for and take action on these issues. | Students are required to and can analyze social and cultural issues from different perspectives; they take action on these issues. | Students critique important social and cultural issues and seek to make national and/or international change. | Students create a plan of action to address a social and cultural issue(s); they seek important social change. |

**Figure 15.2.** Ford's Revised Bloom-Banks Matrix: Gifted education that is rigorous and relevant. *Note.* Adapted from Ford (2011) and Trotman-Scott (2014a, 2014b).

**Figure 15.3.** Ford's color-coded Bloom-Banks quadrants. *Note.* Adapted from Ford (2011); also see Trotman-Scott (2014a, 2014b).

level cognitively, teachers should proceed with caution. Minimal cultural substance is learned (contributions and additive), which can lead to students having difficulty grasping multicultural content and culturally different students in substantive ways. Ford (2011) argued that this quadrant is common in gifted education where critical thinking is espoused but in a colorblind way. Gifted students are thinking critically and solving problems with superficial multicultural content (e.g., food, fun, fashion, folklore).

◆ **Blue/Guarded = Quadrant 3:** Low on Bloom's taxonomy but high on Banks' multicultural levels. This quadrant provides students with opportunities to view cultural events, concepts, and themes through the lens of other cultures; however, there is little critical thinking and problem solving involved. Social action may take place, but the project is superficial, and not likely to have much impact. The curriculum provided to students elaborates on events, facts, and characteristics of culturally different groups, enabling them to become more aware of and gain additional and meaningful knowledge about different groups. In this quadrant, critical thinking and problem solving are higher than the yellow and red quadrants, but the cognitive rigor is low (knowing, understanding, and applying); however, the cultural content is rigorous (transformation and social action). We find this often among social justice educators who present deep cultural content (e.g., Afrocentric educators) but fail to focus on critical thinking and problem solving.

◆ **Green/Go = Quadrant 4:** High on Bloom's taxonomy *and* high on Banks' multicultural levels. Instruction and assignments given using Quadrant 4 allow students to think critically and solve problems (analyzing, evaluating, and creating), and view a multitude of multicultural topics, issues, and themes (transformation and social action). Importantly, they are empowered to make social and equitable changes in developmentally appropriate ways. This, as Ford (2011) indicated, is the ultimate destiny—curriculum is rigorous and relevant! Students are thinking and solving problems at the highest levels and are exposed to content that addresses cultural misunderstandings, stereotypes, and injustices, and that affirms and supports students of color. This is the win-win quadrant for all students and our educational system.

## Pros and Cons of a Few Cells in the Quadrants of the Revised Bloom-Banks Matrix

Following are examples of cross-curriculum social studies and music activities for Quadrants 1, 2, and 3 of the revised Bloom-Banks Matrix, along with possible pros and cons for three of the six cells in each quadrant. There are no cons or disadvantages for Quadrant 4.

**The red Quadrant 1.**

*Remembering-Contribution.* Students are asked to name three Black musicians popular before the Civil Rights Movement. The pros of this assignment are that students will be able to remember the names of Black musicians popular before the Civil Rights Movement. Students may also be exposed to different genres and content of music performed by Black artists prior to the Civil Rights Movement.

The possible cons of this requirement are that students will not be required to provide additional information known about the Black musicians. Also, they will not be required to discuss the genre or the lyrics of the music as it relates to the times in which the music was created. Moreover, students will only be required to identify superficial content (names of musicians).

*Understanding-Addition.* After reading the history of *Precious Lord, Take My Hand* by the African American musician Thomas A. Dorsey, students are asked to summarize in their own words what the song meant to the composer. By completing this assignment, students will be able to identify and summarize the thoughts and feelings of an African American composer via restating. However, the information provided is basic and the information discussed will most likely be less controversial. Also, the teacher will only add to the curriculum and will not have to change the curriculum so that it reflects the meaning of music during historical time periods.

*Applying-Contribution.* Students are asked to create a model of the 16th Avenue Baptist Church in Birmingham, AL, where four African American girls were killed when the church was bombed. Students who complete this assignment will be able to apply new knowledge about the structure of a church (and apply math concepts during social studies class). They will also learn about the system of church design and scaling. Although students will be required to create a model, information about the church will most likely not cover information about the background of the girls or the church members. Furthermore, students will most likely know more about the structure of the church than the congregation and the meaning behind the church being bombed.

**The yellow Quadrant 2.**

*Analyzing-Addition.* Students are asked to choose a song by an African American artist that is popular today and compare the lyrics to those of a song by an African American artist that was popular during the 1960s Civil Rights Movement—analyzing the similarities and differences. Students who complete this assignment will be exposed to and will be able to review lyrics of music from the present and the past. They will also be able to compare past and present lyrics. However, students will not be given the opportunity to learn about the background of the artists or their story behind the music.

*Analyzing-Contribution.* Students are required to categorize the types of music written by minorities during the Civil Rights Movement. Students who complete this assignment may possibly be exposed to different genres of music than those of which they are familiar. They will also be able to identify contributions of minority musicians. However, the information obtained will be basic and will most likely focus only on contributions and not prejudices or injustices that the musicians may have faced.

*Evaluating-Addition.* Students are instructed to rank their choice of music genres during the Civil Rights Movement and explain why they ranked them as such. By completing this assignment, students will be able to identify and remember genres most popular during the Civil Rights Movement. However, information provided about the genres may be superficial or may be comprised of information that students already know.

**The blue Quadrant 3.**

*Remembering-Social Action.* Students are asked what they would have done if they were a musician in the 1950s to ensure that equality existed within the music industry. By answering this question, students will be able to view the perspectives of others who may have been overlooked for their contributions in music. The question requires students to provide an answer that may be packed with multicultural content. However, it only requires students to infer and does not require a higher level of thinking (i.e., analyzing, evaluating, creating).

*Understanding-Transformation.* Students are asked to take on the persona of a musician in the 1960s and describe how they felt when their music was recognized by the dominant culture. Students who correctly answer this question will be able to provide an explanation, from another's perspective, and also communicate an understanding of events surrounding the recognition of minority musicians by the dominant culture.

*Applying-Social Action.* Students are required to write a letter to the local paper unveiling the untruths about the music industry during the Civil Rights Movement. Students who complete this assignment will be able to identify the issues of the music industry during that time period. They will also be able to identify the works of minority musicians and be able to apply the issues to current concerns within the music industry. This activity provides the students with a high level of multicultural content. However, it may not provide them with the necessary rigor, especially if a student is gifted.

**The green Quadrant 4.**

*Analyzing-Transformation.* Students are asked to infer how society would be different if the original artists' faces appeared on the cover of albums in the 1950s. Students will be able to answer the question from the perspective of those artists who were discriminated against, which requires a high level of multicultural content and rigor.

*Evaluating-Transformation.* Students are required to write a story defending the position of artists of color on the record executives' decision to re-record and change album covers in 1950. Students completing this assignment will be able to present facts and provide an argument about the injustice of the decision made by record executives during the 1950s. This activity allows students the opportunity to apply rigor to a situation that is high in multicultural content.

*Creating-Social Action.* Students are asked to form an organization that will safeguard that all artists receive appropriate credit for the songs they write. By completing this assignment, students will be able to create a meaningful organization that will ensure justice for not just minority musicians, but musicians as a whole. Moreover, students will have the opportunity to create on a level that meets the needs of multiculturalism and rigor.

# Summary and Conclusion

The goal of educators must be to challenge and engage all students, especially students like Michael and other students of color who find little connection with what they are learning in gifted education classes. Teachers must utilize resources that enable and empower gifted students to engage in critical thinking, problem solving, and high-quality multicultural activities. As teachers examine the level of complexity and multicultural content in their curricular choices, they will be able to develop and implement differentiated lessons using higher levels of both the Bloom and Banks approaches. The revised Ford-Harris Matrix (Ford, 2011), specifically Quadrant 4, promotes the critical work that aids gifted students as they delve into deep multicultural content that is rigorous.

High-quality differentiation enables students to increase their levels of knowledge and skills in their area(s) of strengths. Differentiation should be based on how culture mediates learning processes. In other words, "all practice needs to be culturally responsive in order to be best practice" (Moje & Hinchman, 2004, p. 321).

Differentiating instruction is a strategy that can be used to teach all students while also maintaining the level of interest and rigor needed to keep them actively engaged. Also, when the curriculum is culturally relevant, students' interest and motivation are likely to increase. Using the original or revised Bloom-Banks' Matrix (Ford, 2011; Ford & Harris, 1999) will help teachers meet the academic, social-emotional, and cultural needs of all students, regardless of their academic skills and intellectual levels.

# References

Adams, C., & Pierce, R. L. (2010). *Differentiation that really works: Strategies from real teachers for real classrooms* (grades 3–5). Waco, TX: Prufrock Press.

Banks, J. M. (2009). *Teaching strategies for ethnic studies* (8th ed.). New York, NY: Allyn & Bacon.

Bloom, B. (Ed.). (1956). *Taxonomy of educational objectives. Handbook I: Cognitive domain.* New York, NY: Wiley.

Ford, D. Y. (2010). *Reversing underachievement among gifted Black students* (2nd ed.). Waco, TX: Prufrock Press.

Ford, D. Y. (2011). *Multicultural gifted education* (2nd ed.). Waco, TX: Prufrock Press.

Ford, D. Y. (2013). *Recruiting and retaining culturally different students in gifted education: Ensuring equity and excellence.* Waco, TX: Prufrock Press.

Ford, D. Y., & Harris, J. J., III. (1999). Multicultural gifted education. New York, NY: Teachers College Press.

Gay, G. (2010). *Culturally responsive teaching: Theory, research, and practice* (2nd ed.). New York, NY: College Press.

Grantham, T., Trotman Scott, M., & Harmon, D. (2013). *Young, triumphant, and Black: Overcoming the tyranny of desegregated schools in segregated minds.* Waco, TX: Prufrock Press.

Krathwohl, D. R. (2002). A revision of Bloom's taxonomy: An overview. *Theory Into Practice, 41,* 212–218.

Ladson-Billings, G. (2009). *The dreamkeepers: Successful teachers for African American children* (2nd ed.). San Francisco, CA: Jossey-Bass.

Moje, E. B., & Hinchman, K. (2004). Culturally responsive practices for youth literacy learning. In J. Dole & T. Jetton (Eds.). *Adolescent literacy research and practice* (pp. 331–350). New York, NY: Guilford Press.

Siegle, D. (2012). *The underachieving gifted child: Recognizing, understanding, and reversing underachievement.* Waco, TX: Prufrock Press.

Siegle, D., & McCoach, D. B. (2005). Making a difference: Motivating gifted students who are not achieving. *Teaching Exceptional Children, 38*(1), 22–27.

Tomlinson, C. (2001). *How to differentiate instruction in mixed-ability classrooms* (2nd ed.). Alexandria VA: Association for Supervision and Curriculum Development.

Tomlinson, C. (2009). Differentiating instruction as a response to academically diverse student populations. In R. Marzano (Ed.). *On excellence in teaching* (pp. 247–268). Bloomington, IN: Solution Tree.

Trotman Scott, M. (2014a). Multicultural differentiated instruction for gifted students. In J. Bakken, F. Obiakor, & A. Rotatori (Eds.), *Advances in special education—Gifted education: Current perspectives and issues* (Vol. 26, pp. 147–166). Bingley, England: Emerald Group.

Trotman Scott, M. (2014b). Using the Bloom-Banks matrix to develop multicultural develop multicultural differentiated lessons for gifted students. *Gifted Education Press Quarterly, 37,* 161–166.

Whitmore, J. (1980). *Giftedness, conflict and underachievement.* Boston, MA: Allyn & Bacon.

# About the Editors

**Kristen R. Stephens, Ph.D.,** is an associate professor of the practice in the Program in Education at Duke University where she directs the Academically/Intellectually Gifted Licensure Program for teachers. Prior to this appointment, Dr. Stephens served as the gifted education research specialist for the Duke University Talent Identification Program. She is the coauthor of numerous books and coeditor of the Practical Strategies Series in Gifted Education (Prufrock Press), a series comprised of more than 30 books on issues pertinent to gifted child education. Dr. Stephens has served on the board of directors for the National Association for Gifted Children and is past-president of the North Carolina Association for Gifted and Talented. She is currently president of the American Association for Gifted Children.

**Frances A. Karnes, Ph.D.,** served as Distinguished Professor and Director of the Frances A. Karnes Center for Gifted Studies at the University of Southern Mississippi before retiring. She also directed the Leadership Studies Program and is widely known for her research, innovative programs, and leadership training. She is author or coauthor of more than 200 published papers and is coauthor or coeditor of 74 books. Her work is often cited as the authority on gifted children and the law. She is extensively involved in university activities and civic and professional organizations in the community. Her honors include: Faculty Research Award, Honorary Doctorate from Quincy University, Mississippi Legislature Award for Academic Excellence in Higher Education, USM Professional Service Award, USM Basic Research Award, Rotary International Jean Harris Award, Woman of Achievement Award from the Hattiesburg Women's Forum, Distinguished Alumni Award from the University of

Illinois, Lifetime Innovation Award from the University of Southern Mississippi and University Distinguished Professor from the University of Southern Mississippi, and TeachTechTopia's Top 10 Most Influential Special Education Professors. The Board of Trustees of Mississippi Institutions of Higher Learning honored her by naming the research, instructional, and service center she founded at USM the Frances A. Karnes Center for Gifted Studies.

# About the Authors

**Catherine Brighton, Ph.D.,** is the Associate Dean for Academic Programs and an associate professor at the University of Virginia in the department of Curriculum, Instruction, and Special Education, Curry School of Education. She is a Principal Investigator with a Spencer Foundation-funded project investigating kindergarten teachers' use of literacy data to inform instruction in diverse elementary school classrooms. Further, she serves as codirector of the University of Virginia Institutes on Academic Diversity. Her current research interests include investigations surrounding classroom-level data use, high-quality teaching and learning (authentic problem solving, differentiated instruction, critical and creative thinking, and teacher content knowledge), and qualitative methodologies.

**Elissa Brown, Ph.D.,** is distinguished lecturer and Director of the Hunter College Gifted Center. As a professor, Brown coordinates and teaches the advanced certificate program in gifted and talented education at Hunter College. She has served as an adjunct professor at several universities, including Rutgers and Duke University. She has been a state director of gifted education, a federal grant manager, a district gifted program coordinator, principal of a specialized high school and a teacher of gifted students, K–12. She is a published author in the field of gifted education and presents widely. She lives in East Harlem, NY.

**Carolyn M. Callahan, Ph.D.,** holds a doctorate in educational psychology with an emphasis in gifted education. At the University of Virginia, she developed the graduate program in gifted education and the summer and Saturday programs for gifted students. She has served as director of the University of Virginia National Research Center on the Gifted and Talented for 18 years. Her research has resulted in publications across a broad range of topics including the areas of program evaluation, the development of performance assessments, and curricular and programming options for highly able students including Advanced Placement and International Baccalaureate. She has received recognition as Outstanding Faculty Member in the Commonwealth of Virginia, Outstanding Professor of the Curry School of Education, Distinguished Higher Education Alumnae of the University of Connecticut and was awarded the Distinguished Scholar Award and the Distinguished Service Award from the National Association for Gifted Children. She is a Past-President of The Association for the Gifted and the National Association for Gifted Children and The Association for the Gifted.

**Bonnie Cramond, Ph.D.,** is a professor in the Department of Educational Psychology at the University of Georgia. She has been a member of the board of directors of the National Association for Gifted Children, editor of the *Journal of Secondary Gifted Education*, and is on the review board for several journals. An international and national speaker, she has published numerous articles, published a book on creativity research, and teaches classes on giftedness and creativity. Her interests include identification and nurturance of creativity, especially students considered at risk because of their different ways of thinking.

**Elizabeth A. Fogarty, Ph.D.,** is serving as associate professor in elementary education in the College of Education at East Carolina University. She teaches both undergraduate and graduate-level coursework in elementary education and gifted education. She was recognized by the National Association for Gifted Children with the Outstanding Doctoral Student Award in 2006 and as an Early Leader in the field of gifted education in 2010.

**Donna Y. Ford, Ph.D.,** is a professor in the College of Education at Vanderbilt University. The majority of her work focuses on recruiting and retaining Black and other students of color in gifted and Advanced Placement classes. She is the author of numerous books (the most recent is *Recruiting and Retaining Culturally Different Students in Gifted Education*) and more than 150 articles and chapters. Dr. Ford consults nationally with school districts, including presentations and evaluations, to desegregate gifted education for Black and Hispanic students. She has served on the board of directors of several organizations, including the National Association for Gifted Children (NAGC), and Council for Exceptional Children–Division for Culturally and Linguistically Diverse Exceptional

Learners (CEC-DDEL). Ford is the cochair of the special interest group called Gifted-Racial Accountability and Cultural Equity (G-RACE).

**Michelle Frazier Trotman Scott, Ph.D.,** is an associate professor at the University of West Georgia. She teaches in the area of special education within the Department of Learning and Teaching. Dr. Frazier Trotman Scott's research interests include special education overrepresentation, gifted education underrepresentation, twice exceptional, culturally responsive instruction, family involvement, and the achievement gap. Michelle has written several articles and conducted numerous presentations at professional conferences. She is the coeditor of *Gifted and Advanced Black Students in School: An Anthology of Critical Works* and *Young, Triumphant, and Black: Overcoming the Tyranny of Segregated Minds in Desegregated Schools*. She has also served as the guest coeditor of a professional journal and has reviewed for journals in the gifted, special, and urban education disciplines. She is President of the Council for Exceptional Children–Division for Culturally and Linguistically Diverse Exceptional Learners (CEC-DDEL).

**Shelagh A. Gallagher, Ph.D.,** is an internationally recognized expert in gifted education. Prior to her current role as consultant and curriculum writer, she spent 13 years leading the gifted education program at the University of North Carolina at Charlotte. She also worked at Illinois Mathematics and Science Academy, one of the nation's premiere high schools for gifted students, where she began her work in PBL. She was also the first manager of the Javits grant that produced the William & Mary PBL science units. She has directed two additional PBL-based Javits grants and is currently serving as a consultant on a fourth. She has received the NAGC Curriculum Award seven times for her PBL units. Gallagher has conducted research and published articles on topics including personality attributes and giftedness, gender differences in mathematics performance, questioning for higher order thinking, developmental and academic needs of gifted adolescents, and twice-exceptional students. She is a Fellow at the Institute for Educational Advancement and works with gifted children at the IEA Camp Yunasa each summer. She served two terms on the NAGC Board of Directors and the North Carolina Association for the Gifted (NCAGT). She has received the Distinguished Service Award and the James J. Gallagher Award for Advocacy from NCAGT, the Provost's Award for Teaching Excellence from UNC Charlotte, and the Article of the Year Award from NAGC.

**M. Katherine Gavin, Ph.D.,** has more than 25 years experience in mathematics education for gifted students, including her role as math specialist as an associate professor at the Neag Center for Gifted Education and Talent Development at the University of Connecticut. Her career also includes work as a mathematics teacher, department chair, and district coordinator. The main focus of her research is the development and evaluation of advanced math curriculum for elementary students. Dr. Gavin received the 2006 National Association for Gifted Children Early Leader award and the 2012 Neag School of Education Distinguished Researcher Award from the University of Connecticut. She has published more than 100 articles, book chapters, and curriculum materials on mathematics education with a focus on gifted students. She works with teachers nationally and internationally who are interested in developing mathematical thinking and talent in their students.

**Alissa P. Griffith** is the Lecturing Fellow in the Program in Education at Duke University where she provides mentoring and supervision support to teachers enrolled in Duke's academically/intellectually gifted licensure program. She also supports service-learning experiences for teachers and undergraduate students as a liaison between the University and Durham Public Schools. Prior to her current position, Griffith was a public school teacher and AIG specialist. She also served as a liaison for a federal grant focusing on positive behavior support. Griffith has presented at local, state, and national conferences on the effectiveness of service-learning as a pedagogy for gifted students. She is a member of National Association for Gifted Children and is secretary for the North Carolina Association for the Gifted and Talented.

**Jessica A. Hockett, Ph.D.,** is an education consultant and ASCD Faculty Member specializing in differentiation instruction, curriculum and performance task design, and gifted education. For the past 10 years, she has worked with teachers and leaders in nearly 70 school districts to improve teacher and student learning. Jessica has published a variety of articles, book chapters, and staff development materials, including *Exam Schools: Inside America's Most Selective Public High Schools*, coauthored with Chester E. Finn, Jr., and *Differentiated Instruction in Middle and High School: Strategies to Engage All Learners* with Kristina Doubet. Prior to doctoral studies at the University of Virginia, she was a secondary teacher in both general and gifted program settings.

**Angela M. Housand, Ph.D.,** is an associate professor and the Academically and Intellectually Gifted Program Coordinator at the University of North Carolina Wilmington (UNCW). As a former teacher,

Housand brings an applied focus to her instructional programs for in-service and pre-service teachers and to her research efforts that test the effectiveness of the FutureCasting® digital life skills framework. Over the years, her work has been presented internationally and published in the *Journal of Advanced Academics, Gifted Child Quarterly*, and *High Ability Studies*, just to name a few. In addition to teaching and research, Dr. Housand serves in elected positions for the National Association for Gifted Children and as a reviewer for multiple research journals. The goal of her work is to support teachers as they challenge students to achieve advanced levels of performance while becoming productive citizens in a global society.

**Brian C. Housand, Ph.D.,** is an associate professor and co-coordinator of the Academically and Intellectually Gifted program at East Carolina University. Housand earned a Ph.D. in Educational Psychology at the University of Connecticut with an emphasis in both gifted education and instructional technology. Housand frequently presents and works as an educational consultant on the integration of technology and enrichment into the curriculum. He is currently researching ways in which technology can enhance the learning environment and is striving to define creative-productive giftedness in a digital age.

**Susan K. Johnsen, Ph.D.,** is a professor in the Department of Educational Psychology at Baylor University where she directs the Ph.D. program and programs related to gifted and talented education. She is editor-in-chief of *Gifted Child Today* and author of more than 250 articles, monographs, technical reports, chapters, and books related to gifted education. She has written three tests used in identifying gifted students: *Test of Mathematical Abilities for Gifted Students* (TOMAGS), *Test of Nonverbal Intelligence* (TONI-4), and *Screening Assessment Gifted Students* (SAGES-2). She is a reviewer and auditor of programs in gifted education for the Council for the Accreditation of Educator Preparation, and is past chair of the Knowledge and Skills Subcommittee of the Council for Exceptional Children and past chair of the NAGC Professional Standards Committee. She has received awards for her work in the field of education, including NAGC's President's Award, CEC's Leadership Award, TAG's Leadership Award, TAGT's President's Award, TAGT's Advocacy Award, and Baylor University's Investigator Award, Teaching Award, and Contributions to the Academic Community.

**David Malone, Ph.D.,** is a professor of the practice in the Program in Education at Duke University. He also serves as the faculty director of

Duke Service-Learning. Malone codeveloped a service-learning/tutoring program that matches about 300 Duke undergraduate students each year with children in Durham Public Schools who need assistance in reading, math, and academic learning strategies. He also teaches courses in educational psychology, literacy, and service-learning.

**Michael S. Matthews, Ph.D.,** is associate professor and Director of the Academically & Intellectually Gifted graduate program at the University of North Carolina at Charlotte. He is coeditor of the *Journal of Advanced Academics* and serves on the Board of Directors of the NAGC. Dr. Matthews also is Chair-Elect of the Special Interest Group—Research on Giftedness, Creativity, and Talent of the American Educational Research Association. His interests include research methods, policy, science learning, motivation and underachievement, parenting, and issues in the education of gifted and advanced learners from diverse backgrounds. Dr. Matthews is the author or editor of five books, more than 30 peer reviewed journal articles, and numerous book chapters in gifted education. He frequently presents at state, national, and international conferences in education. His work has been recognized with the 2010 Early Scholar Award from the NAGC, and the 2012 Pyryt Collaboration Award from the AERA SIG—RoGCT.

**Jean Sunde Peterson, Ph.D.,** professor emerita and former director of school counselor preparation at Purdue University, was a classroom and gifted education teacher for many years and was involved in teacher education prior to graduate work in counseling at the University of Iowa. A licensed mental health counselor with considerable clinical experience with gifted youth and their families, she is a veteran conference presenter and conducts school-based workshops on social and emotional development of high-ability students, academic underachievement, bullying, parenting gifted children and adolescents, cultural values as related to identification of and programming for gifted youth, and prevention-oriented affective curriculum—most of these related to her practice-oriented research. She is author of *Gifted at Risk: Poetic Profiles* and *The Essential Guide to Talking With Gifted Teens* and is coeditor of *Models of Counseling Gifted Children, Adolescents, and Young Adults*, along with more than 100 journal articles, books, and invited chapters. She is a former chair of the Counseling and Guidance Network and also served two terms on the National Association for Gifted Children's Board of Directors.

**Ann Robinson, Ph.D.,** is professor of educational psychology and founding director of the Jodie Mahony Center for Gifted Education at the University of Arkansas at Little Rock. She is past president of the National

Association for Gifted Children (NAGC), a former editor of the *Gifted Child Quarterly*, and has been honored by NAGC as Early Scholar, Early Leader, Distinguished Scholar, and for Distinguished Service to the association. To date, Robinson has generated more than $24 million dollars in external funding, including five Jacob K. Javits projects. Her interests include the use of biography in the curriculum, biographical research methods in gifted education, school intervention studies, evidence-based practices, and teacher preparation and professional development. She is the lead author of the best-selling *Best Practices in Gifted Education: An Evidence-Based Guide.* Her most recent book, coedited with Jennifer Jolly, is *A Century of Contributions to Gifted Education: Illuminating Lives.* Her popular *Blueprints for Biography* guides provide teachers with strategies for differentiating nonfiction reading in a variety of curricular areas for talented students.

**Sarah E. Sumners, Ph.D.,** is an assistant research scientist and interim director of the Torrance Center for Creativity and Talent Development at the University of Georgia. She has led creativity trainings both nationally and internationally, coauthored several book chapters and entries on teaching creativity, has taught graduate courses on teacher education and creativity, and has written several grants to fund research. Dr. Sumners has a wide range of experience in grant writing, teaching, and professional development. She holds an M.Ed. in gifted studies from Mississippi University for Women and a Ph.D. in Curriculum and Instruction from Mississippi State University.

**Audrey Tabler** has taught secondary mathematics in grades 8–12 for more than 24 years and has taught college mathematics for Arkansas Tech University. In 2008, she earned National Board Certification in Early Adolescent Mathematics. During her years as a public school educator, Audrey served gifted students as a classroom teacher, as a coach for both junior high and high school quiz bowl teams, and as a member of the Booneville gifted and talented advisory panel. Audrey is currently a doctoral candidate at the University of Arkansas at Little Rock, pursuing a degree in educational supervision and administration with a coemphasis in gifted education. Audrey served as a member of the Executive Board of Arkansans for Gifted and Talented Education (AGATE). She attends and presents at state, national, and international gifted conferences. A wife and mother, Audrey has helped raise two gifted sons, one of whom attended the Arkansas School for Mathematics, Sciences, and the Arts.